CALLED

TO THE

PRINCIPAL'S OFFICE

Proven answers to today's education problems

Dr. Rodney Haire

CALLED to the Principal's Office

Copyright © 2010 by Dr. Rodney Haire

All rights reserved. No part of this publication may be reproduced, stored in a retrieval system or transmitted in any form by any means, electronic, mechanical, photocopy, recording or otherwise, except for brief quotations in reviews or articles, without the prior permission of the author, except as provided by USA copyright law.

Cover Photo: Roger Lane, Our Living Yearbook

Second Printing, 2010

ISBN 978-0-557-51605-6

Dedication

This book is dedicated to my wife, Judy. She is the most important person in my day, career, and life. Judy is my life partner and my soul mate—she is my everything.

Without her, I would not have been able to survive the emotional pressures of building what has become a model school, Liberty Christian School of Argyle, Texas. She has been there every step of the way.

She and I are so thankful for our two children, Nancy and Rocky, and our grandchildren: Rachel, Hannah, Logan, Rodney, Harlan, and Jett.

Contents

Introduction 9

Chapter 1 23
    How I Made a School Year Seem Eternal—I Hired the Wrong Teacher

Chapter 2 32
    What Foxhole?

Chapter 3 40
    The Deacons Did What??

Chapter 4 52
    DON'T FORGET TO …

Chapter 5 55
    Who Is Running the School??

Chapter 6 68
    Somebody Get A Mop—We Spilled Our School!

Chapter 7 73
    Two Nice Guys—but Board Members??

Chapter 8 79
    Don't Bail—At Least Not Yet

Chapter 9 86
    Make Sure Dad's Powder is Dry

Chapter 10 102
    Shot Fired Over the Bow!

Chapter 11 109
    Guys With the Glass Half Empty Leave!!

Chapter 12 117
    Is Anyone Against Changing A Longstanding Custom?

Chapter 13 123
    It Only Takes a Few Good Men

Chapter 14 136
    Not All Board Members and Parents Who Can Help Wear White Hats

Chapter 15 143
    No Contracts for School Teachers and Administrators??

Chapter 16 154
Perfect Storm Ahead!

Chapter 17 163
TWO BITS, FOUR BITS, SIX BITS A DOLLAR!!

Chapter 18 172
Take the High Road—and Charge For It!!

Chapter 19 178
Who Are Your Heroes?

Chapter 20 189
Higher Salaries—Catch the Wave or Drown

Chapter 21 194
"Choice"—Not Really a Choice

Chapter 22 203
Top Gun

Chapter 23 212
SWATS—"What Are They??"

Chapter 24 222
Are You All Hat and No Cows??

Chapter 25 229
Don't Talk About the Money, Show It to Me!!

Chapter 26 236
Exactly When Do We Want To Start the Improvement Program?
Or What Are You Waiting For?

Chapter 27 247
Prayer Out, Evolution In—We Finally Got it Right!!
(Only if you are an atheistic para-educator)

Chapter 28 256
The Right Guy Runs the School—Wrong Guy Doesn't Get an Offer

Chapter 29 263
All On Board—Hear This!

Chapter 30 270
Are You Sure the Call Was For You?

Chapter 31 280
Wait—Don't Pull the Trigger Just Yet!!

Chapter 32	286
Can We Talk??	
Chapter 33	293
You Been Daddy Wolfed??	
Chapter 34	301
"But What about My Baseball Cards??"	
Chapter 35	308
WARNING—This Chapter Is Going To Test My Credibility	

CALLED TO THE PRINCIPAL'S OFFICE

Introduction

My career in education began in the early 1980s. The experience started out much like one would start up a new company, only the school was never intended to be run by me—I would only be the guy who got it off the ground. The toughest days for any operation are the early ones, but never in my wildest dreams did I ever think that building a school would be the challenge it turned out to be. Now with a bachelor's, a master's, and a doctorate degree later, and too many hours to even calculate, the great story I have named *CALLED* can be told.

I'll begin the book by having a "heart-to-heart" talk with the book. In some ways I feel like I'm saying goodbye to an old friend, and hoping he makes a difference. At the end of the day, *CALLED* has to get it right.

A conversation with *CALLED*...

CALLED, you have really done it now! You could have easily named yourself *How Not to Build a School* or *Ten Blunders Made in Operating a School*, but it was impossible to narrow it down to just ten, wasn't it? You had to get cute, making it personal and even giving a spiritual sound to it. This *CALLED* title has a "from above" kind of thing going on, and it's going to have to be truthful and transparent from beginning to end.

You can't pull any punches, *CALLED*. You can't be a boring book about selecting the best curriculum or the best designs for school schedules. You'd better not even think about giving instruction on how to write the best policy manuals for board members and administrators.

CALLED, I'm going to tell you everything I know about building a school: the memories and nightmares, the good guys and bad, what I wish I hadn't done, and what I'm glad I did.

What you will find in *CALLED*...

CALLED, you have to be practical, and if it is not realistic to expect our governmental and educational leaders to be moral statesmen and to make the tough decisions, then the only other solution is to improve our schools at the grass roots level. That should have been done years ago. So *CALLED,* offering real solutions for solving our nation's school crisis is a task you have to take on, and do it without apology or sensitivity.

CALLED, you can't waste anyone's time—the guys in charge have already wasted too much time. You are going to have to expose the traps, temptations, mistakes, and recoveries I made while building an award-winning school. You have to be about the experiences that were lived out by board members, administrators, teachers, and coaches who not only survived "ground level zero," but won trophy after trophy, and you have to tell exactly how it was done. I'm talking about the decisions and kinds of people who made a great school happen, and those who, probably with the best of intentions, almost destroyed it. We had some "close calls"; tell the reader about those.

CALLED is about the challenges that drove me to psychologists (plural), my heroes and villains, great school board members and bums, wonderful parents and "pains in the rear." It's about the midnight hours when I felt alone in trying to determine when to cut losses, which might include firing that teacher (who is probably miserable in his job anyway) or expelling that student. It means deciding whether or not to hold on to the frustration of trying to teach a parent what **being** a parent means and experience that great victory; or if the student is a senior, just settling for the small comfort that soon the student will "walk the stage."

CALLED is about the heart of a private Christian school: those times that made my heart sing, and those that made me cry. CALLED is non-fiction, but you will have a hard time believing that. If you are a parent, you will find yourself saying: "Surely that parent didn't really do that—no way," or maybe "I wish I had done that with my child," or my hope, "I'm going to be sure to do that while rearing my children."

And in regard to your response to a couple of my experiences related in CALLED, you will say to yourself, "How did that teacher graduate from college, much less get a teaching certificate—or for that matter even a GED?" And I would add a better question: "Why did I ever think of hiring him?" It's all in the 20/20 hindsight of life, my friend.

CALLED is going to say what's on most everyone's mind regarding the quality of education in America. We should have the finest educational system in the world, one that provides a great and memorable experience for our children. Our education majors should go on to enjoy administration, teaching, coaching, or directing a band, but we know that's not happening. I will give you most of the reasons, all of which I have learned from my own experience in the "school of hard knocks." Most of my mistakes could or should have been avoided. I just didn't know any better, had a pride issue, or didn't understand the entire picture as well as I should have. Some of the truths I believe to be essential will be repeated in several different chapters. That is the teacher in me: you tell your students what you are going to teach them, you teach them, and then you tell them what you have taught them. And if I stated an opinion repeatedly, it means I fervently believe that your school will never work without that idea or policy firmly in place.

Every year I tell our students and staff, "Experience is not the best teacher; **someone else's** experience is the best teacher." I learned that little nugget way too late. When Pulitzer Prize winner historian David McCullough was asked what we can learn from the past, my bet is that he didn't even hesitate when he answered that there is no such thing as a "self-made" man or woman. His obvious point is that we are all standing on the shoulders of those who have influenced the decisions that framed our lives. The questions for all of us will always be "**Whose** shoulders will we stand on, and **whose** voice will we hear before making our decisions?" Sir Isaac Newton may have said it best in his letter to Robert Hooke in 1675 when he wrote, "If I have seen further [than you and Descartes] it is by standing on the shoulders of giants."

Solving our educational problems—now there's an original idea.

I run in educational circles with other administrators and board members. I am the president of Liberty Christian School in Argyle, Texas and chairman of the Board of Trustees. That's been my job since the beginning. Solutions to the problems that have plagued our schools since the early 1960s are nowhere in sight. The real answers will be found in hiring the right people who care about their students and love their subject; have a gift and talent to teach (that's a big one); live with integrity, courage, and honesty; and work hard (that's huge). My colleagues are trying to solve our educational problems by paying educators more money, even if they are, in fact, non-educators. Our government is spending hundreds of millions of dollars training math and science teachers—wasn't that supposed to be done in college? How do we know that those being trained will be good teachers?

The administrators of today are charged with making sure their school employs a multicultural staff, taking a nonjudgmental approach to ethics and morals, and making certain that **all** students are awarded high self-esteem ribbons or certificates, regardless of whether or not they have accomplished anything to deserve that self-esteem.

Of course you just recognized that I have defined a large portion of the platform of the political correctness philosophy. It is the political position that most educators are forced to adopt, and the same one that is not appreciated by thousands of minorities who are supposed to benefit—to the minority "race horses," political correctness is a patronizing slap in the face.

Meanwhile, in too many cases where administrators are forced to adhere to the educational laws that pertain to political correctness requirements, we are sending superintendents to prison for theft in almost every state in our union, teachers are being convicted for having sex with students, over 100 ninth grade girls in at least one Massachusetts high school freely admitted to **trying** to get pregnant, students and teachers are being murdered on our school grounds—has anyone connected the morality dots yet?

Maybe we ought to rethink discarding issues in the hiring process that pertain to the teacher's or administrator's integrity and character, and do a better job in the weak or too often absent background check. With murdered principals, teachers in prisons, and sexually abused students in almost every state's recent history—maybe we ought to rethink, like

YESTERDAY, whether there ought to be morals and values brought back into the process.

At this writing in 2010, I believe that most of the solutions are obvious. However, the challenge and real problem is that the establishment seems unlikely to take action. Nobody really wants change; it's just too dangerous. **What if it fails?** Am I missing something here? **It already has!**

In the calendar year of 2007, the high school students in the United States were academically surpassed by 29 other countries. I think the verifiable number is unknown, but it's terrible. The high school students in Belgium referred to the students in New Jersey as "stupid." No one really believed that overgeneralization, but documents supporting similar facts, opinions, and generalities are numerous and maddening.

The emphasis of this book is not throwing stones, piling on, or casting blame. I'm not going to waste energy pointing fingers. I would rather use this brief literary journey to tell a story of how, in a small city in Texas, a really wonderful school evolved. **My hope is that my wrong choices (that I frankly would like to forget—much less see in print) and some hard-learned lessons can be applied to benefit your school, whether public, private secular, or private Christian.**

I understand that the Federal Bureau of Investigation trains its agents to detect counterfeit currency by emphasizing what the **real** bills look and feel like. FBI agents study the authentic so thoroughly that the fake stands out like a school that lost its accreditation. That's the approach I intend to use, and I'm going to be gut-level honest about my personal failures. But in the spirit of giving the reader a vision, I will also share what I believe were the essential factors that made our school great, including my trusted teachers, administrators, and board members who made the hard decisions, regardless of the "fall-out."

Before I began my career in the field of education, I imagined that running a school would be easy. I actually believed it was probably a 10-month job and that parents, kids, and staff would always want to do the right and sensible thing. In fact, the first year, I did not think I would need a policy manual, handbook or paddle. Call me naive, and you would receive an "A."

Can Running a School be that Difficult?

During the first year of my educational career in 1982, I was concurrently the owner of a textile company and part owner of two other related businesses. I had a great partner in Rob Taylor of Dallas, Texas; and we had a good time, made some smart decisions, and made all the money either of us ever dreamed of making. In those years, the total volume of all three companies was approximately $14 million annually, which would probably compute to somewhere in the $30 million range in today's dollars (I didn't do the relative math). For the school year 2009/2010, our school budget was approximately $14 million. The task of running our private school with virtually half the budget of those three companies is at least twice as difficult and complicated.

How in the world could that be? To explain, I'll share some facts, many of my personal stories, and some opinions that I believe to be "spot on." I will also, as promised, offer solutions that have worked for us. I don't know how many educators will have the courage or energy to change their programs, but I will be cheering for the people who read this book and find the heart to take on the establishment in "hand-to-

15

hand" combat. The emperor is buck naked, and somebody has to say so. Guys with a wall full of degrees are in charge of the ship, and our kids are desperate for lifeboats. The sad thing is that we keep re-electing and extending employment contracts to the same really nice folks who are not educators and are in positions of authority way over their heads.

Who Should Read This Book?

A friend asked me point blank, "Rodney, for whom are you **really** writing this book?" What a great question! I am writing for the discouraged teacher who works hard in preparing lesson plans, but finds he is teaching students who don't care, and whose parents have given up. The teacher, whose **only** degree is in education, does not have the confidence he can find a job anywhere else, and knows his cheese is about to fall off his cracker.

I am writing to teachers and coaches who have as their mission statement something like this: "I want to reach the heart of my students and convince them they have potential and can succeed. I want very much to help lift up my students who tried very hard but failed, and encourage them to 'dust off their pants' and get back to work."

I am writing to the administrator who has the credentials, but believes he is fighting a losing battle. Maybe he is exhausted, just too battle weary, and knows he is too weak to face strong-willed parents, teachers, unions, and board members. He is slumped over under the weight of emotional fatigue caused by "faking it."

I am writing *CALLED* in the hope that it is read by every board member in the country. It will emphasize their role in encouraging their administrators, teachers, and coaches. With board support, administrators will lead and direct according to board policy, with a teamwork attitude; teachers will teach with confidence; and coaches will coach from their heart, knowing that even if they lose the big game their job is not on the line.

I am writing to school board members who know if they don't deliver on the campaign pledges they made to get elected, their family will be humiliated and they will probably not be re-elected. Well, on second thought, they might get re-elected if they can lay the blame on the "We are just not paying our teachers enough" garbage. Here's a flash: teachers never majored in education for the money. Do teachers need to be better paid? Of course they do, but all of us know that's not why they are in the classroom.

A Special Note to Board Members...

To all board members I say, "You have enormous power; don't be bullies!" Learn how to use your power to help the children, parents, and administrators whom I know you want to help—in reality, you have been elected to be a servant-leader. Your power flows directly through your administrator. How well you relate to him, the encouragement and support you provide for him, and the tone in which you offer advice and directives will greatly determine whether or not you are a successful board member. Some of you board members are educators; you may be the most dangerous because you think you have all of the answers. There are no two children alike, and, using sound logic, there are no two schools alike. You must stop talking and listen carefully to the questions and problems that your administrator is asking and sharing.

In the boardrooms of private and public schools, there is an enormous elephant in the room, and nobody is talking about it. The board members are the elephant, so they aren't talking. The administrators have their jobs and those of their teachers to protect, so they are keeping their mouths shut. But at the end of the day, our students are being trampled.

In the early years of building our school, I had some difficult board members, along with many good ones. It took several years to work through the process of learning what type of person would make a good board member, and during this process I left many board meetings ready to resign. Most private school boards are self-perpetuating, so when one member resigns or fulfills his time of service, his replacement is selected by the remaining members. This process can become a "good ol' boy" system quickly—has anyone connected the dots between integrity and poorly run private schools? The public school board members are elected, so public school administrators have an enormous challenge in implementing some of the insane policies made by the winners of elections.

I vividly recall leaving a board meeting that was held one night at the home of one of our members. During this meeting, I became so frustrated with the shortsighted opinions of one of the board members that while driving home I literally screamed at the top of my lungs. I sincerely hope that all board members in America will understand the vital importance their support and mature decisions have in the ultimate success of their administrator, and thus their school. Boards set policy and administrators are expected to administer those policies; if expectations are not couched in respect for your administrator, you have failed.

CALLED **will** clearly give many examples of how board members can help, and how they can avoid the landmines that have debilitated so many great administrators, weakened so many gifted teachers, and virtually destroyed so many schools. There are dead schools both public and private; there just has not been a burial service yet. The dead private school will quietly go out of business—families are not going to support an unproductive school. The public school can go on being dead for years, because the school-tax system will keep it in operation indefinitely.

A Word to the Parents and Teachers

CALLED is for parents. You have the responsibility to provide the best education possible for your children; this book will give you some help in making the choice between public or private. In past generations, that was not a problem. Parents simply sent their child to the local public school—few exceptions. If that is the educational plan for your family, you need to remember that your child is going to be competing academically with graduates from the finest prep schools, the best public schools, and with grads from virtually every nation in the world. Before you enroll your child in a school, visit the halls in between classes, the lunchroom, and the playground. Meet the teachers that your child might have, and ask them confidentially if they have support from their administrators regarding classroom discipline. And talk to parents of both the public and private schools in your area. These are some ideas that will confirm one of the most important decisions of your parental life.

Perhaps CALLED is for those great educators who already served in the educational "armed forces," came to the place where they just couldn't stand it any longer, and resigned. I hope this book will give them reason to reconsider, a new resolve, and encouragement to return.

A word of confession:

I am not a politically correct kind of guy. As stated earlier, I believe that political correctness is a detriment to the very people that it was originally intended to help. Political correctness has degenerated into a pack of meaningless words and shadows.

I am a committed Christian because I believe "the tomb is empty," but CALLED is not about evangelism; I just feel it necessary to not try to hide that from you. I am against passing out condoms in schools; let's also give them a beer and cigarette in their "not to take home" packet. I am also against teacher unions and contracts because they are not in the best interest of our kids; and now I officially qualify as a relic. By the way, I am not qualified to speak against **all** unions, as I have never been a member of one; maybe some of them are beneficial, but I'm certain many have to be reined in and given reasonable boundaries.

I can't be sensitive, as CALLED is really for the benefit of America's children, although I suggest your children not read it—it is a book for adults. American students are getting a raw deal in almost all of the country's public schools and in too many of our private ones. Because that is a travesty, I felt this book had to be written and must be **real**—the gloves have come off.

I am going to primarily use the masculine gender for this writing, but that is simply for my own convenience. And to illustrate the point that great teaching or administration is not a profession that is specific to gender or race, I'll give you a couple of examples.

I believe the best English teacher in the country is Dr. Sarah Lippe, and the best social studies teacher is Dr. Martin Noto. Coincidentally, both are currently on staff at our school. And there are examples at other schools. The late Mr. Jaime Escalante, a pro I never had the honor of meeting, was the Hispanic calculus teacher in East Los Angles who taught an entire class of underprivileged minority students to succeed in AP calculus. In 1987, only four high schools in America had more students taking and passing AP calculus than did Mr. Escalante's school, Garfield High.

One of the truly great administrators of our day is Mr. Michael Beidel, the man who virtually built Trinity Christian School of Addison, Texas. (Mike is no longer at Trinity—in my opinion **that** board should be ashamed for letting him leave!) Mrs. Jody Capehart, former administrator of Legacy Christian School in Frisco, Texas is another leading administrator of today. In 2008, to the chagrin of many of her students and their parents, the board of trustees let her get away. In my opinion, they should join that Trinity board in the "Hall of Shame." I hope the entire nation is aware of the great accomplishments of Mr. Joe Clark, the African-American principal who did such an outstanding job of solving many of the problems of one of Chicago's troubled public schools. Have I proved my point that great teachers and administrators in the school business can come from any race or gender?

Also, I will use the term **administrator** to refer to the positions of president, superintendent, principal or headmaster. I am referring to the person who answers to the public or private school board of trustees, or to the church board of deacons or elders. These administrators have similar credentials and job descriptions, and all answer to a board. Our titles vary, but the problems we share are very similar.

That's enough. Let's get to the real stuff; as they say in Texas, "Let's ride."

Chapter 1

How I Made a School Year Seem Eternal—I Hired the Wrong Teacher

Let's have an informal discussion about staffing that will help you make the right hire, assist your teachers with personal needs, and fire those who <u>create</u> issues.

"Who on this staff approved the hiring of 'Mr. Smith'—ME, really?" I think that over the life of my career, I have hired enough of the wrong teachers to staff several schools. These are the teachers who had years of experience, a transcript that should be framed, an impressive professional appearance, and could teach a course that might be called "The Art of a Great Interview." The only weaknesses in their arsenal were that they were a little shy of common sense and emotional maturity, had various addictions—all the stuff that makes the headlines of newspapers, and that shows up **nowhere** on the application form, transcript, or in the interview. I'll refer to many of my small "hiring issues" throughout the book, as the political fallout from this lapse of judgment had implications that stretched from slightly irritated parents to lawsuits.

The success that any school enjoys depends on the hiring of almost perfect teachers, band directors, cheerleading and athletic coaches, drill team directors, etc. The administrator has to hire staff with the right credentials; that is required for accreditation. Further, let's assume he knows to hire staff members who are proficient in their academic area, are good communicators, have strong classroom management skills, are

not afraid of students or parents, have good personal hygiene (I hired a teacher one year who I really don't think owned a toothbrush), and knows how to dress for success. For me, I've learned the hard way that those attributes are the lowest common denominator—your students and parents expect and deserve more.

When hiring, I picture a large cone with holes at both ends. The large circular part is at the top. When an applicant enters, I picture him beginning at the large end. If he has credentials, he keeps moving. If I have a strong sense he loves the Lord and has strong morals and integrity, he keeps moving (in today's legal system, finding out those answers is a little dicey). If he has a proven work ethic, he keeps moving. If I think I would like for MY child to be one of his students, he keeps moving. If he has a nice appearance, he is almost home. Finally, if the school can afford him, he is offered the job, pending a background check. I placed having the academic credentials ahead of a relationship with the Lord not because of that implied priority, but because Liberty is accredited and the educational credentials have to be in place before the interview can even be scheduled. All of us realize that "good Christian character" is no longer a specific hiring criterion for public schools, but in America, our country's heritage demands that it should be, in my opinion.

For a good golfer, experiencing the club and ball connecting at just the right moment in just the right place on the club head happens regularly. Hitting the "sweet spot" in golf is the equivalent of having "teaching moments" to a teacher.

In the year 2000, Robert Redford directed the movie titled *Bagger Vance*. In this movie, Will Smith plays the part of a magical golf caddie who goes by the name of Bagger Vance. Bagger is the golf caddie for Matt Damon, who plays the part of a local World War II hero suffering from post-traumatic stress syndrome. His name is Captain Randolph Junuh, who before the war was a great golfer.

The scene is set for a golf exhibition match between the legendary Walter Hagen, Bobby Jones, and the local war hero "Capt." Junuh—the winner to take home $10,000! The purpose of the match is to raise money to save the financially strapped city of Savannah, Georgia that is trying to crawl out of the Great Depression.

Bagger Vance, the "teacher," is full of wisdom and encouragement that applies not only to golf, but to life, and for this illustration, the classroom. Despite all of the odds against beating the two world-renowned golfers, and trailing by two strokes on the final hole, Bagger will not let "Capt." Junuh give up. Bagger gives his "student" the vision, helps him select the right clubs, but also possesses the savvy to let "Capt." Junuh make wrong decisions. (I won't give away the ending; everyone needs to see this great movie.)

Good teachers are a lot like Bagger, and you have to spot them when you see them. This teacher is a rare find; "greatness" comes to mind, and "teaching moments" seem to be a part of his DNA. These characteristics can't be found on a college transcript. But maybe it is fair to say, when this applicant walks into your office, and you have a feeling he is smarter than you are, this just might be one of your franchise hires—and you need to make the job offer quickly, as these candidates are not on the market long. The teacher you are looking for could just as easily have majored in marketing, as he is indeed selling his subject (product) to a not-so-warm student (customer).

I've noticed that great teachers "move in." Not too long after they are hired and receive the keys to the building and their classroom, they have pictures of their family near their desk; the women might have a table in a corner with a lamp on it or a wall hanging. This is a characteristic that can't be observed during the interview, but when I see it while walking past their room, it makes me smile. This teacher makes her classroom "house" a "home."

A commonly used training method for continuing education is to film a master teacher in the classroom, then show that film to the school's teaching staff. A "master teacher" is a teacher that during the process of evaluation, a qualified evaluator reports, "I suggest this teacher not change a thing. He taught the full classtime, engaged his students, taught to all four quadrants of the classroom, had an excellent level of knowledge of the subject, followed his lesson plan, encouraged his students to ask questions"—you get the picture. Thus, a teacher can have a PhD and still not be a master teacher. One of the popular training theories is that when an average teacher observes a master teacher in action, he will then replicate those teaching techniques in his classroom.

Most great teachers are born with the "X Factor," or instinct. Observing real pros is a good tool, but great teachers will have already observed the "master teacher" on their own time, and the administrator probably never knew it.

Hiring excellent teachers, and that is what separates great schools from the rest of the pack, is a **skill** your administrator must possess. Administrators are going to make hiring mistakes, just like the software manager will hire ineffective salesmen—that is a given. There are many questions that will determine whether your administrator is the man for the job, but two of them are these: first, has he hired **many more** successful teachers than failures; and second, did he recognize his wrong hire quickly, take action, and help the ineffective teacher move on with his life.

Obviously, this is a question concerning your administrator's insight and courage, character traits that the board's search committee has to recognize when **they** make their **only** hire. It takes a very strong and unique administrator to face his hiring error and have the courage to take on the union, board, unhappy parents, and possibly a lawsuit. But the alternative is to leave a lazy or incompetent teacher in the classroom—maybe for years, and very sadly, that is too often the norm. And according to one study, it is also the primary reason that America's public schools' average 12th graders in 2008 were academically capable of outscoring **only** Lithuania, Cyprus, and South Africa.

Firing people will make some of your parents, students, and colleagues angry—a good administrator has to live with the understanding that he just cannot please everyone. The administrator has issues like unions and contracts to negotiate, but whether public or private, if you have to fire a staff member, you'd better have your documentation in order.

I suggest that the main rule in firing is **not** to give a defining reason for your decision on the day of the firing. You have had several discussions with him and have documented all of them with clear objectives, dates, and times; the teacher knows exactly why he is getting fired. **But the day you fire the staff member**, and I suggest it be on a Friday after school, the reason given should simply be, "It is just not a fit." And I strongly suggest that you make that day his last day on campus. (He will ask to "say good-bye" to his colleagues and students, and I suggest you not agree to that.) If you start giving specific reasons, you will dig yourself into a hole that will call for an attorney, and you will likely have to prove your case in court—you have the documentation, but don't have the time or money; plus, you never know what a jury will do.

Firing an employee is one of the hardest tasks that an administrator has, but in all my years I have only regretted firing one staff member—I rehired him the next year. I typically give an employee an opportunity to "resign," and that is to acknowledge that there is always the possibility that we could have done a better job of training, and I choose to err on the side of grace.

One preventative to this excruciating task is not to hire a teacher or staff member who has worked in five different schools in ten years—the odds of your school being the one that makes for a good partnership are against you. Another way to avoid this is to go two or three deep in calling the applicant's references. They are going to give you names of references, usually "upon request." After you speak to the references, ask them if they happen to know another person who might know their friend—you are now looking for references **not on the list**. I have to confess that this has been one of my weaknesses, and if I had taken my own advice, I would have avoided some painful experiences.

Firing the teacher who is lazy, not effective, shows films in class too often, gives too many "study halls," doesn't return graded papers to his students in a timely fashion or enter grades promptly or attend mandatory staff meetings, has too many absences and/or is late to work, is unapproachable to students or parents, does not respond to parents' inquiries quickly, is based on good reasons to take that step. To be a good teacher takes a lot of work, and the teaching field is full of certified teachers who just don't have the work ethic to handle the load and the pressure.

One year I had a classroom teacher who would not return parents' phone calls. After several warnings, I had my exit meeting with him, and he said, while crying and pointing to the telephone on my desk, "I hate that thing!" Life would have been much easier for both of us if he had told me that before the school year started, and allowed **me** to help him return his phone calls; I would have, because otherwise he was a great teacher. But in all reality, his fear of parents had "poisoned the well"; there was a total meltdown of parental confidence, and he had to leave. Firing the ineffective teacher will be no surprise to your great teachers and staff, but it is definitely a two-edged sword. It will improve morale on one hand, and create a low level of fear and insecurity on the other, but that, as they say is "part of the territory."

I have an unwritten balance of scale regarding my heart for our staff. I am very vocal about my praise and trust of them, and will tell anyone who will sit still for a moment that I can be a good president, but without **their** greatness, I fail. I am their biggest advocate, and will do anything within my power to help them.

For example, in our school we have a staff Benevolence Fund. It is a tax-deductible contribution for staff members who want to participate, and with their permission, the amount they choose to donate can be deducted from their monthly check. The amount of deduction varies, but I would estimate the individual donations range from $10 to $25 per month. If staff members have a financial need, they know they can come to me, and I have independent discretion to issue them a check. I realize the huge trust placed in my judgment, and I would never consider violating the trust of the staff I love. There is no committee, no proof of need, just a humble teacher "between a rock and a hard place"—they have the check in fifteen minutes.

The Benevolence Fund program is "on the books," and the receiving and giving of funds is part of our annual financial audit. It is there for all to see. The only part that would not be found through an examination of the audit is the **names** of the recipients. A very important issue for this program's integrity is that neither I, nor any member of my family, have ever received money from this fund. It has been used it to pay for food, a rebuilt transmission, past due utility bills, mortgage payments that are in arrears, family counseling, etc. I told of this fund to one of my public school colleagues and he said, "I need that very badly. Just the other day, one of my teachers needed money because one of his students had run out of diapers for her baby." While the purpose of the fund is for teachers and staff, there are those times when an administrator has to have the flexibility to use this fund to meet an even higher cause—that of helping a student who has nowhere else to turn for help.

Not all of our staff participates in giving to the fund, but that does not determine whether or not they can ask for and receive assistance. My role is to help them through the process without their feeling embarrassed. My sincere attitude is that I know they do not want to ask for help, and I make every attempt to help them with an empathic heart.

Administrators of public and private schools can, from time to time, have the same financial needs as do teachers. The board of the school should be sensitive to that and include in the budget a benevolence fund for their discretionary use to help their administrators. It does not need a large balance, and it doesn't need to grow. This program should work through a very approachable board member, but not be discussed at a board meeting. The amount spent must be part of the financial audit, but otherwise kept confidential. The same principle must hold for this fund—it must **never** serve for the benefit of board members. No "Board Educational Enrichment" trips must ever come from this fund!

A related issue is the use of school credit cards. Our credit cards are held by the business manager and/or her assistant, and they are only given for a specific purpose. If staff members use one, they turn in the receipt in a timely manner.

Chapter 2

"What Foxhole?"

Let's take a chapter to discuss some of the toughest trials that face administrators.

There are so many reasons to "throw in the towel" in the administration of your school that it staggers the imagination. If you are an administrator, the old adage that it is lonely at the top doesn't even come close. At least in the business world, the top position is typically associated with the comfort of a load of money and/or stock options.

For administrators, the fight always seems to come from very well-meaning board members, teachers, and parents. They are supposed to be in the foxhole with us, but instead are on the sidelines making "suggestions." The support we do have is very quiet, from people who don't want to get involved, and thus don't really have a place at the table. They are satisfied to remain a part of the "silent majority."

An administrator is constantly fighting wolves who are after his head, sometimes with only the quiet support of his teammates whispering, "Get in there, Rodney; don't quit now, you can win this fight," or "I'll be praying for you, Bro." If you are the board member or parent who is the exception, and are standing with your administrator, I can't begin to tell you of your great value to him and to the institution that will hopefully outlive you both.

In the early years of building our school, we were past due on almost every bill. (The only category we have never been late on is payroll.) I remember one year we were over sixty days late on paying our utility bill.

I humbly drove to the utility office and pleaded with them not to turn off our service. I wanted desperately to make a phone call rather than go down in person—that was one long drive. I promised them we would pay them in full; we just needed some time. They granted us the needed time.

Within the same week, a strong wind blew a dormer window off the roof of our main building. Augie Zimmerman was, and still is, a man on staff who can fix anything. The bid for repair from the roofing company was $12,000, but Augie said he could repair it for $2,000. In my mind, the check from the insurance company would provide the needed funds to repair the roof, pay the past due utility bill, and pay two of our past due mortgage payments. The problem was that the insurance check arrived, made payable to Liberty **and** to our bank. The bank took all the money. Our plan was to pay the entire utility bill, and catch up on half of the past due mortgage, but the bank would not co-endorse the check unless they got it all. The heartbreaking thing for me was that the banker was one of our parents, and his wife worked at the school.

As the leader, you may have the blood of your own broken heart all over you, and yet there is a force within that just can't or won't give up. Your supporters don't mean to be unsupportive, and your enemies don't mean to do you such harm. But at the end of many days, I found myself very alone and wanting to forget that I ever got involved in the school business. Many of those days ended with self talk like "Rodney, what in the world were you thinking?" But those thoughts were and are quickly followed by, "What would the lives of the thousands of kids and their parents be without Liberty?"

The early years of building any successful organization like a school, company, deli, etc. are the same; there is someone who had to have the heart not to give up. The answer to the questions: "Why do we need this in our life?" and "Why not call in the dogs; you tried and gave it your best, but the hunt is over," is this: "It's not ever going to be over. We just can't give up— not sure why." In my case, I really don't want to—I honestly believe I have been called. I battle every day, and while the battles can be very tough, the payoff is huge. I hope you agree with me, because I know that great public and private schools built on strong foundations of servant leadership have multi-generational value.

The life and experiences of the crucial beginnings of a top quality school are unbelievably challenging. The visionary will have to fight "in the foxholes." Most likely, when he moved from teaching to administration, or in my case, from the field of business to education, he didn't even know there **were** any foxholes. The "foxholes" are miserable, lonely places, and hardly anybody knows about them ahead of time. A couple of my own experiences will give you a clear picture of what I am talking about, but more importantly, will let you know you are not alone.

One year I hired an art teacher who I later learned was bipolar, and was taking the drug Prozac. I assumed it was prescribed, but now have had a chance to reflect, and am not sure. If prescribed, I think her dosage may have been a little too weak or strong, and here's why. I fired her in May, the last day of the school year. The first day before school started the **next** school year, in late August, she came on campus in the wee hours of the morning, and wrote on one of the main doors of the school in a heavy black ink the worst profanity you can imagine. About 7:00 a.m. of that first day, one of my wonderful teachers sensitively asked me,

"Rodney, have you seen what is written on the south door?" Obviously I had not. My wonderful first school day experience that year was immediately destroyed. With sandpaper applied to our beautiful oak door, I got enough of the ink off that no one could read the words. I could have called our maintenance staff, but honestly I was embarrassed and didn't want anyone else to see it.

By the way, I discovered that art teachers can be, actually good ones almost always are, a little "different," but different in a good and creative way. The key in hiring a great art teacher is simple; you are looking for a good artist who is fun and has charisma—the kids just like being around him. Art teachers are typically not too concerned with classroom management, but kids who choose art as an elective tend to be focused because they love to draw or paint, so don't lose sleep over the minor classroom non-control issue. If you make the right hire, just enjoy the product that magically comes from a little "controlled chaos." This hiring approach actually applies to almost the entire fine arts department. My advice? Make the right hires, loosen up, and enjoy the show. The fine arts department at Liberty adds a rich dimension to our program.

Foxhole experience: a few days after a board meeting, one of our members, let's just call him "Doug," sent me a letter saying, "Rodney, you make me so mad I could spit." He had a friend who also served on the board; let's just call him "Fred." I remember him slamming his fist on the desk during a board meeting, saying in a loud voice, "We have to quit spending money!" Both of these men were **invited** to be on our board, and I believe had the best of intentions. But to explain what their harsh and, in my opinion, hurtful words did to my soul would be impossible to articulate.

I think "Doug" perceived a clear violation of what he wanted me to do that I refused to do. In my opinion, he was a control freak, and none of us can do our jobs of having the responsibility without also having the authority. I understand that "Fred" wanted to run our school in a way that I would describe as "on the cheap," but he might have described his strategies as "fiscally responsible." My point is that when you start a school, or move vertically from teaching to administration, you can expect the bullets to fly from within the camp, and that surprised me.

With regard to board members, this scenario plays out very understandably. A guy is invited to be on the board of a private school, or has enough votes to get elected to the board of a public school. He leaves the parking lot of the company he built or runs, and drives into the school parking lot with the same dominant Type A personality for the school board meeting. His mantra has always been, "If you want a job done right, you have to do it yourself," or "I have been elected to fix this place, and that is exactly what I intend to do." The administrator who has the responsibility to actually run the school is rarely a member of the board, and thus doesn't have a vote. By the way, I wonder how long "Doug" or "Fred" would work for a company organized and run that way.

I have learned that if a school is to be successful, there are some basic tenets that must be in the very core of the school's heart—and every school has an identifiable heart. Some are dark, while others are light, but they all have a heart. Some describe it as a culture, but that word smacks of permanence, and the heart of a school is delicate and needs constant attention because it is always changing and evolving. The wrong board can take a school down quickly, and a good board can bring it up—the going up takes a lot longer. A "dark" school has board members who don't understand their highest, best use; a good one has a board full of servant leaders—that makes them heroes in a short period of time. (A dark school also has teachers who spend time gossiping, yelling at their students, always seem to be complaining—and rarely smile.)

A school with a discernable "light" heart is full of heroes. For example, in November of 2009, our preschool director, Mrs. Anna Joyner, had a problem: it was too muddy and rainy for our three- and four-year olds to go outside to play. This is a huge problem if you are three- and four-year olds. I was coming out of a luncheon meeting in Dallas, and a parent of a preschooler called me and said, "Dr. Haire, did you know that Mrs. Joyner allowed the kids to run races in the long hallway of our preschool building?" Before I could tell him that I hadn't heard that, he said "The kids had a great time. My daughter was still laughing when she got in the car this afternoon. Just calling to tell you we love Liberty!!" Doesn't that say so much?

Every board member of your school has to understand that one of his informal responsibilies, while not written in the policy manual, is to **encourage** the administrator. This "not up for discussion" unwritten policy is to make sure the administrator stays mentally confident of board support and has plenty of ammunition for the battles he fights daily that board members know little about. He must know he is not alone, that **every** board member is his ally who, Biblically speaking, "sticketh closer than a brother." Every successful school administrator has to know that the board "has his back." The board has the responsibility to serve the community, but the oversight of their administrator must be done with civility and sensitivity, otherwise they have hurt the community by weakening the confidence and morale of one of their most important players.

In my experience, another primary key to winning the battle is to hire principals and vice principals who are loyal, brave, bright, and possess great communication skills. At the end of the day, the administration team consists of men and women in whom you have complete confidence. At Liberty these administrators are not only competent, they are my friends; and I show and tell them in as many ways as I can that I am their friend, that they are very highly valued, and that I have **their** back. Sometimes I send them an encouraging e-mail and copy all board members. Occasionally I take them out for a nice dinner. (Note to self: "Do both more often.") But more importantly, I give them well deserved public kudos—they are indispensable.

When Liberty opened its doors to the community in 1983, we had little money. In those early years, our teachers earned about half of what they could have earned in the public schools. And rather than a generous budget for classroom décor, our teachers had a $25 per year allowance to decorate their rooms. To encourage our teaching staff, I wrote brief Post-It Notes telling them how valuable they were and that I hoped they had a great day, and put them on their desks before they arrived for school. Even to this day, I tell them that if a parent gets in their face, to nicely say, "Dr. Haire prefers that this level of conversation take place in his office, so please make an appointment with him through his assistant. It has been so nice talking to you." You really can't pay great teachers what they are worth, but you can show them what they mean to you and to your school family through your support, and that has immeasurable value to them and to the majority of families.

And I believe that administrators have an unspoken bond of support between each other that says, "I know you have a very difficult job, and I am your friend." It applies to administrators who don't even know each other. A few years ago, I was contacted by the board chairman of a private school in North Dallas. He wanted me to assist their board in finding a headmaster for their school. I told him I would not do that because I knew that their board had controlled and micro-managed their former headmaster, a talented man who was my friend. I would never send a colleague of mine into that "no-win" situation. He assured me that the board had experienced a mindset change, but I didn't buy it. Last I heard, they were still looking—word gets out.

For those board members who I hope are reading this, while looking for your third administrator in five years, this book, my discouraged board member friend, is for you. If you are the disheartened school administrator, I hope this book encourages you. If you are a dedicated and loving teacher, I hope you know that your students may forget your great teaching moments, but they will always remember **you**. And if you are a parent, this book is going to show you how you can help build a school that will prepare your child to be a success in life—not just in college.

Chapter 3

"The Deacons Did What??"

I think an open and transparent view of potential challenges that a church/school partnership could face would be worthwhile.

For those running schools, there are some issues with which we must deal and over which we have very little control. These challenges will, and do every day, break our hearts. Some of the decisions that boards make for administrators to follow often do serious damage to the morale of the school's leadership. Because of the way our public and private schools are governed and operated, a slippery slope to tragedy looms. There are a few setups that almost always guarantee an overall school performance grade of a "C-," and actually that if the grade is "on the curve."

In public and private schools, the most influential players in the school district are the members of the board. They hire the administrators, principals, vice principals, business managers, directors of transportation, athletic directors, and, in some districts, the guidance counselors. They may even have a committee that approves **all** hires, and that would of course include all teachers, possibly even para-professionals and teaching assistants. This often depends on the size of the district or school, and the traditional and local culture; but sometimes we are talking about the size of the board's ego (couched in the "makes no sense" and outdated policy manual).

Maybe there was a good reason that a former board wrote an amendment to the policy manual that served the school well. For example, "fifteen years" ago, the school may have had an administrator who made the life of the teachers very difficult. He may have even been verbally abusive. To make sure that never happened again, the board wrote an amendment to the by-laws that gave them total hiring and firing authority. But after the board fired the poorly performing administrator and replaced him with a great one, they never removed the hiring policy from their by-laws, nor did they change their way of doing business. And so, by tradition and supported by the by-laws, the board will probably over-manage their really good administrator that they worked hard to screen and hire. My advice: amend the by-laws ASAP.

Most boards, public and private, have strong personalities in abundance, so overstepping the boundaries via micro-managing a good administrator is really very common. I want to share with you some of those stories that you will have a hard time believing. In fact, you are probably going to think I'm "smoking something," or "sharing" with my former art teacher.

There is a private school in a nice little town in Oklahoma. The school is sponsored by a Baptist church, but it could have been any denomination in any town or state. On a beautiful Sunday morning, Sunday School attendance hit a record high, and a large classroom was needed for their adult Sunday School class. The pastor, being the Type A personality that most are, has a great idea: he simply calls his deacons together, and faster than you can say, "The school librarian quit," they empty the school library into the hall to make room for the needed Sunday School classroom. The school's administrator walks in on

Monday morning to find the library stacked in the hall, in random order, and the school librarian "in a puddle of tears."

We all know that in almost every school there are parents who love the library (now referred to as a Media Center), and it is for their love of this cherished place that they donate their energy, time, and, in some cases, money. Jesus was of course correct when He said, "Where your treasure is, there is your heart also"; thus the supporters of the school's library had given of their heart and money. The librarian, her assistants, and their volunteer staff (now a SWAT TEAM after the pastor), consider **their** library to have been violated, actually raided.

Of course the problem doesn't stop there. All of those dedicated staff members and parents have friends who love the librarian and deeply appreciate her sacrificial labor in making the school library a site where young minds are encouraged and empowered to do great things. By Monday at "High Noon," a band of brothers evolves whose sole purpose is to "take out" the pastor; the only question is "how and when." Every English and social studies teacher I know loves the librarian, who is always so helpful to have the right books on the shelves at the right time. By the time dinner is served at home on Monday evening, the topic of conversation is centered on "What are we going to do with that power-crazed pastor and his band of renegades that he calls deacons?"

By the way, hiring the perfect librarian is a tough assignment. You are looking for a person with great communication skills—a lifelong learner who loves books, but loves people more. Your librarian has to have the confidence of every one of your teachers. She is a person in whom teachers can trust, and if she is emotionally mature, I suggest giving her the authority to hire her own staff, determine when to have book fairs, etc. If you make the right hire, your main responsibility as her administrator is to stay out of her way. And a word to board members: if you talk to the librarian, it should be words of praise and encouragement, or to check out a book. (On a personal note: Mrs. Lacy, our entire staff really loves and appreciates you more than you can imagine.)

Did the pastor intend to hurt anyone's feelings? Of course not. Did he make a galactic mistake? Of course he did. He apologized profusely, humbled himself, helped move the library back into place, and did his very best to get everything right with the world. But two things are true. First, you can't unring a bell; and second, the next error in judgment is just around the corner, when it is time to plan next year's school calendar. I can guarantee that the church and school are going to schedule the use of the school auditorium/church sanctuary at the same time and the same day sometime next year.

If nobody steps in with mature leadership, the relationship between the church and school will continue to flow downhill. It's going to take a humble pastor and a forgiving administrator who had better come together fast. When predictable "issues" surface between the supporters of the school and the church and are not quickly resolved, and the operative word here is **quickly**, it will only get worse. I had a great friend who often said, "Rodney, when you have a problem, it's like a burr under the saddle blanket on your horse—it will only get worse if you don't get it out."

There is a private Christian school in California that is a ministry of a large church. The church is so paranoid concerning the school's use of the church equipment that the church charges the school a rental fee for everything, even chairs for school events. A small issue surfaced when the school had its Christmas play in the church auditorium. The school's music director had invited the entire church congregation; he wanted all to be blessed. At the end of the Christmas program, the school administrator needed to take a special offering to pay the church for the rental of their chairs. The church started the school as a ministry, but all too often, the congregation never completely understands that, or more practically, over time, forgets that commitment. When several hundred kids start using their "stuff," it's going to get used up. On this holiday night of bliss, the tuition-paying parents of the students were asking, "The tuition we pay doesn't include the use of chairs?"

There is a church/school relationship in North Texas in which the pastor greatly resented the students' use of the sanctuary for assemblies. The sanctuary was the only large room on the property, so the administrator really had no alternative place for a school assembly. The church started the school as a ministry, the pastor's daughter was a member of the student body, and at first, all went beautifully. The problem arose when the kids started going to assembly in the sanctuary with mud on their shoes. The pastor went to the administrator, telling him to do something about the mud. Now can I ask a question that I hope is on everybody's mind: "What in the world is the administrator supposed to do?" Does the pastor complain when the members of the church attend Sunday morning services with mud on their shoes? My advice to the pastor is to encourage the administrator by grabbing a mop and broom.

I have seen some great church/school relationships. The school serves the genuine need of the parents in the community, some of whom are church members and some who are not. It can serve as a great outreach for churches to meet and serve the needs of families who may not have a church home. The issue is that it must be a united goal in the **heart** of the leadership of the church and school.

My first year in the school business was a "trial run." It was 1982 and the pastor and I were great friends. We were both young and knew nothing about the school business, but we had the wonderful idea to start a Christian school in Denton, Texas that had a population of about 60,000 and, we believed, was in need of one.

I was running my own companies, was 38 years of age, impetuous, and thought I could do just about anything. My wife and I had two children, and we wanted them in a great Christian school. The partnership between the pastor and me seemed to be a natural fit. Very soon the idea took on a life of its own. He and his wife had a young daughter, and they wanted the same for her as we wanted for our children. I had the business savvy, and the pastor had the facility and about eleven acres. While it was futuristic, the basic theme of the movie *Field of Dreams*, "If you build it, they will come" fit our mentality perfectly.

Unfortunately, there was a little factor called the church deacon board, that neither the pastor nor I saw as a problem. The board approved the construction of the modest 5,000 square foot classroom building, but truthfully were so respectful of their pastor that they would agree to virtually anything he wanted.

The church had enough land and money in the bank, so we started "turning dirt." I began interviewing and hiring teachers and coaches, researching curriculum, visiting other schools, and learning on a "straight up" curve how to operate a school.

Some leaders in the educational arena that I interviewed were helpful. I also met some public and private school administrators who should never have been promoted beyond a teaching assistant. In retrospect, I think those administrators from which I sought advice who withheld it, really didn't think that anyone could actually **start** a school, and thus were afraid to get too involved. At the time, their response was very frustrating; now I understand the pervasive lack of courage of too many administrators.

I was a young entrepreneur who thought that building a school had to be a relatively easy project. I was accustomed to making decisions daily that moved thousands of dollars, I loved to multi-task, and I felt that we were going to have a great school in record time.

We worked with a good commercial construction company in charge of building the classroom building. One day, a decision had to be made regarding laying a gas line to the science lab classroom from the church main building. The general contractor called me, and I independently gave him the go ahead; in that same conversation, he asked me if I was sure I wanted him to do that without board approval. I responded, "Of course. You can't have a science lab without a source of gas." He told me he would do it, but I now remember the hesitation in his voice. It was some foreign sound of warning that I was not accustomed to hearing. The cost of running the line was, in 1982 just **$1,000**, and I believed that making that decision was just being a good leader, and was frankly a "no brainer."

What happened next was just short of catastrophic. I didn't realize that the pastor ran everything in the church **but the money**. The money strings were controlled by what was informally (meaning "off the record") an "executive board" that I didn't even know existed—I'm not sure it did until the gas line invoice came through the accounting department of the church. When they discovered that I had spent $1,000 of the church's money without asking for **their** permission, they called an emergency board meeting. The purpose was not to alter my decision to lay the gas line, it was to alter my authority to spend money or make any really relevant decisions whatsoever without their permission. The guys who made up this executive committee were my friends and I respected both of them. The fact that I was getting butchered seemed very surreal.

One of the members of the executive committee came to the quickly-called, beautiful summer evening meeting with an organizational chart for the church/school, and it was one that I don't believe the pastor had ever seen; I know I hadn't. The chart had several levels of authority, but the interesting thing for me was not the position at the top, which was the board of deacons, as it should have been. Second in command was the pastor, then the music director, followed by the secretary, the janitor, **and finally, the administrator of the school**. I was at the bottom of the chart, just below the janitor—and at that time the church didn't actually have a janitor. That placed my position just under a guy who didn't exist! I didn't know that was even possible. These two guys gave "down under" a whole new meaning.

And not only was I demoted off the organizational chart—my wife and I were volunteers. My days consisted of running the school from 7:00 a.m., eating lunch in my car, and running my business in Dallas from 1:00 p.m. until I finished.

They wanted to make certain that I was formally put in my place. I must admit, if they had been dealing with a different person, they would have done an excellent job of discouraging him. In my world at that time, I really didn't care what they thought or what their chart looked like. Today, I admit to you that my attitude was wrong. I lacked an understanding of church governance, but I was young, and the word no was not in my vocabulary. Frankly, I saw it as a wasted night.

What my deacon friends didn't know was that in my business, I was working with thirty-three different Jews, all owners of large manufacturing plants. If you want to know who does a really good job at intimidation, I personally believe the Jews have a corner on that strategy. (In truth, I believe that Jews are just smarter than the rest of us, because they came from the lineage of Jesus, although they would probably disagree about the origin of their intelligence.) These two Gentiles were not even close to equaling the intimidation tactics with which I dealt every day. By my standards, they were amateurs. Strangely, I left their special little meeting with more confidence and determination than ever.

This type of approach to a simple communication issue is so very common in schools, but particularly when a school is associated with a church. It would have been so much better for one of them to call me and explain that the by-laws, or their tradition, required board approval for me to spend money. I would have understood that style to be a bit micro-managing, but would have accepted it. In my opinion, their fear and need to control me ruled the day.

Strangely, I was not the least bit offended. Judy and I left the meeting and had a pancake dinner at Denny's. I felt if that was my place in the "pecking order," and it clearly was, then I would build the school from the bottom up—literally.

There are some events in our lives where we remember everything perfectly: time, place, mood, etc. I remember the next event as if it were yesterday. I was in the hall of the home where the meeting was held, and the pastor, almost in tears, said to me, "Rodney, I am so sorry." I answered, "If you want me to be the janitor, I'll be the janitor. I just want a Christian school for my kids." Of course, based on the organizational chart, the job of janitor would have been a celebratory promotion, but that chart had nothing to do with anything. It was a sign of terrible things to come, but I never saw that chart again, and, honestly, never thought about it until I began reeling in the memories for this book.

These men were good and decent gentlemen, as I think many board members are. I completely understood the arrangement, but unfortunately it was **after** we had begun the school. In March of 1983, I resigned and let them run the school. It is a very common error that men and women don't know the informal questions to ask before becoming the administrator. I certainly didn't.

In 1983, the very next school year, I started another school with another church. I had learned the questions to ask. I was so much wiser for the year I had experienced. I will be forever grateful for **that** board meeting and the many lessons of those experiences, even though God often heard my prayer go something like, "Lord, how could You have done this to me??"

MAIN ENTRANCE OF OUR FIRST CAMPUS

The truth about that whole first year's experience at the church is that I gained a great education in the field of board politics that no formal course in education offers. I learned to look for signs and ask the soft questions that spell victory or defeat. I learned about the terrible effects that a board's ego can have on a school administrator, and those that the haughty attitude of an administrator can have on a board. Partnerships are difficult, no matter who the players are. I learned about power players who really mean to do well, but somehow can't seem to connect their power with the achievement of a desired goal. I learned the enormous value of having trust between the board and the administrator, and of having a humble heart, so commonly absent in both. These principles of attitude apply to both public and private schools, and they are crucial.

In November of 1983, I made the decision to sell my companies and pour all of my efforts into building the best Christian private school my wife and I could build. The opportunity came to me in a very surreal set of circumstances. My company was not on the market, but Mr. Walter Prindle (a complete stranger) walked into the foyer of my office building and asked to speak to the owner. Long story short, I sold him the company—buildings, lawnmowers, and brooms. As of 2010, the company continues to grow and prosper.

Chapter 4

DON'T FORGET TO …

I originally had this chapter at the end of the book. My good friend and author, professor, and counselor Dr. James Kitchens said, "You shouldn't make the reader wait until the end of the book to read this chapter." I hope you agree.

I want to go a little crazy, and tell you in random order thirteen principles that my years have taught me in running a school. These will be of help to the public school superintendent, as well as to the private school president or headmaster.

1. Don't get pushed around. You have the position, the degrees, and the experience, so stand your ground and insist on having the authority to hire and fire all staff members—no exceptions. Outdated by-laws go or get rewritten. Get this in writing before you accept the offer.

2. Don't ever hire an administrator or teacher if your instincts tell you it is a bad idea.

3. To private school administrators: always charge the amount of tuition that it costs to operate. If it is above the amount some of your families can pay, put a financial aid program in place, but don't give your services away.

4. Never allow your staff to gossip. If they do, I believe you should fire them. You may have to teach their class for a couple of weeks, but that is better than having a negative staff member who is

independently destroying morale—doesn't matter if they intended to or not. Gossip is poison.

5. If a group of parents have a complaint, meet with only one family at a time. If a group meeting is allowed, the issue will likely become irrational; if you have a group of parents together, it will turn into a "piling-on session" and constructive ideas will be nowhere in sight. If the meeting is for praise or appreciation, the likelihood of which is unfortunately all too rare, then meet with as many as want to come—have it in the auditorium if needed.

6. Don't get too friendly with your staff or parents too quickly. It is lonely at the top for a reason. You may have to expel a friend's child or fire your best friend; the latter happened to me in the spring of 2008. Don't be afraid to do either; strong leaders don't have a choice as to whether or not to make tough decisions.

7. If you plan to fire a staff member, find his replacement first. The only exception to this suggestion is if you feel impelled to fire a teacher suddenly and unexpectedly.

8. Expect your staff to support your policies. Once you have policies in place, expect them to be followed and check to see if they are. Don't EXPECT what you are not willing to INSPECT.

9. Evaluate your teachers unannounced, especially the new staff members. Don't be a bully or have an "attitude," but this is an important part of your responsibilities. Good teachers love to be evaluated. They are proud of their performance and want you to observe it.

10. If you are in a private school, fundraising is very important—embrace it. You have to remember, the money is not for you, it is

for their children and your students. Realize that some of your wealthiest families are not going to give—not ever. Jesus said, "It is harder for a camel to pass through the eye of a needle than for a rich man to enter the kingdom of heaven." Don't let the wealthy families who don't give make you bitter or sad; they are the losers of the blessing that attends givers.

11. Appoint responsible staff members to turn out all the lights and unplug the coffee-makers; over years, you will save enough to buy a bus.
12. Don't take anything personally, because nobody understands or has a clue as to the challenges you face daily.
13. Always dress for success. Buy your clothes at the best store you can afford; you only get one chance at a first impression.

As your school develops and matures, if you will follow the above suggestions, you will build a great school. During that process, there are going to be some wonderful stories that belong to posterity.

A few years ago, I heard Dr. Jack Hayford, a gifted preacher from Van Nuys, California, refer to the beginnings of his church as "tribal stories." He was referring to the very hard times and blessings that any successful organization experiences that should never be forgotten.

In 2008, I told Liberty's tribal stories to my staff of approximately 200, and they loved hearing them. I told them of the wonderful people, using their real names, that many of them knew personally; the staff had no idea of the sacrifices they had made. For my own therapy, I also told of the "trouble makers."

Chapter 5

Who Is Running the School??

Let's identify some important programs and personnel that are needed for any school to be effective—this chapter is a little "out of the box," as are most of them.

Liberty Christian School began in Denton, Texas, a city approximately 30 miles north of Dallas. The community would classify itself as a college town, and there was a need for a solid academic experience in a Christian environment for students in preschool through twelfth grade.

As is so commonly the case, what is offered in most communities the size of Denton is a public school system, possibly one college preparatory private school, and a homeschool association. The nation's public school system had been adequate in previous generations, but since the early 1960s, public schools began to struggle under the weight of state and federal mandates, including, some would argue, the mandatory removal of prayer. In truth, the public schools that previous generations enjoyed prior to the 1970s no longer exist—they are gone.

Many parents want their public school to meet their child's educational needs for two reasons: first, they are paying for it in their school taxes, and secondly, their own public school experiences were a source of many wonderful memories. Public schools now **adequately** serve only a small portion of our country's school children. Specifically, if your child is in Advanced Placement courses, he may receive an adequate education. Another sector of academic needs are somewhat met on the opposite end of the educational spectrum, those children needing the services of the Special Education Department. But according to many public school teachers across our nation, even those two limited successes are achieved in an atmosphere often described as chaotic, dangerous, and morally bankrupt. There are thousands of great teachers and administrators in our public schools; they are not the problem.

Many of the families who moved to North Texas from another town or state had their children in a private school in the town **from** which they transferred. They thought their children would have a good public school experience because our community was smaller. They hoped to be able to save the tuition costs and have their children receive the same quality of education they had experienced in the private school they had previously attended. However, that has not been the experience of the vast majority. In the current public school environment, it is not possible for a public school to compete with a **quality** private school—if there are exceptions, I have not seen them. Public schools will be able to win in some athletic competitions because they have more students. Their choir and band **may** sound better because the number of students will naturally offer a fuller sound.

That being said, this relatively new and sad phenomenon of limited achievement is primarily the result of two factors: **the underperforming teacher or administrator being allowed to stay because of contracts and unions; and good teachers not being able to control their students' behavior in the classroom or halls for lack of support from administrators.**

Teachers, no matter how effective they are at their profession, cannot teach in an atmosphere where students are not respectful of classroom rules, and that is inevitable when there is an absence of strong administrative support. To my administrator colleagues, the great teachers on your staff **need your support** to be able to do their job. They can't do theirs if you don't do yours.

Further, it has been my observation that the parents of the **disruptive** child choose to defend their child rather than support the teacher or administration because they have no other school option for their out-of-control child. Most families can't afford a boarding school that teaches students the fundamentals of good behavior and solid academics—the cost for most of those schools is currently north of $25,000 per year. The local private school will not accept their child if he has a history of discipline problems, so the parents are defensive at best, or hire defense lawyers at worst. Obviously, the answer is for the parent to be the "parent," and not the enabler or "buddy." Regardless of the cause of the child's dysfunctional behavior, given the absence of support for the teacher or the administrator to discipline a misbehaving student, classroom chaos and demoralized teachers are predictable outcomes. Currently, teacher turnover rate in many schools is above 30 percent.

In July of 2009, I interviewed an applicant for a teaching position who had taught fourth grade in a "blue ribbon" public school from a town north of Dallas. She had been asked to return, and had high evaluations from her administrator—I read them. When I asked her why she would choose to resign, she told me a very sad story. She said that regularly a student or students "thought it was cute" to get out of their desks and roll around on the floor. She would immediately send them to the office, and the administrator returned them to class without having been disciplined. At the end of the year, she said, "I don't know if my kids learned much of anything. I am a good teacher, but spent the majority of my time trying to get my students under control." In a classroom with one child that is a constant behavioral problem, that child becomes a majority—ask any teacher.

I found out very quickly that the demand and market is for a school that is much like the public schools of former generations. Parents visit my office to inquire about Liberty, and have a few very pertinent and common questions. First let me tell you that many of the parents believe they should not have to pay school taxes and also pay the tuition of a private school. A few are not really interested that we are a Christian school, although most of those families greatly value that aspect of our school after a brief time.

The parents simply want a school atmosphere conducive to learning, where students of all ages are respectful to teachers and administrators, and where their children are physically safe. A member of our first board of trustees, Mr. Ed Johnson, told me that the future of private schools was secure because parents would want a safe place for their children to learn. At the time, I thought his opinion was a little paranoid, but he proved me wrong.

And parents want a school that is **not** so highly populated. They want enough students to support solid programs that interest their child, but not so many students that it is impossible for their child to "surface" and have an opportunity to perform in a play or get playing time on a team.

Parents want a school that is clean and orderly. They expect a school that has enough textbooks for their child to have one for each subject. They expect the teacher to know more about the subject than their child knows. Most schools have teachers who coach, but in the interview process of hiring a teacher/coach, I suggest being very clear that the coaching assignment **not** take precedence over their classroom responsibilities. The community in general believes that coaches are categorically poor classroom teachers. In my experience, that has not been true. Some of our best teachers are coaches. They are not only bright, but are motivators. Liberty gives raises to good teachers; if they also happen to be a good coach, everyone wins. Coaches can lose their job at Liberty if they fail to perform in the classroom, not because they lost the big game. I don't deny that the school community wants a coach that wins. My point is that the administrator is responsible to "keep the main thing the main thing," and that can be established at the teacher/coach interview. Liberty's varsity basketball coach for many years was Richard Scofield. Coach Scofield won state championships and was also a great geometry teacher. Coach Scofield went home to be with the Lord in March of 2010. We miss him so much.

Parents expect their child to have homework; not hours and hours of it, but enough to prepare them for the next grade or college. And parents don't want homework to be busy work. The purpose of homework for foreign language, science, and math is to practice what they learned that day; for English and social studies it is to prepare for the next day's class discussion. We expect our teachers of grades 7-12 to assign approximately 20-25 minutes per subject per night of constructive and purposeful homework.

Some parents have children with learning disabilities; the correct term for that is "learning differences." Their child has been professionally diagnosed with a learning difference, and their former public or private school was ineffective in helping with their child's challenges. Most of the parents I meet believe that their former school was trying to help; but because of budget restraints, the lack of awareness of teacher training required, the scope of the problem, and the lack of good diagnostic tests, their child was not improving. And admittedly, working through this issue and producing an effective program is challenging and very expensive.

As I look back, for families with children with learning differences, Liberty Christian has addressed these special needs aggressively. Few schools are able or willing to tackle the great need of really "reaching" children who have learning challenges. This initiative is costly and demands more money than you think it will take, dedicated teachers who are very difficult to find, and continual teacher training. Being a school that really meets this need is very demanding, and I would warn any administrator or board considering adding this program to do careful due diligence. Liberty has taken on the challenge, funded the program, and hired a great leader; but the challenge to improve is always before us. What we know about children with learning differences is constantly expanding, and the challenge for any program designed to meet the needs of students with these issues is to stay on the heels of the newest technology and teaching strategies.

Most public schools have a program that is **average** in helping students with learning differences. Most private college prep schools have chosen not to engage the challenge, but there are private schools that specialize in the field of Special Education. The teacher/pupil ratio is very low; thus, a family can expect to pay a significantly higher tuition.

Regardless of the focus of the school's mission—whether public, private, Christian, secular or a school for children with learning differences, the challenge for all administrators or boards is to hire staff members who are indispensable. Parents should say about your school's teachers and coaches, "I can't believe how wonderful our school's teachers are—my child loves going to school!" Recently a mother told me that her first grader cried when she came to pick him up—he wasn't ready to leave school. That story is true, but isn't it sad that more children and their moms don't have days like that more often.

As important as teachers and coaches are to your school's success, there are some administration and operational personnel that are crucial. I am going to mention some very valuable positions for any school, but private schools may have to grow into some of them. I would use as **few** volunteers in the following positions as possible because these positions need to be staffed at all times.

The business office of your school has to be above reproach. I would not be an administrator of a school that did not have a yearly audit; that's just not smart. Some administrators and board members who are reading this book believe they cannot afford an audit, but I say not only can you **not** afford not to have one, but you had better get a good one. I would use a firm that has absolutely no connections to your school. Offer them a multi-year contract for an affordable price.

As of the fall of 2008, the Dallas Independent School District had a "shortfall" north of $84,000,000—a kind word for financial mismanagement. In my opinion, that tragedy would have been far less likely to occur with a good business office and an independent audit. The people in charge of your business office are indispensable, and this is clearly an efficiency **and** integrity issue. If you are the administrator of a public or private school, organizing a board committee in charge of finance is smart; most universities don't teach Education Administration majors a finance course **at the level** at which they are expected to perform. If there are no finance gurus on your board, don't be shy about recruiting good business minds to ensure that there is never any doubt as to the integrity of your finances. This financial team should give a report to the board at every meeting to inform them how the current operation expenses compare to the board-approved budget. When the numbers are off at a reasonable level, this is not the time to "pile on"; just amend the original budget or cut expenses (if the school is run efficiently, finding budget cuts should be very difficult).

My board gives me the freedom to use funds that were originally designated to be spent in a given department to be spent in another, if the students will benefit by a reallocation of budgeted funds. Further, they give me the freedom to not be concerned if I don't meet our budget "to the penny." They understand that running a budget is an art, not a science, and that the budget is a moving target. I am expected to come close to our projections and to inform them if we are going to miss our targeted budget by any significant amount. A good policy is for administrators not to surprise the board with a projected shortfall before the board has options to make adjustments. Administrators should not be burdened by the day-to-day operational finances, but have a bright business manager to oversee all transactions and advise the administrator of areas that need his attention. For Liberty, the person leading that team is Mrs. Melissa Masten. Both she and her team are extremely valuable.

All schools need someone who is technologically above every computer storm. We have two, David Martin and Tom Shiflet, and we would never consider beginning a year without them. They are great and loving communicators, and have the ability to help those of us who need tech assistance not to feel inadequate—mainly me. They have a great support staff surrounding them and are quick to give them credit for running a technologically advanced school.

In the last ten years, advising/counseling departments have grown to a place of tremendous value in both guidance for college and personal counseling. The counselors serve to assist families with emergency personal counseling when needed. Examples are the loss of a grandparent, a child's parents getting a divorce, the loss of a child's pet, or a child having a hard time making friends. At Liberty, Dee Quick, Toni King, Norm Parker, Tim Sanchez, and Tiffany Taylor have experience and emotional maturity, and they are some of the reasons that our re-enrollment rate is typically north of 95%.

A primary service of the academic advisors is to help our students prepare their college admission packets that will give them the best opportunity to enter the college of **their** choice. In July of 2008, our counseling department attended a summer seminar at Harvard University to gain cutting-edge knowledge of what is required for students to prepare themselves for entrance into our country's most prestigious universities. I suggest a budget line item for continual counseling training.

Another key person on your staff is the administrator's assistant. This person must be approachable, friendly, very bright, and able to anticipate the administrator's needs. In my opinion, an administrator has a partner in his assistant, not an employee. My assistant, Carmen Goodson, has a heart for our school, and that is invaluable to me. She controls my calendar, and I completely trust her judgment. But maybe her most important quality is that she has what corporate America would term a high likeability factor.

We have a friendly, competent receptionist at every major entrance: preschool, lower school, middle school, and upper school. Their primary responsibility is to make all visitors feel welcome and personally answer the phone—I am not a fan of electronic answering machines. I think people interested in your school, or concerned about their child, need to hear a live voice, not a menu, and the voice they hear needs to say to them that we are genuinely glad they called. They are inquiring about the most important beings in their life.

Another factor in running a successful school is that the campus will be more respected by the students and faculty and better maintained if it is aesthetically attractive. When budget is tight that goal is harder to accomplish, but the right person can make a metal building look like a beautiful home. The person who does that for Liberty is Kimberly Kevlin. She is a gifted interior designer, and her love for the school is apparent **everywhere**. If you are a public or private school and you have no budget for this staff person, I would organize a committee, and the chairperson ideally would have the financial capacity or contacts to fund whatever the committee determined your school needed. This project might include new paint, nice paintings or prints, sofas and end tables, etc. It is very crucial in achieving this goal that the committee have the authority to make decisions. Give this committee the project and then get out of their way.

THE COMMONS

Recently, I accepted an offer to consult with a private school. As I drove up, I observed flower beds that were overgrown with weeds, grass on the sidewalk, and trash cans overflowing. Quite honestly, my first thought was, "Why do they need a consultant if nobody really cares?" I spent an entire day making observations and submitting solutions. At about 8:00 p.m. the board met, and decided to put all recommendations on hold; they wanted to think about it. The administrator was brokenhearted; we both knew what that meant. I also discovered the cause of the condition of the school.

When I received the check for my consulting services, I endorsed it and returned it to the administrator. I instructed him to only use my contribution toward achieving the number one goal on the school improvement list of objectives we had submitted to the board. I have no idea as to how my contribution was spent.

It is important to have nice landscaping. The better landscaped your campus, the more pride your parents and students will take in it, and the more they will keep it warm and less "institutional." It also shows that the person running the school really cares about it.

The school must be clean. We have been blessed with a wonderful couple for many years who have made sure our parents and students know the school is cared for and kept clean—Ricardo and Lucy Sanchez are very valuable. They are now assisted by a professional cleaning crew because we have grown to over 225,000 square feet, but whether public or private, it is important to keep your campus clean.

When a school facility grows, a very important person is the building superintendent. We are fortunate to have **the man,** Roy Robertson. He supervised the construction of our campus, and he knows everything about our facility. He and his team are always very helpful to our teachers and staff. This person has to have a servant's heart, which is what makes Roy so valuable to so many. If I were a public or private school administrator with a new campus or major project on the drawing board, I would consider offering the position of building superintendent to the construction superintendent who worked for the general contractor that built your school. It's probably not smart to mention that plan too early; **after** completion would be a good time. In the meantime, get to know him and make sure he is a fit for your school's culture.

Informally, a school must have a team of parents who genuinely care about every facet of the operation. The "key players" must be able to get an audience with whomever they believe will really listen, and that may mean the administrator. For Liberty, those families have always been so important that we just would not have been able to excel without them.

They are more than volunteers; they serve the purpose of "having the school's back." These moms, dads, grandparents, and alumni have positive attitudes, always overlooking the bad and seeing the good. They are very vocal with their praise, and very discreet when they have a "suggestion." It would be impossible for me to name all of the wonderful parents who have helped build our school.

The crucial part of this contribution to your school is that the parents who care must be given the authority to complete their good ideas. That's intended to be a nice way to say to administrators and board members, "Stay out of their way." These volunteers are willing to fund the project and do the heavy lifting, but if you don't give them the freedom to accomplish their goal, you will see less and less of them. These proactive parents are not going to waste their time if they can't realize the victory that attends the achievement of their goals. And I have been blessed numerous times with a single parent or couple who want to make a contribution of positive change, but they actually preferred to work alone. My answer, "Thank you so much. If you need any help, please don't hesitate to let me know."

The administrator of a school must have a plan to fill the above positions as the student population increases. If a private school is associated with a church, some of these positions can be shared, thereby spreading the cost over both ministries. The crucial element in this relationship is that both ministries have a common vision. I'll explain in the next chapter.

Chapter 6

"Somebody Get A Mop—We Spilled Our School!"

Administrators must have very special and gifted staff members in place. Let's talk about "who, what, and when."

The idea of building a private church/school makes great sense. The church actually uses the building only one or two days per week, and the school uses it five, so all should work perfectly well. We can get spiritual and say it's being a good steward of facilities.

I once heard a minister from Pittsburg, Dr. Joseph Garlington, say: "Working for God is always a setup. He shows you the beginning and the end, but never shows you what's in between." I believe that is absolutely true. The school administrator and the church pastor envision their graduates walking across the stage, well educated, having strong Christian values, and equipped to make the world a better place. The challenge is that there is a lot of "in between" that takes a considerable amount of common sense, love, and wisdom—there really are no free lunches or shortcuts.

There is a fine school in Fort Worth, Texas that is related to a wonderful church. The school is presently desperate for classroom space and has the opportunity to grow. In 2006, the church completed a beautiful educational wing, but it is **off limits** to the school's students. If you are the school administrator, a member of the school's staff, or a parent trying to get your child off of the waiting list and accepted into the school, you are not a "happy camper."

On the other side of the "aisle," the church members are saying, "We don't remember any of the school parents donating money to our new educational wing." Of course both believe they are right, but if the church starts a school, it has the responsibility to invest in it.

One commonly used solution is to have a Building Use Fee as part of the school's enrollment process. It is collected upon enrollment whether your school is part of a church or not. If you have a new family who was not present to help pay for the facility, a fee is fair and easily understood. Our fee is currently a one-time fee of $4,000 **per family,** and I have not had one family question the legitimacy of this expense. For the incoming family, the Building Use Fee is not tax-deductible because it is technically not a gift, it is a fee. But for the hundreds of families who participated out of their own generosity and during the time of the capital campaign, it was deductible because it was a "gift."

Another key component in the school's success is for the administrator to possess the common sense and experience needed to lead intelligent people effectively. Whether the school is public, private, or church-sponsored, all of the leaders must have the emotional maturity to understand the real issues, which are often **not** the ones verbalized. The administrator has to have the savvy to hear what is **not** spoken. If you have a broken school, you may not need to look any further than to examine the emotional maturity of your leader.

Your administrator has to have spiritual maturity and academic credentials, but having those is not enough. These guys have to be leaders who possess the "X factor." The best description I can give is that the parents, faculty, and students believe he can handle any problem, that all will be treated fairly, that his integrity is beyond question, and that he is not afraid or intimidated by anyone. He understands he is not ever going to please everyone, and being concerned and sensitive, he makes the right decision almost every time. He believes there is a **best** answer to most situations, and his direction and decisions are **never** for sale. But his maturity and ability to make bold decisions have to be so well and humbly communicated that few parents will be offended, because the administrator takes the time to express his decisions with great empathy for those who disagree.

In the study of sociology, we have learned that all of us make **ideological** choices. We decide what we will believe, then study and believe everything that supports that belief. Some of our choices are not easy; one can take one side of a certain issue and actually not be able to prove his decision is absolutely correct.

For instance, if someone asks me if I can prove that Jesus is the Savior and Messiah of mankind, I must admit that I cannot. I choose to believe that He is by faith. Then I read and study supportive materials, in this case the Bible being the primary resource that reinforces my decision. I read Christian authors, listen to Christian leaders, etc. to confirm my own choice to believe in Christ. And I admit that if I read atheistic authors, I have a predetermined opinion that, while the author may be bright, he basically missed "the only question on life's test."

But the exact same process holds true for an atheist, humanist, Buddhist, Jew, Muslim, etc. One simply cannot prove that his belief is the only correct one. We can argue and even go to war, but one side is right and the other wrong; **that belief** is not ideological—it is pure fact.

And the same holds true for a parent who believes ideologically that his child should receive an "A" because he tried and did his best. If a parent believes that a standard should not be objective and consistent, it will often cause the parent to believe that his child's teacher and administrator are insensitive and don't really care. These parents may be very vocal, even expressing their discontent with you in the "open to the public board meeting," which, remember, I strongly recommend **never** take place. Whether a public or private school, closed board meetings are much easier and more efficient than are open meetings. A public school may be required to have one or two open meetings a year, so the by-laws may need to be changed to eliminate that. Basically, the parents will have to have enough confidence in the school's leadership, and that comes with successful decisions supported by emotional maturity **and** time.

But after saying that, I know the reader appreciates that we administrators and teachers are going to make mistakes. I remember making a particular decision years ago that I would love to retract. I was just ignorant and hardheaded or a combination of both. I have regretted it often. We have an award at the end of each school year for students who make the "A" honor roll. We had a wonderful third grade girl who had consistently made the "A" honor roll her first and second grade years. During her third grade year she broke her right arm, the arm with which she wrote. She made a "C" in penmanship and her mother requested that we waive that grade because of her broken arm. I refused to grant the waiver based on my belief that, "If I make an exception for her, then I would open the door for kids who had other excuses for a drop in grades." In my mind, the "good excuses" would never end. But after saying that, I believe I made the wrong decision. Don't try to justify, defend, or deny your mistake; just apologize to the appropriate people and move on to the next victory. (Andrea, I humbly ask for your forgiveness.)

The valuable lesson I learned from that experience is to always give your administration the freedom to make exceptions, because the world is indeed not "black and white." If you are a public or private school board member, always try to write your policies to allow your administrator to make exceptions. This is a unique business because none of our "widgets" are the same.

In regard to Andrea, I was a young administrator, actually in my third year. If you are unfortunate enough to serve a board that will fold in the face of parent or political pressure, then you may not have the option to change a decision that is mandated by policy. Nonetheless, I would always attempt to make the decision that is right, and "let the chips fall where they may."

Chapter 7

Two Nice Guys—but Board Members??

There is so much to say about school boards that I have chosen to mention the issues and solutions in several chapters. The position of a board member is very difficult to define. One can write a job description, but it is not that easy. A board <u>and</u> administrator position is more like a mosaic. I've defined those positions in several ways, not to be redundant, but because they are complex.

As I reread this manuscript, the book sounded a tad cynical. But if this is just another book of observations of the obvious condition of our public and private schools, then nothing has really been accomplished. I have seen too many first-rate teachers and administrators get a raw deal. My heart and intention is to change the system so that a different story **can** be told. It will take a paradigm shift. People in high places who are doing all the talking are going to have to start listening. (God gave us two ears and one mouth for a reason.)

I recently had lunch with two board members of a private school in Texas. Our school has been ranked number one in the state of Texas in its division for six years out of the last seven (2003-2010) by the Texas Association of Private and Parochial Schools. Not to brag, but we honestly do have a great school. The school represented by these board members is ranked much lower. Over a two-hour lunch, do you know how many questions they asked me concerning **how** our school was winning?—Zero! I don't pretend to have all the answers, but they were board members with good hearts, very nice men, but didn't have a clue as to how to lead their school. Anyone needs a certain level of understanding of the issues to ask good questions, and they did not have that.

They called the meeting because they thought our school had recruited **one** of their families. I cleared that misunderstanding up in about five minutes, explaining that the family had approached us, and we made small talk for the rest of our time together. After they realized we had not recruited, we parted friends. I left thinking, "Their poor administrator. These two men are in leadership over the school for which he is giving his lifeblood. They had two hours to pick my brain, and didn't have enough knowledge of how to run a school to ask a single question." Not to oversimplify, but if you want to stop families from leaving your school, set clear goals and communicate the process your school's leadership will take to achieve those goals. I would then give the parents a timeline as to when each goal will be completed. As you begin the process and real progress is made, your parents will not want to leave a school on the move—but I wasn't asked to share the details of how a school begins that process.

Boards should expect re-enrollment to be above 90%, and teacher turnover less than 7%. While these metrics are general, they will give you an overall evaluation of your school at "30,000 feet." Board members, if your school is near those metrics, I strongly suggest spending most of your time encouraging your administrator and asking him how you can help. He has to have made a number of very difficult decisions. Encouragement to the staff who have created a school with those numbers is a vital task, and you can bet they all need an "atta-boy."

The members of public or private school boards actually have the authority to make whatever decisions they want to make—with little accountability. Even when their decisions don't make sense, the administrator has to implement the mandates. Some of the mandates come from your state's capital, but that doesn't really matter to the administrator who has to enforce them. This is driving good administrators crazy! Administrators stay for a very brief time, and the main cause of turnover is that they are forced to follow directives that make absolutely no sense.

Private school administrators move from one school to the next, each time hoping to find a "hands off" school board, one that macro manages. The administrator will stay until the "honeymoon" is over, and will then submit his resignation. A school system in which the administrator has **the authority** to match his responsibility is very rare. Without the proper authority, he can't solve real problems, and the result is a leader who is not respected, and predictably, a school that is poorly run. In the meantime, too many of our kids are graduating from high school, many public and a few private, unable to write a complete sentence or paragraph.

In reality, there are some wonderful civic-minded citizens serving on both types of school boards. However, far too often their voices are drowned out by a few loudmouth members with larger than life egos and/or a load of money and plenty of informal strings attached. There is never enough money in the private school budget to support the school's vision. The public schools are always top-heavy in the administrative costs that are needed to support unnecessary state and federal mandates.

So, many times it is the board members with money, or those who can obtain money, who rule the day.

There are some public and private schools that are run very efficiently. My point is that there are far too few. For instance, the Catholic Church is often an exception, and is generally doing an excellent job of education. It has a very definite agenda to Catholicize their students. That agenda is straightforward, and if that meets with your family's approval, the academic education is typically excellent. The Jesuit School and Ursuline Academy, both in Dallas, Texas are two great examples.

The Episcopal schools are another category of effective denominational schools. One example is the Episcopal School of Dallas. In my opinion, it is a great school. I know the administrator, who is highly respected by his board. Father Steve Swann has been given the authority that is equal to his responsibility, and just as in the business world, that is the crucial point. And the reason is simple, both public and private schools **are** a business.

Bureaucratic entities like public schools, most board-run private schools, governmental offices, etc. are run by committees that hardly ever get anything done except waste time and spend other people's money. In the years 2008/2009, both the government and businesses in the USA were burdened with the problem of losing money. Corporate America announced layoffs in the thousands, and after the blood-letting will predictably return to profitability. The federal government chose to solve its deficit by adding more departments and increasing "pork programs"—WHAT??

By the way, I have an idea. Americans are desperate for financial heroes in Washington. Suggestion: whoever is in charge of government spending, instruct all departments, except the military, to cut their budgets by 10% in 12 months or less. If the department fails to meet that directive, the top 10 heads of that department get fired—two-week severance, and no letters of recommendation. To the military, a financial swat team will be going over invoices and contracts, and if any form of fraud is found, the top person serves ten years in Leavenworth Prison. (Do they still break rocks at Leavenworth? If not, send them to the one that does.)

And one more "by the way," I am strongly in favor of a national sales tax. We can then capture all of the taxes that are currently not being reported when the tax cheat buys something—anything. Our Department of the Treasury captures the taxes from drug dealers, illegal immigrants, prostitutes, thieves, gamblers, basically all recipients of America's blessings who deal in cash and who are not declaring their income—my guess is that they don't know what their income actually is. For the drug dealer who wants to buy a $1,000,000 cigarette boat because he thinks he can outrun helicopters, he will pay 17% sales tax, or $170,000 to the Treasury, and we all hope you have "fair sailing" through the sudden and unpredicted storm. If you lose your boat in the rough seas, or it gets blown out of the water by the "slow" helicopter, please buy another. For those of us who are reporting correctly, we get massive help in what is an outlandish number of income tax cheats. One immediate reduction in government overhead is that the number of IRS agents can be cut in half, as they will only be auditing businesses.

I have never seen a **successful** educational institution that is run by boards and committees with virtually no one taking responsibility for failures. If a corporation loses money, it is likely that the board will demand the resignation of the chairman, fire the CEO, and make deeper budget cuts. If an independent public school system turns in poor scores, suffers high drop-out rates, sends fewer graduates to college, etc. virtually nothing happens. The superintendent has to have committed a felony before the board is forced to take action—hardly any exceptions. "But our school is a Blue Ribbon School!"—please, give me a break!

If you are the administrator or on the board of a public school, so much of your authority has been taken over by the government that you may justifiably feel helpless. Administrators are drowning in directives and memos coming from the district's legal counsel, state mandates, union officials, or the school board's dusty old policy manual. The administrator is sitting in the back of the boardroom thinking, "These directives and instructions give moving targets a whole new meaning." And a word to board members, your administrator has to live with these mandates every day—please appreciate the fact that he lives with a lot of frustration.

Administrators, please don't walk out of the boardroom—at least not yet. I know you are ready to bail! But at the risk of sounding simplistic, try not to get discouraged. You **may be able** to get the authority that correlates with your responsibilities. I have some ideas that may actually help.

Chapter 8

Don't Bail—At Least Not Yet

School boards can be a huge help; let's talk about how that can happen.

Administrators, please identify the board members who are making your life more difficult than it should be. Remember from your Psychology 101 class, there is power in **naming** the problem—he has a name, **write it down**. Many of you have changed or are considering changing school districts, which is probably a mistake. The same "suit" is in almost every boardroom, and they usually have a personal agenda that surfaces at every meeting. First, please identify and **name** the member who is making your life miserable. Most likely every one of your board members has been to high school, some have college and post graduate degrees—they are not totally unfamiliar with the operations of a school. The issue is that they don't understand that running a school has a nuance and a personality that makes it more difficult to run than one could ever imagine. They don't understand that the issues may involve the union leader who has an ego; a well-entrenched, highly educated teacher who should have been fired years ago; and maybe a parent who is very argumentative. Moreover, most board members don't understand that every year the list of challenges and people issues change.

Some of you are thinking of changing professions. Please reconsider, at least for a few more chapters. You may be some of the great administrators and educators, and we don't want to lose you. I remind you, "naming" the person will help you more clearly define the problem.

That exercise gives one the power to stop feeling so "wiped out" when the harsh words come or the really nonsensical board motion is made. If you have the guy's "number," then you can actually anticipate and expect the dysfunction. If you know what to expect, there is power in that knowledge. Additionally, there are some proactive things you can do to help your colleagues and you survive, and actually change things for the better.

First, let's take a look at the individuals who comprise your school's board. Let's begin with the good guys, and give one of these types of board members the benefit of the doubt and assume that he has good intentions. He genuinely ran for the office or was selected in order to help the cause. Granted, he may not have known exactly what the "cause" was, he just knew there had to be one. Let's call a guy like him "dear ol' dad—(Dad)." Dad does not have to have his ego fed or his name in the newspaper.

Dad desires the public school to be a technologically updated version of the one that he attended in his elementary, junior high, and senior high years. He had good teachers, maybe a wonderful band director, maybe a coach who "changed his life," loved his principal, and in all of that, earned a good education. He then probably attended a good university and may have even graduated.

Now a board position opens, and his wife and many of his friends say to Dad, "You can do this; we need your common sense approach to solving problems. You have to go for it!" Dad spent his own money, plus what little he could raise from those who talked him into running, and got into the political arena because he **did** want to make a difference. By the way, for you supporters of Dad who have serious financial capacity, don't think that $50 is going to help; there are just too few of you who will actually write a check. For those who can, please think in terms of $500 or more; for those who can't, keep the $50 checks coming. All gifts are tax-deductible, and Dad doesn't need to fight the financial aspect of the election process alone.

Maybe this is a good time to mention something that is on the mind of every board member, administrator, and development director. Most every week in any major city newspaper we can read the section acknowledging the capital campaign that is underway at a given non-profit organization. It may be a private or charter school, local university, art museum, concert hall, etc. There the names of the "major donors" are listed. But the "elephant in the living room" is that the donations are not major—not relative to the family's capacity, and everybody knows it. We all know of movie stars who make $10,000,000 to $20,000,000 **per movie**, and see a photo in a weekly magazine of them handing the oversize check to the director of the "animal shelter" for $5,000. We all know that the movie star spends more than that on a purse or shoes. Can we do something about the hypocrisy? Not really, because the shelter needs the $5,000, and without the photo-op, the $5,000 goes away. But the amount should be embarrassing to the donor. It is a disappointment in the heart of the smiling but resentful representative, and everyone knows it. It is the reason that when the parable of the "widow's mite" told by Jesus 2,000 years ago is referred to and appreciated, we all know the heart and value of the real "donor" to which Jesus was referring. To you really wealthy guys, I'm trying to help you here—not being unappreciative. If you are giving "pocket change," then I respectfully smile and say, "Thank you." None of the non-profits of which I am aware can make it without your gifts, including ours. Another issue is that relatively small gifts from wealthy donors causes administrators to get discouraged and ask themselves the question, "How can I do a better job of communicating our need to those families who can give us serious traction?" The answer, my administrator friend, is "you can't." Perhaps they are just not givers or do not realize the importance of gifts that are relative to the person's capability.

Before I realized the spiritual issues that attend giving from the heart, I told a board member something that was weighing heavily on my mind. Liberty was in a major capital campaign, and the wealthiest family in our school simply did not care for me—for whatever reason, it was very personal. (Not to imply that there is only one family that does not like me. I've been the head of the school for a long time, and my chances of only having several that don't like me are slim to none.) This family had a reputation in the Dallas community of being major donors. I told this board member and good friend that if I resigned, I thought the family might give Liberty a very large gift, maybe as much as a million dollars. The board member told me to get that thought out of my head, but I'm not sure I ever did. We administrators take resources for our kids and teachers really seriously—we all know **they** are the beneficiaries.

And the heart of the gift does not only apply to the rich. Jack Hayford, the former senior pastor of the Church on the Way I referred to earlier, tells a poignant and personal experience that is probably applicable to all of us. I heard him share this experience years ago, so a couple of the facts may be incorrect, but I'm close. A homeless man was walking on the sidewalk in front of the church as Pastor Hayford was leaving to go home for the day. The man was obviously in need of everything and anything. Pastor Hayford gave the old man his shirt and $10. After getting back in his car, he knew he had given the old man too little—he had a $20 bill in his wallet, but had chosen to give the homeless man the $10. He drove back, got out of the car and gave the man the $20 also. Pastor Hayford, as best I can remember, said, "I will make another $20; this man doesn't seem to be able."

The principle of giving according to one's capacity was **the point** of the widow's mite. It was also, of course, the point of Pastor Hayford's story he told on himself so transparently. The truth is that all of us, no matter our station in life, can be just as guilty as the rich. ("Father God, I plead guilty to a greater charge—I didn't get out of my car." Signed, your child Rodney.)

Back to "Dad." He understands about the changes in our new "age of information" technology (IT), and is all for adding all of the computer science labs needed to see his school soar. Maybe it's **his** alma mater that prepared him to excel at the next level. Things are going well—Dad is elected and can't wait for his first board meeting. He gets there early (Dad actually gets everywhere early), and is full of excitement and anticipation.

Here comes the proactive part for the discouraged administrator, who at present may be YOU. Dad is a board member who, after the first board meeting, is ready to sit down with you, the school's administrator, **privately**. Dad's wife and friends were right on the mark; he just happens to be the kind of guy who **can** get things done. Your strategy is really very simple: tell him the names of the members on the board who are really hurting the school. This is where you name names. Dad will not be surprised, as he is very intuitive. Ask him to put his entrepreneurial skills

83

to work, do some lobbying with you, run interference, and explore ideas to solve the problems caused by the board bullies—at least get them under some manageable level of control.

This is not going to sound very spiritual, but you are in this battle for the kids and your staff, not the egos of board members. Tell Dad that you **want** to remain employed by the school, but must have his help to solve the school's board problems. HIS school system has to stop the revolving door of principals, vice principals, teachers, coaches, etc. Be very emphatic when you explain that you and your colleagues are depending on **his courage and leadership.**

Your next strategic move is to ask him to invite another likeminded board member to join you **and** the athletic director for lunch **off campus**. The AD is probably one of the most influential colleagues not only in the school and/or district, but in the community. Did you know that 95% of the leaders and owners of companies have one of two things in common: they were either high school athletes or were on their school's debate team. If he has a couple of board colleagues with whom he identifies and also trusts, let him invite them. Yet, you want this meeting to be very private and very exclusive. For this crucial project, you, my friend, have **gone dark**.

The agenda is simple: you must get the board members out of the business of running the day-to-day operations of the school. Among other operational decisions, that means they have to release control as to who is hired or fired. Follow this **important rule**: don't send your new best friend Dad and one or two of his board friends who are solution-minded thinkers into the next board meeting alone **or** unprepared. Remember, the problem board members are well intentioned men and women who actually believe that they are going to "fix" the school; they just need "one more" term in office—NOT! All new ideas are normally rejected, and don't think you are going to get more than one opportunity to move this very old "we've never done it that way before" mentality. Unless you are prepared, the establishment, without giving it a second thought, will totally reject any proactive solutions that are not theirs. Without a blink, they will throw Dad, his board colleagues, you, and the AD under the bus. They have the votes to do it, and the revolving door will just keep on swinging.

To you discouraged administrators, Dad and his first tier of trusted friends are leaders you need to meet with "yesterday." They will help you get the control you need because they are now truly enlightened and desperate for change. Remember, your first meeting must be for lunch, and a time for you to garner, or frankly lobby for, support. Bring the facts, have them in writing, well organized, and remember, bring a copy for all.

Chapter 9

Make Sure Dad's Powder is Dry

The bad news can become the good news for change.

Why can you expect Dad and his buddies to be so supportively passionate? Because they will have realized that things are a little more complicated than the district just needing a few more computers. The district is in real trouble, and unless the bold and the brave take charge, you are giving notice that they will serve a very long "whatever" length of term in office, spend hundreds of hours in boring committees, yet will have honored virtually none of their campaign promises and not really changed a thing.

Your inspirational, proactive, and informational tools for your meeting must be solid and well organized facts. You give them the bad news, and don't spare their feelings. If these are the guys you believe they are, your bad news will motivate them. These leaders are energized by problems revealed in a frank and straightforward manner.

First, explain that there have been a few changes since Dad and his board friends graduated from high school. The school is very crowded. The classroom ratios are roughly 32/1 (or whatever they are in your district), not 17/1.

In past generations, teachers were in charge of their classroom—now it's the kids with the **attitudes**. In former years, principals were respected by students and their parents, and coaches had authority just a notch just above the President of the United States. Humbly explain to them that in their local high school, too many teachers are afraid of the tough kids, and tragically, so are most of the parents.

Give them the teacher turnover rates; in some districts that number is north of 30%. Remind them that in their "day" it was closer to 5%, some years "zero." List the **names** of the teachers and coaches who have resigned over the last five years who were doing a great job—**be specific**.

Explain that too many kids are **not** graduating, much less attending college. Of those who do, too many are dropping out after the first semester because they are academically unprepared. You can get the names of the former staff from the Human Resources department, and the figures of students who dropped out or didn't finish college from your school guidance counselors; this information is required data that accredited schools must maintain.

Explain that the reason the district has fewer lawsuits than it actually could have is that the present administrators, you included, deal effectively with litigious-minded parents before their lawyer is called. Explain that **their** school leaders represent a strength and an authoritative presence that the district simply can't afford to lose. These heroes save the day regularly, and the board seldom realizes it. They are district principals, teachers, and coaches—all heroes that **no school** can lose. Here are a couple of Liberty's.

In the summer of 2008, Chris Searcy was in charge of our summer camps and he had a situation that will make my point very clearly. Our summer camp program was led by Chris, one of those franchise players that a school is blessed to have on staff, and he proved it on a given summer afternoon in 2008 at about 4:00 p.m.

A young boy was in our summer camp program under the supervision of a very mature counselor. The counselor had a very soft foam bat, and he was behind the line of kids, gently tapping them when it was their turn to "run." The game took place about 2:00 p.m.; we know that because "Searcy" runs our summer camp on a very structured and organized schedule. When the boy's father came to pick him up, the boy started to cry. Naturally, the father was extremely angry, and immediately found Chris to ask, "What did your counselor do to my son?" With maturity that attends a great leader, he patiently walked the dad through the game, showed him the steps, and we had a "successful landing." The father was gently told that his son might have issues with which to deal, but the problem wasn't the game. A less capable leader could not have talked through the situation calmly. These are staff members that schools must not lose.

There are usually two sides to every issue. One morning I had a ninth grade boy sent to my office. He was sent by a teacher and while crying, tried to say, "Mr. Haire, you can't even wave a flag in this school!" A few moments later the teacher followed the student and said, "Mr. Haire, (Bob) was hitting students on the head with his flag." "Bob" got paddled for hitting other students **and** lying. His parents called me to thank me for assisting them in teaching their son valuable lessons.

Here are some additional facts that you have armed Dad and his colleagues with, to make copies of for Dad to give to all of the board members. Today, our schools are fighting some battles having to do with basic respect for authority that we should have never had to fight. If our schools are an **independent** system, then how and why does our state and national government have the right to stick their big noses in our

independent school's business? Let me share with you a few of the issues that are currently of major concern, that Dad will need in his very well prepared and organized "information packet" for the board meeting.

In most of our public and a few private schools, a healthy fear and respect for authority are all but absent. Respect has been replaced by guard dogs, drug tests, metal detectors, politics, and law suits. School boards have to deal with unions, and the board's consultant is normally a local attorney on retainer. Ask almost any question in a school board meeting, and all heads look to the attorney before answering. Why? Because the state and federal government have instituted so many regulations that prohibit the local schools from making logical, rational, and independent decisions. The term "independent school district" is an oxymoron.

Boards are choked with legal issues. The situation is crazy, and it is time to push back. Build several courtroom battles into your budget, because it is the only way to change laws, and our kids are worth it. By the way, in our Student Parent Handbook at Liberty, we state that if a parent sues our school, the plaintiff pays all attorney fees. I suggest you get legal wording for this policy from your attorney, and write it in your handbook. Since 1983, only one family refused to enroll their daughter because of that paragraph in our handbook.

Our public schools have state-mandated curricula, and receive very little in the way of state financial support with which to teach the required courses or meet the mandates. They have mandated programs required to meet state standards, but the money to pay for these "great ideas" is just not sufficient. Here is a place for the established school board members to earn their keep. They have influence because they are the **incumbents**. They need to be in the state capitol, lobbying their state representatives to eliminate the Department of Education, both in Washington and at the state level. The federal government sends little money to the states, and has people on payroll who know virtually nothing of the needs of the local districts.

The issues just never seem to end. Some board members are concerned that prayer and religion have been removed from our public schools. They would agree with Patrick Henry, who in the Virginia Bill of Rights, June 12, 1776, wrote, " That religion, or the duty which we owe to our Creator, and the manner of discharging it, can be directed only by reason and conviction, not by force or violence; and therefore all men are equally entitled to the free exercise of religion, according to the dictates of conscience; and that it is the mutual duty of all to practice Christian forbearance, love, and charity towards each other." Most liberals, and perhaps some conservatives, don't agree with Patrick Henry and are not concerned. But Christians, who make up the majority of our nation's culture, have had a main artery cut. Liberals see the removal of prayer from schools and the falling of standardized test scores beginning at approximately the same time, as a mere coincidence. Liberals see prayer being removed from schools and the birth of gangs, once limited to inner cities, jails, and prisons but now a reality on our campuses, as again, just a coincidence. Are you **kidding** me? In our school, we pray every day, and while I don't know for sure that prayer in and of itself is a silver bullet, it sure sets up the God of peace to rule the classrooms and halls. We have no gangs, metal detectors or guard dogs—probably just a coincidence, RIGHT?

Mandated standardized tests are a debilitating requirement to good educators. I interview parents all year who are applying for their child to be admitted to our school. I'd like to believe it is for the religion **and** academics, but honestly, it is mostly for the academics. The parents, many of whom are public school teachers, are concerned because public schools spend a lot of time teaching to their standardized test, and that means less time in the textbooks. The schools that do poorly on the test receive a lower evaluation, and in many cases, less money from the state. The administrator's job is on the line, the principal's job is in question, so guess what happens? The teachers pass answers to students, and the rumor is that this problem is at an epidemic level. They are ashamed, embarrassed, and demoralized.

An Associated Press writer, Kate Brumback, wrote an article on June 20, 2009, in which she reported that two administrators in an Atlanta, Georgia suburban school had resigned. She reported that the principal and the assistant principal were charged with altering public documents, which is a felony. These two administrators are **accused** of changing scores on fifth grade State of Georgia public school standardized tests— each state has its own tests.

In July of 2009, a staff writer for the Dallas Morning News reported an unbelievable story. Tawnell D. Hobbs reported that a high number of erasures on the Texas standardized test from Lang Middle School "tipped off state and district officials to possible tampering, according to the Texas Education Agency." The story continues to state that about 400 eighth grade students took the standardized math exam in the spring of 2009. When students who supposedly scored in a higher category were retested, their scores fell from 79.5 to 43.7; the students in the lower academic category scored 62.8 on the original test, but 3.8 on the retest. Hobbs stated that if the allegations are found to be true, some administrators could be facing criminal charges.

I really do not know if the school officials mentioned above are guilty or not—I hope they are all false allegations. But I do know that "the word on the school street" is that school teachers and administrators all over the country have similar stories, and all of them feel very ashamed and frightened because they **are** doing what these school officials are charged with doing. It doesn't make it right, but it does make it very sad. If true, my **guess** is that not one of the hundreds of teachers or administrators feel good about what they actually believe they are forced to do to ensure continued government funding, and all must be very disheartened. While students in private schools are studying material that is "scope and sequenced" year by year from the textbooks, public school students are studying for a **single** standardized test.

Let me do my best to say this scripturally and with great sensitivity: STATES, GET THEE THE HELL OUT OF THE SCHOOL BUSINESS, IT IS NOT THINE!! Come on, Mr. Gutsy Governor, close your State Department of Education YESTERDAY! If Washington doesn't have the courage to eliminate the dumb idea of a Department of Education, the states can. Then when the Washington bigwigs call your state's Department of Education, they will hear, "This is not a working number." And when the government sends their money for your school's "pound of flesh," it gets returned with "Return to Sender" stamped on the envelope. Which of you governors have the courage to become our next national hero?

Could we demoralize our teachers any more? Try to make sense of this story. I recently asked a student making application to our school why he would change schools in the middle of his tenth grade year. His answer was that he was tired of the students in his classes openly disrespecting his teachers. He went on to say that students used profanity in the classroom, and the teachers did nothing about it. In fact, he said that some of his teachers got so frustrated that they used profanity in response. He stated that many students in the classroom thought it was funny. He failed to see the humor.

Another student applying from another public school, but for the same grade, told me that in his chemistry class, a student "did a line of coke" on her desk during class. I asked where the teacher was, and he said she was sitting at her computer, eating a bag of chips, and never looked up. She either never saw it, or chose not to address it; he wasn't sure which. This event holds three probable answers: first, the teacher should be fired, and second, the principal who allowed it should be "reassigned" and report the next day to his new boss—the groundskeeper. (Actually, our groundskeeper would not be interested, but I'm sure he could find work somewhere.) The third solution is probably at the root of the problem. My guess is that the teacher was hired by an incompetent person or committee. It is also a good guess that the board is running the school, and the administration has given up and is just going through the motions.

A student from a nearby high school applying for our eleventh grade told me there were forty kids in her science class (this could have been in almost any school district, in any class). She explained that on the previous day, several boys were having water-tube fights in the back of the classroom, and other students were using their cell phones. I asked,

"What did the teacher do?" Her response, "She just kept on trying to teach." She told me that her father was a physician and expected her to make good grades. She was not going to be able to accomplish her father's expectation in that learning environment. I have to say, I considered that a very mature observation from a high school junior.

The main issue in all of these scenarios is that we have a lack of control at the top. No matter the school district, stories like the above are common—so sad. If students are permitted to say and do virtually anything in school, what chance does a student have of receiving a competitive education? And how discouraged must the dedicated teachers and administrators be if they have lost the ability to make and implement difficult decisions? (My hope is that the board establishment is now taking notes like crazy!)

I also know that it is heartbreaking to good administrators to be required to include courses that are NOT age appropriate. Is anyone buying the idea that sex education should be taught in early elementary school health or science classes? I'm sure in most schools it is "taught very tastefully." However, do any moms and dads of first graders want a teacher they know virtually nothing about teaching their six-year-old about sex? Move up a few years, and the teacher may pass a banana around, with the day's teaching objective being to securely place a condom on it. This is a common practice in many public school fifth grade health classes. "You know, we just cannot be too safe, and besides, you never know at what age your child will become sexually active."

That is the enlightened rationale of the liberal teacher unions. Discussion of sexually transmitted diseases is held in health classes starting in very early elementary grades. Class discussions regarding homosexuality start in some first grade curricula. It is a part of the progressive school district's mandates. Open and frank dialogue is something that **the school** must make sure happens. "You can never trust those narrow-minded right-wing Christian parents to do what has to be done." This liberal agenda is expressed in books like "Heather Has Two Mommies," and "The King and the King," so the message can't be missed.

I know there are many liberals who are good administrators, but in my opinion, they are wrong if they believe we should teach **graphic sex education** in schools. I believe educating children about sex is the role of the parents. My liberal friends and colleagues, the fact that our moral climate is at the bottom of the chart and the fact that we are losing many great educators are the facts that prove you wrong.

Many good teachers are leaving the field because, among other reasons, they are being forced to teach material that is not age appropriate. If my position is wrong, bring a solution that makes sense—and I hope you are not going to insult every fiber of intelligence in my brain with the argument, "We just have to pay our teachers more money." That argument has nothing to do with solving the real problems. I will prove it in a later chapter, but my bet is that you know it. Teachers never entered the field of education for the money. If they did, they are not smart enough to be a teacher.

To further convince the board establishment, Dad can inform them about the "revisionist history" curriculum presently being taught. Dad and friends are going to hear it from a couple of their more conservative constituents, so better that truth and information come from Dad. Dad explains that many of our state-mandated social studies textbooks have actually been rewritten to conform to a liberal agenda. Dad will be asked by some of his conservative supporters, "What are you going to do about my child's history book that is teaching slanted, negative ideas? I helped you distribute yard signs. May I ask you to do my child and our school, FOR GOD'S SAKE, ONE FAVOR??!! Do you know that my kindergartner, only five years old, was taught to mock Christopher Columbus?? Make sure our social studies textbooks are teaching truths, not innuendos!" Unless Dad and board members are armed with this information ahead of time, they will have no answers, and may not have a clue as to what this concerned parent is talking about.

During your first meeting with Dad and friends, some time after they think about it for a moment, one of them will respond, "This surely must be a simple misunderstanding. Our state curriculum committee would never have approved a textbook that even remotely tried to rewrite history—is that even possible?" Dad's argument and concern don't fly. However, the person with the experience or facts is rarely at the mercy of the person who has only an opinion.

The case made by the "educational gurus," the ones that taught us New Math, eliminated phonics as the primary method for teaching reading, haven't taught diagramming sentences since the late 1980s, and introduced us to "open classrooms" is simple. They really believe that the old history books, the ones taught to them, were actually filled with lies, and greatly distorted the truth. But fortunately, they have rediscovered the "truth" in time to ensure that the next generation will learn the real history of our nation, not that which has been taught in our public schools for generations (can you liberal progressives spell g-a-r-b-a-g-e?).

Dad now has some serious facts with which to convince his colleagues that there must be some changes, and very fast. By the way, a great source of facts regarding the absolute truth of our nation's history is David Barton's organization, Wall Builders, in Aledo, Texas. He has indisputable and documented information, and I strongly suggest you invite him to speak at a PTA meeting. I'm guessing his calendar fills quickly, so it will take some planning. He is a Christian, so if you are in a public school, you may want David to "tone it down," but I'm not sure he can—he is solidly dedicated to telling the truth.

You must honestly explain to the board that the school they loved as a kid really only exists now in the form of bricks and mortar. Explain that nobody in their school district was on a clandestine committee, but that, in fact, some of the new textbooks do actually have four pages dedicated to the Ku Klux Klan, and one page dedicated to Abraham Lincoln—NAW—YEP! What about George Washington? He is covered on page 145; why would we need several pages to glorify his simple achievements? And Thomas Jefferson is now described as an avowed atheist who slept with his slaves, accusations that would never hold up in a court of law. In William G. Hyland's book, *In Defense of Thomas Jefferson*, Hyland documents that it was likely Jefferson's younger brother Randolph who was the father of Sally Hemings' child.

Nobody disagrees that **some** parts of revisionist history are correct, but are we sure that we want that to be our focus? The Klan was a very sad part of our history, and that needs to be said. Jefferson's early Christian faith is in question, no argument. But if we place emphasis on the negative, is it not hard to imagine that there will be birthed an anti-American philosophy in the new curriculum? It is presented in the spirit of historical honesty. Yet, in the end, it is the true American spirit that survives, not a season of horrific greed and a lack of concern for human dignity that was so prevalent in the pre-abolitionists years of the South. Lincoln is one of our national heroes, and what is important is not only the shamefulness of the plantation economic system, but the courage of Lincoln in winning the day.

Are we certain that Jefferson was an atheist? He did write in a letter to Robert Skipwith on August 3, 1771, "A lively and lasting sense of filial duty is more effectually impressed on the mind of a son or daughter by reading King Lear, than by all the dry volumes of ethics, and divinity that ever were written." But he also wrote a letter in 1774 to Benjamin Rush his Summary View of the Rights of British America, "I have sworn upon the altar of God, eternal hostility against every form of tyranny over the mind of man." My point is, let's teach the whole truth. It is possible to make the argument that as Jefferson got older he came to have a relationship with God? If I were teaching US History, my students would engage in a lively discussion. The assignment would be "Prepare to discuss the evolution of the worldview or religious philosophy of Thomas Jefferson during the last ten years of his life. Please read pages 145 to 155 to prepare to contribute to this discussion."

Are we sure that Washington's leadership can be adequately discussed on one page? We know that task is impossible. None of those assumptions is absolute. Why must we present them as such? This is the urgent heart and call of parents using a measure of common sense, and preserving the dignity and respect for our Founding Fathers. I recently had lunch with a delegation of leaders from a foreign country. I asked them, "Who are your nation's heroes?" They couldn't name one. We have hundreds; they make up the fabric of our country's heritage. Our kids must know who our heroes are, know of their sacrifice, and learn that we all have the privilege to be proud Americans; and that the privilege was paid for by the blood of men and women who loved our country enough to die for her.

Prepare Dad and his new best friends, in the nation which has "In God We Trust" on its currency, for the questions that will surely come from their patriotic supporters about what the Federal Department of Education did with Easter and Christmas holidays? Do we really have to call it "Winter Break"? (I'm not sure what various districts call Easter, but my bet is that it has little to do with Jesus' resurrection.) Remember when Dad was in school? Fish was served in the lunchroom on Fridays in honor of the Catholic tradition. His teacher prayed a Christian prayer before his class had lunch, and the pledge of allegiance was said with pride. He most assuredly learned that the tradition of covering his heart with his right hand while saying the pledge was to protect his heart in case a bullet should be shot at his heart before he finished saying the pledge. That, my friend, **is** allegiance. Our children, when studying US History, should learn that John Hancock wrote his name in large letters when signing the Constitution so the King of England would know who to hang first. Like it or not; Christianity, family, and patriotism were our nation's foundational cornerstones. Anyone discounting those sacrifices to serve their own anti-American or liberal agenda should be deported to the country of their choice!

In an article in the Dallas Morning News a few years ago, Mr. Joshua Benton wrote a very interesting article in the Metro section entitled "Principal Concerns in Schools." In his excellent research, Benton said that the folks who study how kids learn say that stability is an important key to a good learning environment. When you have to replace a third of your teachers each year, you can't maintain stability. He went on to say about principal turnovers, "If you're running through them like Kleenex in hay fever season, best of luck improving your school." A teacher interviewed for the article was quoted as saying, "Each one (principals) had their own unique shortcomings. The first year, students were literally running the halls in gangs. They'd burst into my classroom, screaming and laughing, throw candy at the kids, then run out. Nothing would happen to them. There was no discipline." Any job applicants want to work in this school environment? Local boards, as well as state and federal educational department members are blaming teacher turnover and the shortage of good candidates on low salaries. I agree that salaries need to be raised, but that will not solve the problem. If that were true, the schools in Washington, DC, who pay the highest salaries in America, would have more applicants than could be interviewed, and the lowest turnover—neither of which is true.

Give Dad and his colleagues a chance. The district deserves it, and frankly, you have to win the battle against micromanagement from within that room. Otherwise, you are going to have to fill more openings for principals next year, and do it with men who probably were demoralized at their last school, or promote someone who can't handle the job. "The hits just keep on coming."

NOW you have Dad's and his colleagues' undivided attention. It is not so much that this is all new information to them. But it is going to be a huge concern to them that **you** are upset enough to gently threaten, or rather advise, them that this could become their problem "solo" if the board does not drop the micro-managed style government immediately. They have to hear the truth that those with the responsibility, you and your staff, **have** to be those with the real authority.

Dad must be prepared to go into this very special board meeting armed with organized, well written, clearly understood facts. He will need to be reminded that Andrew Jackson wrote a letter to the troops who had abandoned their battle positions during the Battle of New Orleans on a cold January 8, 1815, saying," The brave man inattentive to his duty is worth little more to his country than the coward who deserts her in the hour of danger." This group will need the mental support and comfort Andrew Jackson offered to all Americans when he said, "One man with courage makes a majority."

Chapter 10

Shot Fired Over the Bow!

Now "This is what I'm talking about!" This is the time to speak to the important issues that will determine your school's future direction—you have nothing to lose.

I told you from the outset that I am not politically correct, and I am about to prove that point—big time. In my opinion, **this** board meeting has one huge agenda, and it is going to require a paradigm shift and elevation in the minds of the board establishment paralleled only by a space launch. The purpose of this particular board meeting will require a "closed to the public" session. The administrator and the AD are in the meeting because you are on the agenda. You may never have another chance to present your case. You will indeed be fortunate if you can accomplish this mind-altering event. But you have to take the ultimate risk, laying it all on the line.

Your selection of "guns"—the guys you have chosen to be your mouthpiece, the small group led by Dad—have to be franchise players who are proven winners. The goal that Dad and his team are trying to achieve is to **make sure the people who know how to run a school have the freedom and authority to run it**. These problem board members do actually have a major role to play, and I will cover their best and highest use in this chapter. But first, you and your team of board members and staff have a job to do, and your selection of players is crucial.

This board meeting must "stay on point." It is not the meeting to fight for equal rights or establish a tighter policy for making sure your school is multicultural. This meeting is the place to solve a big problem, and you need "clean-up hitters." This may be difficult, and lightweights who got out there and knocked on a lot of doors are to be admired, but being listened to in this board meeting is at a different "pay grade." In my opinion, it is like hiring a male to teach a kindergarten class or a female to coach the boys' football team. When you have to begin the conversation with, "I'd like to tell you why I hired 'Mr. Bow-tie' to be your child's kindergarten teacher this year," you are in an uphill battle before you start—a luxury our schools, public and private, lost decades ago.

You are going to need some serious ammunition, and there is no better place to start than from a perspective that Dad and his colleagues (other like-minded board members and school district VIPs) **can** and **are** going to solve the problem. Once Dad gets the floor to speak, he will be equipped with enough artillery to win the battle, because **you** have prepared him. If all goes as planned, your team will experience an event that is bloodless. At least that should be the planned strategy. Sun-Tzu said in *The Art of War*, "The best victory is when the opponent surrenders of its own accord before there are any actual hostilities… It is best to win without fighting."

Having the element of surprise can be a good thing in a board room full of incumbents. You have to have a recognized and very real power. If you have board members who are reluctant to make positive changes, they must understand that Dad and his one or two board friends have the support of you and the athletic director, whom you have brought in as a special guest for this meeting. If not, you have "hung Dad and friends out to dry." And if you go in alone, without the AD, you, with few exceptions, are just not going to have the needed political clout. This may go without saying, but be sure all members **in your camp** attend this meeting. That will add a huge measure of strength to your position. I'm using the AD in my illustration, but in your school it could be a highly respected department chair, the head football or basketball coach, or the band director. It's whomever the school board knows the school can't lose.

My bet is that Dad and his friends will respond with hope, and will be appreciative of your initiative and courage to face the board. If Dad knows he has you and the AD in his corner, he and his colleagues should come into the meeting with confidence and humility. They will tell the establishment that they have to be **the** Board that raises school morale and convince them that: "**We** must do whatever it takes to stop the revolving door in our school's leadership positions." Remember, at the end of the day, the board members have donated hundreds of hours of their time and that must be genuinely appreciated and respected.

Dad and his friends have been elected to a situation that is far different than what they anticipated, but it certainly could be described as Jackson's "One man." With your assistance, Dad and his fellow board member friends are prepared to **shout** your concerns from the boardroom table. With your assistance, the board has come to realize that the changes that need to be made are gargantuan. Sadly, nothing really substantial can be changed without legal advice, and everything will appear to move at the speed of a glacier, but you are now on your way!

The board establishment should now be receptive. And now they are empowered to do their best, and more importantly, will remember that they have given their word to their community and supporters. If they have the stuff from which leaders are made, some very big things can and will begin to change. **In about three meetings, they will realize the depth of their dilemma. These are now the good guys and your friends, and now you're not alone.**

Another good board member who may quickly join Dad and his team is from the Generation X age. This person would have been, in 2009, 35-45 years old. This man may or may not be part of your first "luncheon," but will most likely join the cause very quickly. Here is why. He has bought into the new secular humanism school philosophy (which is actually a **religion**, but that is generally categorically denied by the public school unions and state and federal officials.) That is one of those ideological beliefs you will have a hard time winning, so my advice is that you not die on the hill of proving that secular humanism is a religion.

Most in this **enlightened** group don't believe or realize that secular humanism is masked atheism, and that it is just as much a religion as Christianity or Hinduism. But this candidate is right on with the new everything. He is actually OK with revisionist history; he doesn't believe it is a real problem. Anything new has to be good to the Generation Xer. He is fine with not teaching phonics in the lower grades, dealing with teacher unions, and not having prayer in schools. He is a pure believer in separation of church and state, not because he is necessarily an atheist, but because he doesn't want education watered down with religion. We can argue his core values, but that is not the purpose of this book.

His real concern is that the school's standardized test scores are too low, and nobody seems to have a clue as to how to raise them. The best he can do about his "I promise you that if I am elected, our SAT and

ACT test results will soar" campaign platform is to celebrate with the local liberal newspapers. The Dallas Morning News, in August 2007, featured a headline story entitled "Texas gains on SAT as scores fall nationally." The author was celebrating that Texas scores on the SAT rose from 506 to 507 in math, and rose from 491 to 492 in reading, the largest increase for the state in a decade! Let's all hear it for our great educational victory! GIVE ME A BREAK! Our state schools are competing with students from private schools, most of which are increasing their scores every year. They are competing with kids from Taiwan, Korea, and China who study twelve hours a day. The Generation Xer is looking for a place to hide, and your private luncheon would be a safe harbor, but he may be too slow on your "movement" to get that privilege. You will just have to see how quickly he finds out he's in trouble.

The Xer's second agenda issue was to add additional Advanced Placement courses, maybe more teachers with advanced degrees, and tutorials for kids having learning problems. Those solutions should take care of the standardized achievement test issue, but none of those ideas survived the budget cuts this year. "We will see about it next year," says the school board chairman with all of the old answers that obviously don't work.

Now the Generation X guy also understands that "Big Brother" from the state and federal education departments is in the local school's business, but there appear to be a few more mandates than there is state money to finance them. That is why home owners have a huge "number" beside their yearly property taxes labeled "Local and State School Taxes."

These Xer guys are typically bright, so it doesn't take him many meetings to see that his agenda and platform just went up in smoke.

He also promised his supporters he would lower school taxes. Now he learns that the promise is an impossible goal if his agenda to add more academic courses is ever to become a reality. Depending on his guts and determination, Xer may have to make Dad an ally. Dad may be the only guy he knows who wants to move the power source from the incumbents to really almost anyone else. Xer, if lobbied by Dad, you, and the AD, may become **really** enlightened.

Further, he will be able to see that scores can be raised if the teachers are actually allowed to teach. Maybe there **is** a solution that will **not** cost more money, but just requires board and administrative support for the teachers that will lead to better classroom control and management. ("Teachers in control of their classroom"—there is a novel idea.) You may finally have the attention of two or three board members because the source of their frustration has just been exposed to the light of their own awareness. Others at the next board meeting may, no guarantees, get on board (no pun intended). It may also be possible that each of the new guys has a small circle of influence. **Now** you have a shot at getting something done, maybe before the next school year.

If a publically traded company reported financials that compare to the terrible test scores of our public schools, a couple of very predictable things would happen. An aggressive management team would develop a proactive plan to change things quickly. Poorly performing employees would be fired, some departments eliminated or combined with others for better efficiency, etc. But too many schools just keep trying to pay higher salaries to the poorly performing employees, add new departments, build more of the same models—it's just crazy! The new school board members are going to bring fresh ideas, but the establishment must listen and act, "bag" their egos, and overcome their fear to make changes.

Every year our team of administrators pores over every aspect of our school to find ways we can make positive changes and improvements—any good business does the same. The board insists we have no "sacred cows." We work tirelessly to revise our Teacher and Student Handbooks, to make sure we aren't wasting our parents' hard earned money, and to be proactive in making any changes in time to inform our parents. Our board not only trusts me to make sure this happens, but if they sense that our team of administrators does not take this initiative, their responsibility is to hold me accountable. I am their representative in leading the charge to make sure we deliver for the parent body the best school possible.

Chapter 11

Guys With the Glass Half Empty Leave!!

Let's talk briefly about the <u>only</u> way to run a good board meeting, and "connect the dots" with the real reason a person might run for a position on the school board.

I said earlier that the board has a purpose in lobbying your state officials to get out of the independent school's business—the state's Department of Education serves no valuable purpose, just gets in the way, is a hindrance to **real** progress, and costs taxpayers money. One of the most important roles for an incumbent board member is to lobby his state representatives to eliminate the Department of Education. Everyone working in the DOE gets a "pink slip" and 30 days notice; remember, we are serving the students, not providing bureaucratic job security. This is just one department of our government that serves no purpose, and it is a good place to start.

With the board now informed of the serious and complex issues facing their school today, and understanding that they are to set policy and give the administrator authority over daily operations, **it is now time for the huge paradigm shift. You, the administrator, need to lead the board meetings.** There is a chairman on the board, but under this new meeting agenda, his highest and best use is in two other roles. His most important assignment will be that of keeping his fellow members on point. Members may ask questions for clarification, and secondly, may ask to speak to submit a good suggestion or solution to a problem.

Droning conversation and opinions that have no point are out, **solutions** and **ideas** are in—and no more "echo chambers."

There will be an agenda written by the administrator, published and distributed by the **chairman** to every board member two weeks before the meeting. All members will have one week to add their requests to the agenda. They will get permission to add their requested agenda item from the chairman. Before the chairman adds the item to the agenda, he calls the administrator to see if the agenda item can be resolved in a one-to-one meeting with the board member. That will allow the board member with an issue to have communication time with the administrator, the goal being to resolve that issue before the meeting.

There will also be an opportunity to explain to the board member that Dad and friends, the AD, and you need him to help move the board's purpose and focus from daily school operations to school policy. A good way to measure whether a board member is being too intrusive into school operations is that if the moment he leaves the board room, he ceases to have board authority. The authoritative boundary for all board members is the board room door—both coming in and going out (you could literally say it is an open and shut case).

If this scenario goes as planned, YOU now have leadership responsibilities in the board meetings, and you MUST use that newly acquired authority with integrity and a humble spirit. Board members have allowed you lead them for optimum school operations effectiveness. If you do that, three predictable things will happen: there will be no more "white knuckler" meetings for you, the kids will win because the board is now focused and moves into the next year **without** the horrendous turnover in personnel, and the board meetings will be more enjoyable for the members. These guys are bright and will embrace the improvement; they just had never seen this boardroom model. When a school board functions as I have described, there will be a direct and positive effect on staff turnover—I'll bet that is a surprise. The only turnover will be teachers whose spouses are transferred, those who are retiring, women who become pregnant and choose to stay home, and a few who have to be fired (I hope not).

One board member's motive to join was that there was no "color" represented on the board. We are seeing more and more of this motive surfacing. He ran for office with the idea that if his "people" had more opportunity, received genuinely fair treatment, and gave kids of color a good role model to follow, things would magically improve. He most likely grew up in an America that was prejudiced. This problem has been resolved in the "smart rooms," but memories of a cruel injustice were so branded on his psyche, he can't take a chance that his children will not be given a fair opportunity. Depending on the district, this candidate may win only because of his color. I realize that statement is not politically correct, but please remember, this book is about real issues and honest observations. This candidate may well be the best candidate, so if that is true, he should receive the majority of votes in the election. If the white voter votes against him because he is a minority, then the intelligent hope is for that ignorant white voter to stay home. Your school board needs to be made up of statesmen who represent the entire district. All votes that help students succeed are good votes, and any board member who votes against helping any student in the district should be forced to resign.

Assuming he **did run** to balance the race issue, he will do everything in his power to make sure a person of "color" is hired as the administrator because if that were true, the universe would come into proper alignment. He may also ask, "And by the way, how many top administrators are female and/or of color, and is that number in balance with our community demographics?" This is a cause he is passionate about, and will become the board meeting mantra from him **if** permitted. That is one of the reasons the agenda has to be published two weeks prior to the meeting.

Please don't misunderstand. Our nation has a responsibility to make the playing field level for all. It's not only in our Constitution, but it is right on the highest of moral ground. My issue is not whether this board member has a solid point. It is that he is fighting the issue of racial equality on the wrong field. Our schools are in very deep trouble, the competition for good teachers is fierce, and the best technology we have is way behind the international curve in contributing to the quality of education for our kids of all races. **Education** has to be the battle cry— not equalizing race or gender.

If the minority candidate gets on the board's meeting agenda to spew his doctrine of fairness and his accusations of bigotry, everybody will be rolling their eyes, and he will have lost what may have been a worthy cause. It certainly was coming from a sincere heart—but his cause is just not a topic for the boardroom. If his colleagues try to get focused on the real issues, he will play the race card, which is always followed by a call from the ACLU or NAACP or both. Dad has about had it, the Generation Xer guy is even getting his fill, and the board meetings are now a political brawl over everything **but** improving the school. You don't think this could be true? Just attend the next board meeting in any major city—I'm scarily on point. All board members have to understand that there is only one boat, and all members are in it.

But the guy of color may not be through. He will drive home the issue of "balance of race" on the teaching staff that has to be in proper ratio to the school district. First, we all absolutely have to be certain not to violate any laws having to do with discrimination; because one **avoidable** lawsuit will destroy everything we are trying to do morally, not to mention the effect of the legal expense. But if your teachers are hired because of their color, your good teachers will leave—even those good teachers of color will leave. Administrators have to have the freedom to hire the **best** teachers and coaches regardless of color, gender or nationality; otherwise, your turnover will rise and low scores will just continue to fall.

The discrimination card will play for any good cause. Again, I actually have no argument with the cause of fairness. I just know our school boardrooms are the wrong place to attempt to fix the "equal opportunity" problem—assuming there still is one, and I do concede there are pockets of ignorance in every state in our union.

And being gut level honest, we all know that most social problems must be won in the heart first. In our homes, it happens when the father changes his mind and soul—not when he starts swinging a belt in anger. In any company that needs improvements, it happens when the president sees things from a new perspective, and communicates the new direction effectively and with compassion—not when he indiscriminately starts firing people who are making a contribution. If bias and bigotry are keeping some highly qualified people out of the field of education, then that needs to be changed "yesterday." But if we are correcting our race problems with policy that paves the way for incompetence, then we have brought a knife to a gun fight, and lose the war we will.

Now "Dad," "the Generation Xer," and probably a few of the incumbents are thinking to themselves, "I'd like to get my head out of this trap; you can keep the cheese." It doesn't take long after the first public board meeting is held, for the voters who care enough to attend to realize that possibly with the exception of the administrator, this is a room full of agendas. Dad is in disbelief that the school he remembered as being so wonderful has disappeared. The Generation Xer guy is shoving his newfound power around with an agenda that now has more to do with hoping that the scores don't go **south**, and the cultural genius is wondering why his colleagues are so biased, bigoted, and narrow. If your power lunch has not happened yet, you are sitting in the corner thinking, "I should have gone to law school. What was I thinking?"

By the way, please don't write me letters telling me about the person of color on your local school board who has an advanced degree in education and is a great problem solver. I am very aware that there are some wonderful exceptions; I know many. But again, don't confuse advanced degrees, gender or **any** nationality with competency. In my opinion, they are not related, not even distant cousins. Competency is truly a color and gender blind issue, and school leadership has to "get that."

The board at Liberty expects me to deliver, and are on "stand by" if I need help. They are supportive, and as long as I do the job which they hired me to do, they simply oversee the expected progress. At this writing we utilize two board committees with specific projects. The first is the Financial Committee. The chairman will give the latest numbers at every meeting or may defer to the business manager to make the presentation—his choice. The second is a Master Plan Committee. Their task is to present facility scenarios that comfortably fit the ultimate population of the entire campus.

As the administrator, if I have a unique challenge for which a board member has expertise, I will call to ask for their help—it is on a project by project basis. I know these board members respect me, are praying for me, and have my back. I also realize they have a serious responsibility to replace me if they know I am not delivering a quality educational product for the parents who depend on them—and it's nothing personal. I am chairman of the board, and this system has proven to be the most efficient and productive way to govern our school. If you are in a public school, make your superintendent the "ad hoc" board chair and let him facilitate the meetings. I realize that ours is a business model, but I ask you, "Is that all bad?" Our country's most productive sector is greatly run companies; our least efficient are public schools, churches, state and federal government, and many private schools.

In the current school year, I serve as chairman of the board with ten additional members. I have served with many boards with many personalities. I am blessed at this time to serve with ten very bright and creative members. I am a lot smarter with **these** ten members in the room. We are friends who love and respect each other—to the member. We don't always agree on an issue, but that is the way it should be. Our school families are well represented, and when we make a decision to spend money, we understand it is not our money and we take that responsibility seriously. In the last meeting held in January of 2010, one of the members commented how well this board worked together. He has served long enough to know when that was not the case.

They have never asked me to compromise my integrity, and will stand by me in tough situations. I love working with this board because they let me do my job, and I let my staff do theirs—and that is the point.

Chapter 12

Is Anyone Against Changing A Longstanding Custom?

There are some customs that have been very destructive to schools for decades. The board can fix those problems—let's talk about one of them.

There are some very important responsibilities that can be filled with the right school board members, board of trustee members, and PTA board officers. There is enormous talent in these leaders, and they desperately want to be of use. The important point is that they need to be "plugged in" where the administrator has specific areas of need. These willing leaders want to be given purposeful direction.

The usual scenario is for a PTA or board officer to assume that what the administrator needs is what **he** wants to accomplish—also known as his personal "agenda." If you are the PTA president, and really want to help, ask the administrator, "How can I be of service?" and you have just earned your stripes. You have just crossed over the "agenda" bridge to servanthood, and have placed yourself in a position to really help students. It is not a question the administrator has heard often, maybe not ever. It may take him a few days to give you the answer, so have patience. In fact, I suggest you leave him with, "Why don't you think about it and get back to me." I'm telling you, for a parent in a position of influence to ask the administrator, "What do you need me to do?"—are you kidding me?? HOME RUN!! I have had several outstanding PTA officers, so I know they can make a tremendous difference in the morale of your school when it is not a position of power or pride for them.

For starters, what **every** school administrator needs to clearly communicate to the leaders of the board and PTA may be hard to appreciate, but it is this: your school needs parent leaders to squelch all gossip. It is the single most effective poison pill ever introduced into any organization—especially a school or church.

If I can give parent leaders a tip for **any** occasion or situation, it is to stop all gossip the minute it hits their ears. Gossip is **not** defined as discussing areas that can be improved, but is discussing those areas with a person who can do nothing about them, usually the person in front of them in the carpool line.

The next opportunity to help your administrator is to anticipate his needs and meet them before he has asked for your help. If you have taken the time to get to know him, look for ways to serve him. He is always going to need parent leaders to encourage his teachers and staff. He is always going to need parents to provide resources. Most administrators are hesitant to ask for what they really need—so offer.

It is money and good volunteers that are needed in public and private schools. By the way, if you are a wealthy parent in a public or private school, and you see a financial need, I have a suggestion. Make an appointment with the administrator or development director and ask him, "What are your most pressing needs?" If he doesn't tell you right away, be obnoxiously persistent, and if the need aligns with your heart and vision, then just write the check. Maybe God blessed you so that you could bless His children. No bands need to play, no fancy dinners need to be served—just a giving parent taking care of his child's school business.

Some wealthy parents are afraid of giving too much, or of being the only one who is solving the school's financial problems—why not be the answer to the problem, and stop worrying about help that you don't need. Some wealthy parents work very hard at staying below the radar. It's "God, please don't let them know I have a lot of money." A very wealthy parent told me one time, "Rodney, do you expect me to just give it all away?" From my experience, that is not a problem for any wealthy parent I have ever known. However, I can identify with the feeling that they are the only one really sacrificing, but the truth is that none of us is alone.

If you want an athletic field, classroom, or gymnasium named after your family or a loved one, don't be bashful in asking. Leaving a legacy is a legitimate desire. If you are a financially blessed family who really wants the school auction to succeed, tell the chairperson he can count on you for $50,000 in donated auction items, or fewer items and a check for the difference. In 2001, a private school in Houston, Texas raised $1,200,000 in their annual auction! Parents who had financial capacity "stepped up," and students will be blessed for generations.

Good schools, both public and private, are expensive. Having teachers spend their time organizing cookie sales or car washes to raise $500 is crazy. They need time to prepare lesson plans, and because we really value them, let's give them time to just rest and be with their families.

Your administrator always needs parents who approach challenges as seeing the glass half full. He needs parent leaders who are very vocal about the things the school is doing right. A good administrator rarely needs a parent to tell him what the school "really needs"; there are only a few minutes of every working day that he doesn't think about that. He needs resources, creative ideas, and people who are problem solvers, not problem finders. If you are an officer on the PTA board, or an informal leader, always try to find ways to encourage your administrator and staff. Good suggestions from parents are valuable; I would try to balance the suggestions with words of encouragement.

According to one study, an administrator makes 67 decisions a day. Some of them on a given day **will** be wrong. Don't worry, he will realize the mistake soon enough and make every effort to correct it. But if you are a board member, don't even entertain conversing with a parent who calls you to fix his child's problem—even the one caused by the administrator. Tell the parent you will be happy to talk with him after **he** calls the appropriate person. Explain nicely that the board doesn't deal in the day-to-day issues of the school. If your administrator finds out one of his board members has been discussing an issue with a parent, it will be tremendously demoralizing to him. And I promise you he will know, as the parent who called the board member will tell the administrator that the two of you **talked**, and the board member told him he was certain the administrator would fix the problem. My advice? If you return the call, handle it like one of our board members did in September of 2008. I was so proud of him when a parent called him about an issue, and he told the parent, "Liberty's Board of Trustees manages the school at 30,000 feet—call Dr. Haire." (Thanks, Andrew.)

With regard to the president and officers of the PTA, the president needs to be handpicked by the administrator. Then the supportive officers need to be selected by the newly appointed president and the administrator. You should never allow these important positions to be elected ones; the risk of having an emotionally immature leader is too great. And if politics comes into play, it will take another full-time staff member to keep the PTA from destroying the morale of the school. After you select the president, then discuss with her/him the people with whom **she/he** wants to serve. Sounds a little bit like a good ol' boy system, doesn't it? It can also be called making sure the right people are in charge. This new way of organizing the PTA is another function the school board can serve; it is a simple board motion, second, discussion ("I see no hands"), and unanimous approval. DONE! The motion passed that "The president of the PTA will be appointed by the administrator."

In Christian schools, the PTA is customarily named the PTF, Parent Teacher Fellowship. For the two school years 2008-2010, Liberty has chosen not to have PTF officers. We have a well-loved staff person, Sandra Garoutte, who is in charge of delegating all PTF projects. She may choose to place moms of lower school children on lower school projects, and another group of moms of upper school kids to work on projects that mostly benefit upper school students. This leader must be an emotionally mature staff member who has excellent people skills. I suggest the administrator take time to make this hire.

All PTF presidents at Liberty were appointed; I asked them the names of the moms with whom they wanted to serve, we discussed them, and they made the phone calls to recruit. These presidents did everything in their power to help me and our school. They never tried to overstep their authority, were never part of a gossip ring, and were always doing whatever they could to make my job easier. Other parents greatly admired them, respected them, and perhaps most importantly, were glad to see them coming. I will take with me to my grave a very deep appreciation and love for our "presidents." (Thanks, Roger, Dorothy, Patty, Tonya and Barbara.)

A message to officers of the PTA, PTF or school board: your position of leadership does not preclude your right to express a legitimate concern when it involves your child. You have a parental responsibility that supersedes the civic one for which you have so graciously volunteered. Just make certain it is a legitimate concern that is not self-serving. If you are a leader, you will know what that means.

Chapter 13

It Only Takes a Few Good Men

There are strong leaders in your school. I suggest taking the time to get to know them, and offering them a project which they can get their teeth and heart into.

So here you are, administrator of a public or private school, and most of the problematic issues are the same. You are blessed with all of the responsibility and little real authority—violation of basic Management 101 principles. And the sad truth is that most everyone on the board knows it, but egos, politics, and tradition will keep all mouths shut. It smacks of, "There is an elephant in the living room, but if we don't say anything, maybe it will go away."

If our schools and government were run more like an ethical and efficient business, we would have better schools, and our taxes would be considerably lower. Abuse in spending by people in power is at an epidemic level. Examples with which many are familiar are the athletic complexes in mid-size towns across America. They are beautiful, first-class facilities. The home-side press box is typically soundproof, with a full kitchen for guests and VIP's. Most have a football field, track, natatorium, and meeting room suites. Cost to the taxpayers in 2010 dollars is typically north of $120,000,000. Why the lavish expense? Because it is other people's money.

By comparison, Liberty Christian School completed Phase I and II of construction in 2005 and will start Phase III in 2011. When completed, we will have an athletic complex (probably minus the natatorium and

VIP suites), a preschool, lower school, middle school, high school, a beautiful sanctuary, all on 76 acres, and the total cost will be approximately $45,000,000. Our board will have obtained competitive bids on every expenditure, and in my judgment, stretched our supporters' money as far as possible.

MAIN ENTRANCE OF OUR CURRENT CAMPUS

In the first two phases, the board acted responsibly, made no sweetheart deals, and at the end of the day, delivered a campus at a cost that had financial integrity. Most of our parents and many of our grandparents gave as generously as they could. A vast majority of the teachers and staff gave sacrificially, and 100% of the Board of Trustees participated. I know they will do so in future phases as well.

However, some pledges from parents were not honored, and others were not paid on time. We stopped the projects that could be stopped, but a portion of our tuition increase for the school year 2008/2009 had to be used to cover the additional mortgage caused by unpaid pledges. When the money came in, we resumed the unfinished projects. The board set the priorities, and we began working as pledges came in. Phases I and II were virtually completed in 2007, but at that time, we still had projects to finish in the approximate amount of $750,000.

I have served with board members over the years, who, if they were in Congress, and had real authority, I honestly believe our highest income tax bracket would be in the range of 15%. They would need only one term in Washington (four or six years), and would select their handpicked team of like-minded capitalistic patriots (nice term for efficient financial barracudas) to help them.

Men and women who know how to run large companies would be recruited, and my guess is that they would clean up Washington's financial mess in record time—and probably would not accept a salary. These patriots just love America. There would be no pork, no unproductive departments, no fat on anyone's payroll, and certainly no "I'll vote for your pet project if you'll vote for mine." That level of deal making would be beneath the integrity of every one of these American patriots. None of these civil servants would even consider selling out their integrity for re-election.

Our board members have helped with the finances in running our school. They have asked the hard questions, and I greatly appreciate their supportive role in making me accountable. They serve the parents of our school with diligence and integrity, and our parents are the beneficiaries. Each year we have an outside CPA firm perform an audit, and have always received a good report. I will tell you that if it were not for these board members, Liberty would not have even come close to being a great school.

It would be very easy to simply list names of the members who have served faithfully on our board, but I think that mentioning their names is not the point. I think the value is in telling **what they did to make a difference.** The benefit for you, as the reader, is to not have to reinvent the wheel. I'm going to tell you some key components in the makeup of your board that will make your school great. For parents voting for your public school board members or boards, the following are qualities you should be looking for in the men or women you elect. Admittedly, these qualities are difficult to measure, so you must rely on their reputation in the community and on your instincts.

One characteristic is that they always ask the hard questions in a kind way. That made me appreciate their character and honest heart to be the best board members they could be. (Jeff, you are a dear friend.)

They are thoughtful and generous. Several board members were commercial pilots, but always did their best to be off duty the day of the board meeting. It seemed to me that after every payday, one member always brought an addition to our first and very humble computer lab. This showed me that he really cared that our students had good technology with which to learn. (Dennis Lyons is with the Lord now, and we miss him.)

A member of our first school board was one of our prayer warriors, something every Christian and public school needs more of. If Barbara had an issue for which she had passion, she would do two things. First, she would pray fervently. Second, she anticipated that there might come a time in a board meeting when, in her words, she would have to "lay it down"—her term for not insisting on a lengthy argument in the board room.

Several members have become very dear friends. Some always gave me the impression that they thought I was a great leader—that always gave me a boost when I got discouraged. One day one of them saw that I was emotionally drained. He walked into my office and wrote a check to the school for $100,000 and asked, "Feel better?" (Thank you, Craig.)

During a capital campaign, we really wanted a statue of our mascot, the Warrior, at the entrance to our campus. The statue was 15 ft. tall at a cost of $100,000, and I really didn't think it was a realistic goal. After a breakfast meeting, one of our parents who would later serve on the board said to me, "And Rodney, get that horse." Of course gifts of this size are enormously helpful, but the knowledge that I was not in the proverbial foxhole alone made days like those even more encouraging and memorable.

When we needed land for our new campus, the same generous family donated 50 acres to get our new campus off the launching pad. They followed this gift with a six-figure cash gift, and another pledge for the next thirty years. (Jack and Debbie—thanks.)

Liberty Christian School

THE WARRIOR

Some valuable members were truly bright businessmen who brought a very sound simplicity to what seemed like an endless sea of complex financial problems. When they talked, they spoke with a calm authority that made all of us know that at the end of the day, it was going to be all right.

For school administrators, there is a desperate need to have a board friend with whom you can be gut level honest. Over the years, a few of these men have called me every couple of weeks to "check my temperature," and never have an agenda. They just want to know how I'm doing. (I appreciate you too, "Reece.")

Some board members always presented a calming effect to our board meetings. I don't think they ever knew how soothing their very presence was in our meetings. I noticed their very deep love for their family, and anyone could see that it was for the best education for everyone's children that they served. Humble strength is always disarming in a room full of strong leaders.

Private school leaders, you have to start wherever you start, and never lower your expectations or compromise your dreams. The larger the vision, the more likelihood that you will find board members and parents with resources to join you in the pursuit of the larger goal. "Heavy hitters" are not really interested in small projects.

I believe you need a good accountant on your board. He will give the board confidence that your financial direction is "true north." But look for an accountant who is a peacemaker, because most private schools will experience seasons when you have "more month left than money." (Thanks, Robby and Steve.)

As private school board members, their financial gifts are expected to be of a larger amount than others, although not always. Some board members may not be able to offer large financial gifts, but can contribute significantly in other ways. The important issue is that they are leaders as "givers."

When your private school embarks on a capital campaign, it is important to communicate to your parents that there are **no** small gifts; but there **are** large ones. A capital campaign is necessary when a private school builds a building, purchases additional land, adds on to the present facility, begins a major program, etc. The chairman of the capital campaign must communicate to all parents that it is important to not wait on the groundbreaking celebration before they give; the ground can't be broken **until** they give. Great schools must have the financial support from as many families as possible.

If you embark on a capital campaign, I strongly recommend that you employ a consultant. Consultants differ in many ways; all have different styles, and I would suggest you interview several. Their philosophy must be compatible with your school's heart. At the end of the day, they will help you identify those families who are willing and have a desire to help **their** school achieve great things; in our case, it was build a new campus. The consultant will guide you to meet with those families who will likely have the capacity to give the campaign financial traction. I'll give you a few examples to help you get the picture. As the administrator and board member, you are going to be on personal visits and have lunches with families who have capacity **and** a willingness to help you achieve the goal (not always the same). The names may come from your consultant, but more from your knowledge of the families.

One day a board member and I met with a dad who is an attorney in Denton, Texas. This dad and his wife have three boys in the school, soon to have four. The board member, Don Lovelace, made the "ask," and the parent said it would be an honor to give the school $100,000. If you are the one doing the "ask," an immediate response is valuable as it builds confidence—it makes the next "ask" easier; but let me stress, none of them are easy. Thanks, Rocky and Andrea.

On the way over to Rocky's office, I remember telling Don, "This 'ask' is a little uncomfortable for me; would you do it? Asking my son for a gift seems awkward." Don responded that he would be glad to. After the meeting, as we were walking out, Don said to Rocky, "I have a large rug that you might like for your office and I'd be happy to give it to you." That struck me as a very warm gesture; Don is a seasoned and very successful businessman who was making the "ask," and Rocky, a young successful attorney, who was making the very significant gift. And as we left, the tables turned in a good way.

The administrator and board members are crucial in the success of any capital campaign. Normally the administrator and one board member visit with a family. One evening, a member and I went to a family's home to ask for a six-figure gift. I really didn't know what to expect from our meeting. This may sound a bit strange to those reading this book who are not Christians, but board member Don Reece and I spent over two hours in the man's home just talking about the Lord and the wonderful things God had done in the lives of his children through Liberty.

At the end of our time together, it just didn't seem right to talk about money, so we told him we were just going to leave some information with him, and he could talk it over with his wife and call if he had any questions. Sometimes it is just not the right time to talk about money. In a few days, his wife brought in a six-figure check and dropped it at the front desk; the next week, she brought another. (Thank you, John and Michele.)

I've given just a few examples of donors who are necessary to give a campaign financial traction. These parents are givers. They made large six-figure gifts to the campaign, but their support didn't stop there.

One family observed that our band needed the instruments necessary for a drum line. There was not an ask from our development team; I got a call from the dad making the offer to help. Maybe this is what Jesus meant when He said, "God loves a cheerful giver." The offer to buy the instruments needed for a drum line gave the band the momentum to grow. This man works for a company that matches gifts, so we received the same amount again! (Bruce and Shellee, your gift changed lives—our band grew from nine students to ninety in three years!)

We have a wonderful parent who is a widow and a single mother of three wonderful children. She continues to be an enormous help to our school as we take on the huge task of constructing an entire campus. She provided the funds to construct the library at the beginning. (Mary, you are truly an encourager.)

If you want to help make your school a great one, become a positive leader in any way you can. Maybe you have a special talent, gift, or money—but the payoff is in the **giving**—odd, isn't it. I've noticed over the years that there are givers and takers, and I've never met an unhappy giver, no matter their station in life or amount of the gift.

There have been hundreds of men and women who have been a huge help in building our school, and I would love to mention every one of the over 900 families by name, but no one gave donations or encouragement so their names could be mentioned in this book (at the time, nobody knew there would be a book); they gave out of their love for a cause. Don't ever think your gift of money or words of encouragement don't count; they all do! **There are no small gifts**!

Warning! If your **Christian** school embarks on a capital campaign, expect "all hell to break loose"—literally. Expect some huge disappointments; I guarantee they will come from the most unexpected people. Here are some examples at the other end of the spectrum that I would love to forget.

On our first campus, we were in the early stages of a capital campaign to build a lower school classroom building. In the beginning years of a private school, normally there are not many wealthy families, maybe not any. In our case, we had several. One of my really good friends was one of the wealthiest. His kids were having a tremendous educational experience; they had exceptional teachers and coaches, and one of his daughters was a great athlete. His family could not have been more pleased. I showed him the drawing and plans for a modest 7,500 sq. ft. classroom building with a total cost in 1992 of approximately $500,000. He loved the plans, but his first question was, "Rodney, how in the world are you going to pay for it?" I can't begin to describe the disappointment I felt realizing that he and his wife were not going to take a lead financial role in this project.

My experience covering four capital campaigns is that gifts normally don't come from where you expect them. I received many great surprises, and just as many disappointments. I really don't know if the highs are as high as the lows are low. During each of our capital campaigns I developed stress-related diverticulitis. While painful, I'll use one of Jack Nicholson's lines in *The Bucket List*: "I'm pretty sure I'd do it all again."

I want to share with you the strategy that Liberty Christian School used to build our new campus. I wasn't sure it would work. First, we had a feasibility study done by a professional development company. It told us that **if** we had a capital campaign, we could expect to raise a low of $2,000,000 and a high of $4,500,000. We then hired an architect and general contractor. Secondly, we divided the new campus project into seven major sections (upper school, lower school, science labs, computers and technology, library, athletics, and fine arts). I would be used to help wherever needed (I'll explain). Each board member chose the category he felt he could really get excited about.

We then drew numbers from one to seven out of a bowl. The board member who drew #1 got to pick his first choice of a co-captain family from the entire parent body that he wanted to work with in raising money for his project. We then went through all seven, each man choosing his co-captains (each member had two "draft" choices). At the end of this first stage, we left the room with seven members who each had two co-captain families. Each board member was to contact his co-captain family and invite them to meet for a briefing on strategy. Their task was to cover the total cost of their project.

Then we met with the board members and their two co-captain families in the gym for an **all-school** "draft." The name of every family was printed in large letters on a long sheet of paper, about 25 ft. long. We had seven tables of six people each—the board member and his two co-captains (husbands and wives).

Then we had a drawing that evening to see which team would get first through seventh choice of any family that was on the 25 ft. long list. As a family was chosen, it went on the board member's "ask" list, and was marked off the large sheet of paper. After the draft, every family in the school had been chosen and was on a team. Each board member and their co-captains were responsible to contact each of the families on their list. If a family they contacted did not want to give to the specific project that the board member had signed up for, the giving family simply designated his gift to the project of his choice. The board member receiving the gift would then make a very happy phone call to his board colleague who had **that** project, celebrating a surprise gift to the other board member's team.

At the end of all of the calls and visits, we had a meeting of the fifteen "heavy hitters" from all projects to let them know where we were in the overall goal, and almost all of them made another contribution. This program took almost two years to complete. Some of our board members had to call families three or four times, and some never received returned calls. But at the end of the day, we had commitments totaling over $10,000,000 and a gift of fifty acres of land on which to build our campus. There were some things we would have done differently, but we experienced a very successful and unique campaign.

I honestly do not understand why it is so difficult to raise money. The adage in the fund raising business is that the most common reason that people don't give is that they are not asked. Why do we need to be asked to do something as worthwhile as giving or helping the school where our children and grandchildren are being educated and trained? In the heart of every administrator, unsolicited gifts hold at least three times the value of solicited ones, and my guess is, that's also true for the Lord. Thoreau said, "Philanthropy is almost the only virtue which is sufficiently appreciated by mankind." Amen, "Bro" Thoreau!

Chapter 14

Not All Board Members and Parents Who Can Help Wear White Hats

Board members and families with financial capacity who actually help a school "move the ball across the goal line" are rare. Let's try to get into the head of those who don't.

A **few** board members just want to talk about the school's problems. Their approach to representing their constituency drives their board colleagues crazy. In my experience, the helpful board members begin to lobby for shorter meetings; and during many meetings I found myself wishing I was on the teaching staff. One of my board members was president of a large corporation. He told me that his board meetings became so painful and unproductive, he had his board meeting around a large conference table—but removed all chairs from the room.

We administrators must always keep in mind we have chosen a great profession, and understand that problems exist in every field. The uniqueness of the school business is that most of our problems originate from our superiors, and a major purpose of this book is to help solve that frustration.

During my really tough board meetings, I had to remember **those** families who stood with me in building our great school. I remembered that those families understood it is always about what you "do," not what you say. Remembering their sacrifices gave me the strength to continue the grand purpose, and experience those meetings in perspective. In Texas, the saying about a guy who just talks a good game is that he is "all hat and no cows." If you are that person, board member or not, do your school family two favors: stop complaining, and only make promises you intend to keep. Empty promises and fault finders are very cheap, and have no real value because there are so many of them.

I believe every administrator or development director would appreciate from a family who is not ever going to give to any campaign a simple phone call saying, " Rodney, you and I both know I have a lot of money, but you need to know that I have no intention of giving Liberty Christian School any of it." That has happened to me three times in 28 years. My response was, "I really appreciate your saving me time—I hope your child greatly benefits from our school." And under my breath would say, "Good for you that other less fortunate families picked up your check—because there are no free lunches." (I just realized how therapeutic writing a book can be.)

In the early years, one board member believed that the more he complained about the expenses, the lower they would suddenly become. Another often accused me of wasting money. For example, he said in one meeting, "What's wrong with our yellow dogs?" He was referring to our fleet of buses that were very undependable. He actually is a bright guy, very wealthy, but his micromanagement of our school's finances drove me crazy. If I had been wasteful, the following paragraph could not have been written.

It is important to know that in the first 20 years of our school's existence, we purchased almost all furniture, including student and teacher desks, at auctions. Normally, you can find out about these events in the Sunday edition, back page of the classified section of your local newspaper. I had what was actually a hay trailer that I used to haul our purchases. I went during the summer, after I inventoried what furniture needed to be replaced or purchased for the next school year—it was my shopping list.

If you are not familiar with auctions, you'll need to bring your tax-exemption document, a credit card, a blank check, and a few hundred dollars in cash. Arrive an hour early to survey the inventory to be auctioned, and mark on the auction sheet provided by the auctioneer those items that best match your "shopping list." All items will be numbered. Often I attended two or three auctions during a summer, as it is rare to find everything you need at one auction.

I have three suggestions: stay away from electronics, stay in clear sight of the auctioneer, and always be the last to bid on the item you want to purchase. You will only have 24 hours to remove your purchases from the auctioneer's warehouse, so either get your own "hay trailer," or ask the auctioneer for the name of a mover who he knows is dependable and honest. The dress is casual, and I suggest wearing comfortable shoes. You will save money, normally 60% or more. For the **first** fifteen years, the average cost of our student desks was **ninety cents each.** During an auction held at the University of North Texas in Denton, we were able to purchase 450 desks at fifty cents each!

My experience is that these irritating and pessimistic board members and parents seem to run in pairs. Mr. Stingy had a friend who heartily supported his every psychotic attempt to step into the day-to-day operations of the school. That principle of "pairs," while not documented by a double-blind study is, in my opinion, true of boards universally. I believe it is true of negative and critical-minded parents, public and private school boards, church boards—and maybe boards of every kind. There is something about power that can breed a very dark kind of synergy. The two of them seemed "balanced" when they were invited and agreed to serve, but once in a position of authority and power, their contribution and value went south. That is a common occurrence. Administrators, in selecting or appointing board members or committee members, you are looking for emotional and spiritual maturity—**then** givers who have capacity.

These power-hungry "duos" will have many opportunities to take a clean shot at any administrator. One of the hardest aspects of running a private school is that you have to hire teachers, purchase textbooks and student desks, etc. before you know for certain what your enrollment will be, which is the primary source of income for the next fiscal year. That inability to adequately plan for a balanced budget drives private school administrators crazy. If you serve in the same school for fifteen years or so, your experience will get you ahead of the curve, but it is **always** unnerving. In fact, you have to set almost **all** of your school's expenses before your income is known.

There is no other way to run a private school. No school administrator has a crystal ball, and projecting enrollment is a very tough aspect of the business. And if you have members with control issues on your board, this will provide them with large amounts of fodder for their verbal cannons, enough to last until the next election, the time they resign (which will seem like forever), or until the administrator resigns from the relentless humiliation and stress (which is almost always the case).

It must give negative board members some sort of sordid joy to see their administrator twist in the wind. The administrator will have to admit that he hired too many teachers, ordered too many textbooks, bought too many football shoulder pads—the list is exhaustive. Board members do have a serious fiscal responsibility, but becoming a productive board member is a process and an art, not a science; but more importantly, it is a matter of the head **and** heart. If you have a competent administrator, he will not get better if you continually criticize. The same general principles are true in the lives of pastors, but one of **them** can write **that** book.

It should be the goal of every private school to operate exclusively on tuition dollars. In the early years of a school, fundraisers may be a necessary part of meeting the budget. Get free of that dependency as soon as you can. I'll give you a hint: we are talking about setting a realistic tuition, **and** instituting a financial aid program—don't leave home without either.

In the words of a popular television hostess, "This is a really good idea." In the early years of Liberty, we added a paragraph to our handbook that became invaluable. Simply stated, it read something like this: "Liberty Christian School will make every effort to establish tuition rates that cover operational expenses. However, if for some unexpected reason, Liberty experiences unanticipated expenses, an assessment of up to $25 (in 2010 I would recommend $100) per student may be needed to balance the school's budget. The board will make every attempt to limit the number of these assessments."

An assessment has been instituted approximately twelve times in our school's 27-year history, but when needed, it was invaluable. I trust that your school will build up a reserve of cash, but until that happens, this may be a valuable paragraph added to your handbook. If you impose it, make sure it is accompanied by a letter clearly defining the unexpected expenses that the assessment will cover. If you explain it adequately, you will hear complaints only from the families who could not afford a private school in the first place—or from those families you should never have admitted.

The board of trustees, whether public or private, must get the hiring of the administrator right, and then have the confidence and wisdom to let him do his job. By some studies, the average tenure of a school administrator is 18 months, and most leave out of frustration with the board. The reasons are very easy to understand. The administrator normally can't fire a teacher, can't hire that special coach, and can't really do much of anything without board approval. In most cases, all he can do is ask the board members for permission to do his job. That is not exactly a recipe for success. Advice to board members, when you find a good administrator, remember two important rules: first, he can easily be overmanaged, so avoid the temptation; and secondly, he must know **during meetings** that you have his back.

I have to believe that most boards **try** to do it right, and some are close, "just no cigar." They want to hold the administrator accountable, and that is their responsibility. The issue is all in the attitude with which they perform the accountability. If it is with encouragement and support, asking, "Do you need anything from any of us?" they are on target. If it is holding up numbers and asking questions that he can't answer, they are being bullies and need to stop it, resign, or be voted off the board.

For starters, you are not dealing in widgets. You are dealing with kids, and in many cases, very hard-to-please parents. From my observation, demanding parents are a more difficult issue with which to deal in private schools than in public. In private schools, there is an ownership factor that is not present in most of the public school arenas. In fact, often it is a generational mentality. A parent recently told me he couldn't wait to have grandchildren, and that he was hoping to see them at Liberty.

And the demand for excellence is higher because the parents are paying for a product that may be best described by a question asked of me by one of our parents: "When my child graduates from Liberty, will she be ready for Harvard?" The bar is very high.

On the other hand, if the board has hired the wrong administrator, the best decision it can make is to replace him with one the board can trust to do the job right. First, define the job description, the soft issues and the hard ones. Then find the person that fits. I think it is best to hire an administrator who already has a job, whose school does not want to lose him. Don't find the person, and then define the job around him. That can't work. Not **probably** won't work, it **will not** work.

Chapter 15

No Contracts for School Teachers and Administrators??
(I Know, I Know…)

At the end of the day, our schools have to be about educating kids. Let's talk about some of the current issues that keep schools in America from accomplishing that goal.

Running a school carries with it an enormous awareness of responsibility on the part of all of the administrative team. It offers a euphoric high from being able to accomplish great things for kids. The win is truly indescribable. But also present are the gut-wrenching pains of having to live with bad decisions, many of which administrators have to own. There are joys from having hired a great teacher, but hiring the wrong teacher or coach is terribly debilitating. You know whether you hired the right or wrong staff member in the first few weeks of school, because the "honeymoon" period is very brief.

The way we solve that problem is by not offering contracts. Not one person has a contract, including me. Contracts are a great method to protect employees from abusive employers, but the character and integrity of the head administrator and board should provide that protection. Contracts are just not in the best interest of the students.

One year that policy seemed to backfire on our school. Our choir director resigned two weeks before school started. If she had been under contract, her resignation would have been less likely.

As it turned out, and it usually does for a school that genuinely prays for the right staff, we were able to quickly hire a uniquely gifted and more experienced choir director. Several times over the years, I have hired the wrong person and that person has not fulfilled his obligation to teach, thus allowing me the opportunity to make a change for the better.

In this instance Mrs. Ann Smith, our new director, took our choir to sing in the National Cathedral in Washington, in a church in New York City, and in a Manhattan homeless shelter. In the spring of 2009 and 2010 she took them to Ireland to sing in some very old, beautiful churches. That never would have happened without her gifted vision and leadership. By the way, our choir doubled in size after she arrived.

If you make enough hires, you are going to make some mistakes, and a "no contract policy" is the only failsafe. If you decide that this idea is a good one, it may take several years to allow the implementation process to take effect through attrition. I suggest beginning your next school year with a board-approved policy that says in effect, "New hires don't receive contracts." A benefit for the teachers is that if their spouse gets transferred or they find that they don't like teaching or a new opportunity opens up for them, they are not impeded by a contract. This new hiring policy must be made by the board, and the reason given to new applicants is "It was a board decision." Public schools are trapped by teacher unions, and until our politicians become statesmen, a no contract policy will be a "front page" issue because the mainstream media is liberal. If your board has the courage, as soon as the present union contract expires, I suggest you get in front of the media and call the educational editor of your local newspaper for a photo-op of you tearing up **your** contract.

Let's address the crucial issue of evaluating staff, and how board members can help. Liberty's board members are emotionally mature. If our administration is conflicted about the value of a staff member, any one of the board members would be helpful as a sounding board (no pun intended) if we needed another opinion regarding that staff member's contribution to the overall good of the school. We are not seeking an evaluation regarding the teaching competency of the teacher, but rather the emotional and spiritual maturity of a parent's point of view. But here's the caveat: there has to be an understanding that the administrator can talk freely of his thoughts and options, but has no responsibility to follow that board member's suggestions—not in this private meeting. He is just using his friend who happens to be a trusted board member to hear his thoughts. In this type of scenario, the board member ideally should offer ideas only when asked. Members of boards can be a huge help in this area, but rarely are asked for fear on the part of the administrator of having to implement the board member's "suggestions."

The truth is that the administrator is not always looking for someone to give him the answer, he just needs to talk through an issue. Confucius said, "When you know a thing, to hold that you know it; and when you do not know a thing, to allow that you do not know it—this is knowledge." The people that worry me, both administrators and board members, are the ones who always seem to have all of the answers.

Boards have more to do with the failure of schools than any other entity. I realize the huge role supportive parents play, the impact of a teacher, and the tremendous influence of a coach. There's no argument from me on any of these absolutely crucial roles. But at the end of the day, it all flows from the top, and here is how it works.

The administrator really works for one organization, the Board. It may be a church deacon board; it may be an independent private school board or a publicly elected one. The administrator of the school must have board support in order to keep his staff on task, to deal with very difficult parents, and to motivate kids. I just can't emphasize that enough. If he is without verbal support, or even feels alone, he will fall—it is just a matter of time.

The administrator knows, as does the whole world, that teachers and coaches are underpaid and overworked, as of course is the administrator. If the administrator knows he has board support, he can support that staff person with the full knowledge that nobody is going to go over his head. Trying to do so will just be a waste of time for that overprotective parent. I gave an example in an earlier chapter, and here is another very sad one.

It was about 1989 and our school was just beginning to get traction when a group of parents decided to meet privately at the home of an influential family. The original purpose of the meeting was to have an informal discussion on the SAT college entrance exam in relation to other schools. My understanding is that the meeting quickly turned south and became a gossip session. At the end of the meeting, a list was produced of 15 grievances that one of the organizers committed to writing.

The group decided that one of them would deliver their "15 Theses" to each board member the very next day. They actually had one of our teachers in their meeting. This man also served a local church as their pastor. I know he was there because several of the "15 Theses" were on an administrative list of goals that had been shared with staff. Obviously he was not a loyal staff member, but he was an excellent teacher.

The next day, each of our board members, except me, received a copy of this document. An emergency board meeting was called with everyone but me being invited, and a "state of emergency" was declared. After that meeting, one of the members asked me to meet with him and a couple of other members to discuss a strategy to deal with an issue of which I knew nothing. To be honest, I was in the mood to let **them** run the school. I greatly resented the board for having met without me, but that was obviously not my decision.

That night I lost respect for **most** of the members of our school board. I wanted to resign, but we administrators can't really do that quite so easily, because children, loyal staff, and an institution are involved. So I met with the board, and we went over the carefully written "15 Theses." It was decided that I would face that group of parents, and also invite **all** parents to the meeting who wanted to attend. Sadly, but predictably, we had the largest percentage of parental attendance in the history of the school. If we had been visited by the fire marshal that evening, we would have been in violation of every occupancy code in the book—it was "standing room only" in our gym. When I saw the crowd, it reminded me of the traffic slowdown at the scene of a traffic accident. The crowd was the onlooking traffic and I was the accident; at least that was the anticipated scenario.

The board decided that I would address the general meeting from beginning to end, speak to each of the 15 points, conclude with an open forum for question and answer, and hopefully, my wife and I would get home alive. I went to Dillard's department store, bought a new suit, and remember telling my wife Judy, "If I am going down in flames, I want to look as good as I can."

147

One of the parents who formed the original group of "caring parents," was passing out what was, in my opinion, very negative and inflammatory literature in the back of the room before the meeting began. My wife saw him and immediately asked if he had permission to pass out his "relevant information." He admitted he did not, and, very honorably, "folded his tent." (He could have started a fight with Judy, but she was so mad he would have been pulverized, and I doubt been able to be identified with dental records.) This was an emotionally charged night.

As I went through their list, point by point, it became very apparent that the list was essentially without substance. "Armchair quarterbacks" exist on every front in the school business, public and private. Toward the end of the meeting, I will never forget one of our very loving and faithful parents, Mrs. Irma Thomas, raising her hand during the Q and A with a very simply-stated observation. Irma said something to the effect of, "We have a great school, and I know it is not perfect, but it is truly wonderful. Recently, our church was considering starting a school, and I asked Rodney if he would mind sharing with me the important issues we should be aware of before we began the serious due diligence process. When we received his twenty-page report, we closed down all thoughts of starting a school. Further, it made us appreciate what a blessing we have in Liberty, and the great sacrifices made by so many."

After the ovation, there was a very strange atmosphere in the gym. The board was surprised that I had survived. The critical group of parents tried to find a place to hide.

I felt very alone that night. I would either be God's man for the job, or He would replace me. I knew I was alone after I discovered that I had not been invited to the first and last secret board meeting in the history of our school.

After Irma sat down, the meeting was virtually over. I closed the meeting with an awkward prayer. I'm not at all sure that the Lord was impressed with my halfhearted prayer of reconciliation after so vicious an attack by a group of, in my opinion, self-serving control freaks. They wanted to control me, our school's government, and to a dangerous extent, their children's lives. Administrators must beware of control-oriented parents—they are real and present weapons of mass destruction. Caring parents are wonderful; it's just important to realize the difference.

One of my friends refers to the "controllers" as "helicopter parents," hovering everywhere their child happens to be. Sadly, at the end of their child's teenage years, they will likely have been "too big a parent." These parents are so afraid that their child will do something wrong, say something inappropriate or make a mistake, that if you ask the child a question, the parent will answer for them. Psychologists have seen so much of this recently that they have a general term for the child's emotional state: "There is a house there, but it has no furniture."

These overprotective parents may try to use the school board when they can't get their way. I've had phone calls at home when their daughter didn't make cheerleader. I got a phone call from a dad when his second grade son made a "B" in physical education! (As I remember, the secret parent meeting referred to earlier was held at his home.) If we administrators fail to support our teachers or coaches and get involved in subjective decisions, it will destroy the morale of a good staff. If the overprotective parent can't get the "right" answer from me, he will likely call his board member friend. If the board member will **not** entertain a conversation, much less a meeting, the school wins.

If the cheerleader director kicks three girls off the squad for drinking alcohol, the team has three fewer cheerleaders—period. When the starting quarterback is ineligible to play in Friday's big game, there is not an emergency board meeting called to evaluate the teacher's grading system. These are all very real problems in the life of an administrator.

Discipline issues are almost never "black and white." Here is a common scenario and the predictable fallout. On one occasion of recent memory, a very good student came into my office with his parents. The student and his parents were emotionally shaken to their core because their son had experimented with marijuana. The son didn't get caught by his parents, but confessed his potentially dangerous decision to them. The young man had excellent grades and had never been in trouble—he just did a dumb weekend kid thing. I did not choose to punish him. On another occasion, a young lady got caught cheating and forging her parent's signature on a discipline report, and I gave her a three-day "in-school suspension." To make matters seem more unfair to an outsider, the boy was a great athlete. It appeared, from the outsider looking in, that I had clearly "played favorites."

These circumstances and experiences were different in that the boy confessed from his own conscience, and the girl got caught. The fallout is that the girl's parents called a board member, I was accused of favoritism, and I couldn't defend myself because I couldn't break confidentiality with the boy and his parents. I would have resigned before I would have told anyone about that young man experimenting with drugs. (By the way, he later attended an Ivy League school, and may not have been accepted had this experience been on his record.) He repented and I forgave him—end of story. To drag him through the mud would just not happen on my watch. If I had not had the reputation of moral integrity and sound judgment, I would not have had the support of the board. Administrators and staff, as long as you protect your integrity, you retain the privilege of doing the right thing, and not having to bend to the politically correct thing.

Every year we have a mandatory Parent Orientation prior to the beginning of school. I take about twenty minutes to share my heart, and one point I make is that running a school is a job that will often appear to be unfair, and that rarely ever will the whole truth of a matter be fully disclosed; they are simply going to have to trust our judgment. If we don't have a reputation for making good decisions, we can't expect the support that we must have to operate our school in truth and fairness.

The board has to make the quality decision to support the authorities who are running the school. Again, if the board has the wrong administrator, they face a problem that can only be solved in a closed board meeting in which a very difficult decision has to be made. Does the administrator go or stay? If the board can't support and trust his decision-making skills, he has to go. But the decision had better **not** be dependent on the board member who let his arm be twisted by a discontented parent.

If you want examples, check out two of the public schools in Plano, Texas. They experienced well-documented cheerleading fiascos in approximately 2006/2007. You will not believe your eyes. It does not apply only to cheerleading. Grades, athletic eligibility, discipline decisions—all these connected issues have emerged due to school boards "blinking." School districts are going to get sued, and if you are on a board, you are going to lose some friends. Don't make decisions based on your fear of a lawsuit or because an unhappy parent is going to talk about you. Frankly, you have to be stronger than that. But you are going to encounter some litigious parents, and all schools should purchase a "Directors and Officers" insurance policy. It covers board members, administrators, teachers, and coaches, and is relatively inexpensive. (And don't forget to include in the handbook legal protection written by a good attorney that states clearly if a parent sues the school, the parent pays for the school's legal fees.)

A very basic truth remains: you never will get the full story from half of the parties involved. There is the parent's opinion, the teacher's or coach's opinion, the administrator's opinion, the child's opinion, and then the truth.

We administrators are always going to make mistakes, but if we have character and integrity, we will generally make decisions boards can trust. To board members, I say it will be in the best interest of the students, teachers, and the school if you will just allow administrative decisions to remain. In the end, you will have a more stable school. If you don't support your administrator, he will be reduced to a puppet in the eyes of his staff, parents, and students. If you have the right guy and go against his decision **just once**, you can measure the time of receiving his resignation with an egg timer. If he is weak, he will stay and you have an administrator whom nobody respects. The problem will escalate to an inmate-run asylum, and you will be responsible for a situation you don't even want to think about.

Board meeting days are typically the hardest days that an administrator has on his calendar. There is not even a close second. One reason is that some of the issues that the board deals with are **not** the issues for which the board has all of the facts. For instance, assume the board member has been called by a parent who could not get the answer he wanted from his child's teacher or coach. Because the parent helped in his board election campaign, he feels he has a "friend in high places, who is only a phone call away." The very best thing for the school is for the board to have agreed on a policy of non-intervention and respond to any parent by quoting the "party line." That will mean telling the concerned parent that the board has a policy of not interfering with the decision of the administration. Note to administrator: have that meeting with Dad, hopefully one or two of his board friends, the AD, and hopefully the Generation Xer YESTERDAY!!

Chapter 16

Perfect Storm Ahead!

If your school is not getting traction, there are some gut-wrenching decisions that you must make. Let's talk about some of them.

By now you know that all administrators are going to deal with difficult board members; since 1983, I've had my share. Without question, the board that gave me the hardest days came in the early years when I did not know what to look for in a board member. I thought the primary qualification was that they needed to have the capacity to give money. I don't believe that anymore.

My greatest pain has come from members who wanted to micromanage. In the early years my board conflicts got so heated that at one point I tendered my resignation. Today I know that was a mistake, but at the time I didn't understand that controlling board members are often a part of the territory.

I mailed my resignation to all of the members so that they would receive it a couple of days before what I anticipated would be my last board meeting. My wife was packing my office during the board meeting, and the strangest thing happened. One of the members who I actually believed did not like me **at all,** asked, "Rodney, what would it take for you to stay?" You could have knocked me over with a feather.

After an extended meeting, we came to an agreement and I stayed. The major point for me was that I insisted on hiring a person with the accounting background to serve as the school's business manager. Every meeting was laced with accounting questions, and I was getting very tired of their attitudes regarding questions that only an accountant could answer. I really thought that when they received my resignation, they would be ecstatic about finally getting rid of the guy who was keeping them from running things. I remembered feeling abandoned and was willing to leave quietly and peacefully. I told them at the meeting, "My wife and I don't want a going away party, we just want to leave and let you guys run things." I remember being caught off guard with total surprise that they wanted me to stay. That request came from the same guy who, in an earlier meeting, pounded the table in anger. Who knew?

Productive school boards can offer the community invaluable leadership. In the public school arena there is a destructive movement emerging that could gain traction. The proposal is a four-day week for public schools. The goal is to lengthen the school day, thereby giving the children the same number of classroom hours as in the five-day week. The primary motivation is cost savings derived from running the bus system four days per week instead of five, serving less food, and saving utilities. This is a terrible idea which I believe will move our public schools even further down in the world's academic pecking order. Kids have a limited attention span, and lengthening the day will only adversely affect their ability to learn and comprehend the material. Additionally, a three-day weekend will mean taking longer for students to recall their previously taught lessons. Public school board members have a wonderful role to play in stopping this craziness—which is all in the name of **progressive education. By the way, "progressive education" is an oxymoron.** Also, if your state is facing a budget deficit, rather than cutting the school week to four days, just eliminate the Department of Education—nobody will notice.

Incumbent school board members have another important role to play that is going to be very difficult. It is to keep your state's Department of Education from instituting policies that will cause good teachers to leave. (Remember, your first objective is to eliminate the Department of Education in your state, but assuming that can't be done for a couple of elections, your next objective is to keep them from making decisions that will place more demands on your teachers.) I recall a congressman who ran for a state office in Texas because he wanted to close it; I wish I could give this statesman's name, rank, and serial number, but I honestly can't remember.

In August 30, 2009, the Dallas Morning News printed a very sad story of a great educator, Sarah Fine. The reasons for resigning are now clichés: "I'm just burned out" or "I want to spend more time with my family." We have heard the same ones over and over. But *CALLED* is committed to telling the truth. Sarah Fine, a great teacher in a Washington, DC high school has, in her words, "thrown in the towel." The writer of the story cites that "half of all new teachers leave the profession within five years." That, my friend, is not "burnout." Boards, don't let anyone expand your teacher's bureaucratic workloads. You want them preparing creative lesson plans, encouraging their students, and assisting those students who need help. Don't let any state official micromanage your school.

Sarah Fine recalled one of her lesson plans in which she had her tenth grade students walking around the room as part of the assignment. Her class was interrupted by an administrator who came into her class and told Ms. Fine to "get the class seated and silent." Dedicated teachers need freedom and encouragement. My guess is that this administrator did not have experience with observing Mrs. Fine, and reacted poorly to what was most likely part of a creative lesson plan.

Another factor that Ms. Fine mentioned is the lack of professional recognition extended to the teaching profession. The teaching pros that I work with could have been doctors, lawyers, or virtually any profession they chose. I have a number of great leaders on my staff that I wish were in Congress, but presently our elected officials make far too many compromises, and my friends would just cause trouble.

In America we are blessed to have good teachers who want to teach. And we can't afford to lose any of them because we added meaningless tasks to their already busy lives. And, I am aware that we have teachers in the classroom who should be fired. In a televised conversation with Reverend Rick Warren in 2008, Presidential candidate Senator John McCain may have put it best when, speaking of teachers who shouldn't be teaching, he said, "**Those** teachers just need to find another line of work."

Ms. Fine also pointed out the tremendous value that experienced teachers bring in offering ideas that can have a positive impact in the field of education. The educational profession has to be proactive in terms of improving methods, discovering new ways to help kids learn, etc. The problem is that too many of the "improvements" made in our educational system have been made by political appointees and not experienced classroom teachers or school executives.

I mentioned that board members who brought real value to the table did so in their own unique ways. That same principle holds for parents who surface as leaders. Administrators can spot parents who are valuable assets from those who just do a lot of talking in less time than you can say "flake." Particularly in preschool through fifth grade, parents can play an enormous role in assisting teachers. Every teacher is looking for "Room Mom of the Year" to surface.

Too many parents think that their monetary contribution is not valuable because it is not a large financial gift. Gifts come in all sorts of packages. Large financial gifts are crucial, especially in private schools; but small ones have their own kind of value that speaks of "sacrificial giving" to administrators, bringing to their heart a dimension and depth that some large gifts can't.

For instance, I recall a single mother of a third grade student who always paid her tuition on the last day of every month. The unusual aspect of this story is that the amount was never the exact amount owed. She always sent in a few dollars more than the amount due. I called her to ask why she never paid the exact amount. She told me, "Mr. Haire, the amount I send over my tuition is the amount that I have left in my checking account at the end of the month, and I want to give it to Liberty." I don't think it was ever over $5, but I'm telling you the story, and it happened almost 30 years ago. Administrators never forget "foxhole buddies."

I have many memories of families who have brought gifts that have contributed significantly to the success of our school, and they will always be remembered with great fondness. One day a check came in for a very substantial amount from a new family to Liberty, whom I did not know. I called to ask if they would have time to come in and visit, and to allow me to thank them personally. During that meeting, they told me that their eldest son had been helped tremendously during our football camp by some of the other players. That helpfulness spoke volumes to them about the leadership of the coaches, and they wanted to invest in it. I will never forget that conversation or the gift. It was of the size that gives schools enough financial traction to move forward. (Thanks, James and Karen.)

If you appreciate your private school, please show your appreciation in as meaningful a way as you possibly can. Parents who are not able to give financially will greatly benefit because gifts of larger amounts allow the school to cover expenses that tuition can't cover, such as the construction of buildings. If tuition can increase in the minimal range of 3%-5% annually, it will allow the children of parents who have financial limitations to remain. Additionally, your school will offer an element of reality because it will not be a school just for "rich kids."

I had a parent tell me recently that she was willing to work in any capacity to provide tuition for her child to attend Liberty. I recall some moms and dads who got their commercial bus drivers license so they would be available to drive children on field trips to earn a portion of the tuition that their current job did not provide. And I have had some parents give monthly gifts of less than $10, some for years, and I am telling you that private schools can't make it without all levels of sacrifice.

Our board members are very sensitive to raising the amount that parents pay for tuition. But the fact is that as expenses increase, tuition has to increase or the quality of programs has to decrease. In a board meeting a few years ago, we were discussing whether or not to have an increase in tuition. A really good, smart member made the case for why we **had** to have an increase; higher cost of insurance, need for higher salaries, higher fuel cost, etc. After a very organized presentation, he voted against the increase! Had the other votes gone south, that school year would have been almost impossible to operate.

It would have meant that I would have had to explain to all of my teachers and staff why, in spite of their comparatively low salaries, they would not be receiving a well-deserved raise. Boards have such tremendous power which, if used unwisely, can cause unbelievable damage. Had the other members not have acted prudently and in the best interest of our school, I would have kicked myself for not having had a "Dad meeting," you can bet your report card on that one. This board member served Liberty wisely for many years; he is highly respected. This example of a great board member attempting to take the school in the wrong direction, with the best of intentions, is why board meeting days are the most difficult for administrators.

It is difficult to work with board members who want to run a school in a financial way that is impractical. It is one thing to be frugal and responsible; it's another to be "penny wise and pound foolish." If you are a board member who is afraid of zeroes at the end of dollars, you'd better resign. Good schools are expensive and in demand. Bad ones are inexpensive, but nobody wants to be a part of them—probably not even the member who voted against the tuition increase. Don't be afraid to charge what **your** school is worth!

I will never forget a board meeting held at the home of one of our board members. I'm vividly recalling this meeting that was held in approximately 1990. The host was a member who is a very bright guy and, given my tendency to be a little liberal in the area of financial risk, his conservative nature brought a good balance to the board.

One of the board members who made my job so hard took off his boots, revealing a really big hole in his sock. We all got a good laugh out of it, and he laughed with us. But, at some base level, it seemed sad to me that his personal standards were so low, just like his vision for our school. If you are on the board of a school, and I know this may sound very superficial, I think there is a level of "class" that should attend your presence. You represent an institution and there is an appearance standard that I believe should be maintained by both you and the staff.

If your private school is producing good results, and the population is growing, **don't be afraid** to do the following as soon as possible:

1. If justified, raise the tuition. One year we raised our tuition 22% and only lost five families. That increase would have been too high had we not been priced far too low for the product we were delivering. A board member who was the president of a bank looked at our financials and said, "We have to raise our tuition if we are going to continue to provide this level of education." A relatively easy way to effectively raise your tuition is that if you are charging on a nine-month basis, keep the monthly tuition amount the same, and go to a twelve-month pay plan. The school's expenses are on a twelve-month cycle, and it will make good sense to your parents.

2. Don't be afraid to enter into a capital campaign. If you need to build, begin a capital campaign. I suggest using a good consultant to help you through the process. By the way, trying to reduce debt through a capital campaign is a bad idea. There are very few parents who will give to something they

are already receiving; you are facing an "entitlement factor" that is nearly impossible to overcome.

3. Offer financial aid to families who need it. The most expensive student desks are the empty ones. I'll get into the details of all three in later chapters. All are large topics on their own.

Chapter 17

TWO BITS, FOUR BITS, SIX BITS A DOLLAR!!

If your school doesn't have a football team, you are missing an opportunity for some fun and for exciting growth.

My wife and I started our school for the academic rigor **and** spiritual growth that we knew the next generation desperately needed, neither of which our community offered. But during our due diligence study, a fellow school administrator told me that unless a school has a football team, it will never be a **real** school. The suggestion didn't sound at all spiritual, nor did it sound academic, but I discovered it was absolutely true. Athletics will drive a cheerleading program, drill team, band, and most importantly, school spirit. It will also drive up enrollment.

The keys are to have a vision, obtain the necessary financial support, and hire the right head coach. Our athletic director and head football coach from 1983 to 2009 is one of the most loved and cherished men in our school. Coach Bowles is respected by our parents, our students, and our alumni. He joined us in building Liberty in 1983 as a science teacher, AD, and head football coach.

One of the most important contributions that Coach Bowles brought to the table was his ability to hire excellent men and women coaches. He hired coaches that he instinctively knew were going to add integrity and character to our athletic teams. Looking back over the history of our school, Mark Bowles was a crucial contributing factor. For you, your AD must be a man of character and possess great leadership, because you need him to assist in setting the tone for good citizenship that will pervade your entire campus.

Can't afford an athletic program? You need to rethink that conclusion. In fact, if your AD is good, you will need to hire an assistant for him. If you make the right hire, you will have parent and community support at a level of which you never dreamed. And guess what? The fathers and grandfathers who love athletics are often the same guys who are running large companies. They will be some of your major donors for new labs, buildings, busses, an endowment, etc., and will make great board members.

Roger and Teresa Lane are parents of three great kids who graduated from Liberty. Along with hundreds of other families, the Lane family fell in love with Liberty's athletic program, and Liberty fell in love with them. They bought a large and very loud horn, powered by an air compressor and mounted on a trailer, and pulled it to all of our games. Roger sounded the horn when Liberty scored points. Roger is also a gifted photographer and took candid photos at games. That led to taking photos at related events, and that led to taking class photos. He now has a very unique company, Our Living Yearbook. Parents can go online to order photos of their kids' life at school, all birthed from Liberty's football program. If you want Roger's company to cover your school's photos, visit his website at ourlivingyearbook.com. (The front cover and many pictures in *CALLED* were photographed by Our Living Yearbook.)

BOWLES STADIUM

WARRIOR FOOTBALL

CHEERING FOR THE WARRIORS

BAND MEMBERS AT A GAME

In the public school arena, the same principles hold true regarding athletics. But don't make the mistake of insisting that your coach win in order to keep his job. Expect him to make good and decent men out of immature, testosterone-driven boys to keep his job. Hire a man who is a role model, and don't worry about his won-loss record; that will take care of itself. You obviously have to have a man who knows X's and O's—we all want to win games. But this man has to be a man all will admire. This is an integrity hire!!

Your football coach is going to influence your school leaders like nobody else can. If he is the right guy, he will have influence, I'd have to say **strong influence**, over the very kids that will test the disciplinary standard. Think of it this way. It takes a certain kind of young men to put on football pads and run at each other, **at full speed**. It takes a certain kind of kid to tackle a player twice his size, and it takes just the right coach to keep those same boys under control in the halls and classrooms. If you hire or fire the coach based on whether he wins games, you may end up with a trophy (although I doubt it), but more importantly, you will end up with prideful football players who are arrogant bullies. Get the right coach, and the players will be taught how to display humility and show the character that their coach models. I understand the dynamic of having a great role model who doesn't understand the game well enough to compete, but the point is your school can have both. Like the administrator, this hire already has a job and his school does not want to lose him.

In 2008, Liberty needed Coach Bowles to move out of coaching and into administration, but we wanted to wait until he was ready. Mark wrestled with the decision and felt it was time. He had trained the right man to replace him, and his legacy continues. Our athletic program is now led by Coach Greg Price, and in the words of his players, "He is an awesome coach." I agree.

I was sitting at the lunchroom table recently when one of the teachers told of an incident that had happened earlier that morning. For any reader who believes that private schools are a "bubble" and unlike the real world, I'm about to rewire that idea.

We had a substitute teacher in a classroom in the upper school. The substitute had been subjected to disrespect by a group of eleventh grade boys. Coach Price heard of the incident, called the boys into his office, and paddled all of them. These were all good kids; they just needed reminding that students are to respect anyone in authority. We have a great leader in Coach Price; all of the boys understood the punishment.

I want to relate a story that I promise will challenge your belief that this book is non-fiction. Staffing events occurred in 2008 that created an opportunity for Liberty to put in place a new principal **and** vice principal of the upper school at the same time. Normally this would be a harrowing experience, but we had two seasoned men ready to fill those positions.

Mark Bowles and Ed Cook were the two qualified men. Now you have to get this picture in your mind. The three of us were in my office, and our objective was to decide which man would hold which position. Mark began the discussion with "Ed, I think you would make the best principal." Ed responded, "Mark, you have been here longer, and I think **you** have earned the position." I'm keeping my mouth shut, just watching two humble leaders discuss each other's careers, both wanting to do the right thing for the school. I was observing an unbelievable example of Christ-like behavior at a level seldom seen anywhere. I don't know why I was surprised; both men display this type of leadership every day, and I am humbled to work beside them. They decided that Ed would be the principal and Mark the vice principal. I don't remember casting a vote—there was no vote. I immediately advised the Board, as I wanted them to be the first to know. But there are situations in some schools that are not as pretty.

It broke my heart to read about a school board in Louisiana that had to fire its head football coach because a judge ruled that the school district did not have the right racial quota. It is my understanding from what I read that a federal judge forced a school board in Louisiana to fire their white coach, and replace him with a man who was an African-American. If the black coach is the better hire, then in my opinion, the board should have done a better job in the hiring process and given him the job in the first place. But if the board did make the right hire, the black coach should enjoy the dignity of earning a head coaching job on his own merits. If the ruling came down that way, I truly hope for the kids' sake that the black coach led the team to a state championship, but that is hardly the point.

And what in the world is a judge doing getting into the school business? In my opinion, this black coach faced an uphill climb. And maybe this school doesn't require the head football coach to have classroom teaching assignments. But if it does, the black coach had better be a superior classroom teacher to the white one, and the judge had better know the difference. FAT CHANCE!

There is a Christian school in Texas that is associated with a certain denomination. Recently, a parent transferred his children to Liberty from that school. The reason was not that the parent wanted to uproot his kids. It was that an influential board member rallied enough votes to get the head football coach fired, and that power play reduced the morale of the entire staff to a new low, so the parent felt that his family had to leave.

This Christian school has had, and may still have, a policy that the administrator has to hire teachers that belong to a certain denomination. The **students** can come from any Christian denomination, but not the teachers. This makes the hiring pool so shallow that the board just can't compete with schools that hire the best teachers and coaches, regardless of their personal choice of Christian denomination. If a board is persuaded by a member that a teacher or coach should be removed for personal reasons, good families will leave until a dramatic change is made. This family did not want to leave their school, but were so disheartened they felt they must.

One mother from this school was in my office applying for acceptance at Liberty for her child, and actually cried at the interview because she didn't want to leave their former school. If your school is losing good families, find out the reason or problem and fix it! The natural tendency is to throw stones at the families who leave, and I promise that will **only increase** the bleeding. If we were losing good families at Liberty, and I did nothing to stop the losses, I would expect our board to find a leader who would.

Good teachers and coaches are difficult to find. We interview as many as twenty-five applicants for every hire. If I had to hire by any criteria other than academic, character, spiritual maturity, and work ethic qualifications, we would come in last in any kind of school competition.

Develop a good athletic program that includes football and features coaches who are good role models for the kids, and have fun while watching your school grow!

Chapter 18

Take the High Road—and Charge For It!!

Let's discuss some ideas that will help your school improve—beginning next year!

Most private schools are underpriced for the value that their families receive. Humbly explain to your families that you really do not want to increase tuition, but it is necessary in order to continue to offer the high level of education that their child is receiving. Plato said, "The direction in which education starts a man will determine his future." Sacrificing quality in education must not be open for discussion. Most parents will wholeheartedly support a tuition increase if it is justified, explained honestly, and will improve the overall quality of their offerings. Most of us understand "there are no free lunches."

At the same time the tuition is increased, offer a financial aid program for those families in need. You will have to determine a very ethical and fair way to make this program absolutely confidential and credible. The aid must be distributed according to need and be above reproach. In 2009/2010 we had a $1,000,000 line item for financial aid in our budget, and it was a matching program that served about 165 students. For that fiscal year our total budget was approximately $14,000,000 and total enrollment approximately 1,270.

We offer a matching program, not necessarily a 50/50 match, but with the receiving families paying as much as they can afford, which averages about a 40% discount. We use a third party company to make the determination of family qualification. You will be accused of favoritism, giving athletic scholarships, etc. but as long as those accusations are false, you can easily live with this good idea.

Instituting a financial aid program is a courageous board decision, and so is raising tuition rates. It is also important to realize that if you are underpriced, it is primarily at the expense of your teachers' salaries and benefits. As salaries and benefits comprise the largest part of your total budget, underpricing tuition is ultimately a burden that will be carried by your teachers and staff, and is not fair. Another important point is that your families **want** your teachers to make more money. None of our families would want a lower tuition if it meant lower teacher salaries.

A few years ago we had a unique assembly. Beginning with the kindergarten class, we had the teachers sitting on stage, and had appointed twelve or more kindergarten students to share from their hearts why they appreciated their teacher. Each student had a microphone, and we let them say whatever they wanted to say. The students from each kindergarten class talked directly to their teacher for a minute or so—we didn't time them. We invited all of the parents.

We went through all thirteen grades with the same format, students praising their teachers. This assembly took several hours, as one grade would leave and the next entered. We gave out a card and envelope to each parent, and let them share what **they** appreciated about their child's teacher, **any** suggestions on how we could improve the school, and gave them an opportunity to give a tax-deductible gift to the school. The giving opportunity was actually an afterthought; the assembly was strictly planned to encourage our teaching staff. After all cards were collected and totaled, we received over $600,000 in pledges and gifts, and got some great ideas on how our school could improve. From the parental ideas we made a list of the achievable projects, and started marking them off as we accomplished the goals. Some ideas did not cost money, but the gifts received at the assembly allowed us the funds for those that did. Cost to the school for this activity—zero! Some teachers told me the encouragement from that assembly got them through the end of the year. And the kids and parents loved it. (Note to self: Why in the world have you not had another assembly??)

If you raise tuition to the level it needs to be to continue offering quality programs, you may still hear complaints from families, but at the end of the day, you will not lose the families that are in your school for the right reasons. In all of my years, I really don't think I've lost over twenty families because of a **justified** tuition increase. We have lost families because they couldn't afford the tuition, but they probably should never have tried to add private school tuition to their budget in the first place.

But here is the key: you have to be delivering the educational and extracurricular programs worthy of the increase. Your school also has to offer enrichment courses in grades kindergarten through fifth, and solid electives in grades sixth through twelfth. The more offerings you have, the higher the number of families that want to enroll. You just have to be honest in your evaluation of your school, because ultimately the marketplace will give you an objective grade. If you are fearful and running your school with too few offerings, then improve it or close your doors. But if you are delivering a great product, then charge accordingly. This is not high math. Total your costs of operations, estimate a conservative enrollment of student population, and price it. I would estimate enrollment on the low side; for example, if you project an enrollment of 500 students, price tuition on the basis of 475.

And if I had a chance to roll back to 1983, I would begin an endowment fund of 2% and add that number to tuition. Warning to boards! If you are a relatively new school and take this advice, in a few years your endowment should be in the six or seven figure range; invest it conservatively. A great school that has been in operation for over 100 years lost $20,000,000 in the stock market "adjustment" of 1984. Not learning from that lesson, they lost about the same amount in the "dot-com" meltdown. Both times, the board thought it was investing the endowment wisely, and this was a boardroom of very bright men and women. Sadly, there are examples like these all over the country; we just rarely hear of them. They are understandable; the board of trustees is trying to gain as much return on investment for the endowment fund as possible, and some risk is necessary—my point is that they should be very conservative risks because it is not the board's money.

Programs that add great value will bring your school the asset you need to justify a tuition increase. After you have developed a solid athletic program, I suggest adding Advanced Placement courses before you **expand** your foreign language offerings. I realize that this priority is academically misplaced; you have to be thinking, "Rodney, surely you mean to add AP courses, expanded foreign language courses, and then build a strong athletic program." Your argument is very sound, but it won't work. It takes students to build **any** program, and you have to meet that enrollment target goal through meeting the priorities of your students from grades six to twelve. Did you know that parents almost always determine the choice of school when their child is in the age range from 3-year-old preschool through fifth grade; but from sixth through twelfth, it is almost always the kids who decide on the school? And most of the exceptions are the families with kids that good private schools refuse to accept. The student has gotten into trouble, and normally the parent will come to the interview without the child. The parent may have great interviewing skills, but remember, you are not enrolling the parent.

I suggest adding a well-structured physical education program to your elementary school, and offering it five days a week. I also suggest adding a foreign language in elementary. We switched from Spanish to Latin a few years ago and most of our parents loved it.

We added a choice of band, choir, or drama to our fifth and sixth grades many years ago, and required all kids in those two grades to choose one. The reason? Not every girl can or wants to be a cheerleader, nor every boy an athlete. So now we have kids that the varsity band, choir, and drama teachers are recruiting in junior high and high school—all have a place to be wanted, and that, my friends, is added value!

I suggest adding programs as your enrollment grows. Don't reserve all of the money—invest it by spending it wisely; you are essentially strengthening the infrastructure of your school. The strategy is simple: as you add offerings, both your population and tuition will justifiably rise. A school that keeps its infrastructure growing will attract families that want to grow with it. **But your hires are the key**; programs with weak teachers or coaches are not value added assets—they will, in fact, be a very expensive mistake.

Hires are the key. I was invited to speak on the importance of the interview and hiring process to a group of graduating university seniors who hoped to be hired by schools for the fall. There were about 300 students who were education majors in the audience. One part of my lecture addressed the importance of their first impression in an interview that they would have with a school board or administrator. I told them to bring their "A" game. Dress nicely—men, wear a coat and tie; ladies, a nice dress or pantsuit. Sit up straight, look the interviewer in the eye, answer the questions in a straightforward manner, and show ENTHUSIASM. I suggested responding with "Yes, sir" or "No, sir" because that would show respect for authority, and separate them from the other applicants. Six of the students stormed out of the auditorium and slammed the door. I called the head of the education department the next day to apologize for offending her students, and she honestly responded to me saying, "Dr. Haire, those students stay offended. My guess is that they will never be able to hold a job longer than a year in any school district." That lecture would be part of my Education 101 course in "Preparing Teachers for Success," which I will describe in greater detail in Chapter 28.

Chapter 19

Who Are Your Heroes?

At any given time, we can focus on those families and friends who have helped and are helping; or on those who did or are doing us harm—your choice. I'll give you my experiences of both.

I'm writing this as I'm in my 28th year in the school business. By that time, we educators have joined one of two camps. Some are like the politicians who want to be re-elected and are too cowardly to abandon the "politically correct" camp. Others have courageously and emotionally joined the group formerly inhabited by many of our great forefathers, who said "The only issue is that we must be right—period."

My father-in-law, the late John Robinson, is one of my personal heroes. If he were still alive, I'm certain he would say, "What in the hell is this giving away your product about? What is that nonsense? Is your school worth the money or not?" My friend John was in the Navy, later made his living working in the oil business, so his language was not exactly out of the King James, if you know what I mean. At his funeral there was standing room only, and I believe it was because John was unashamedly bold, honest, and very courageous. If we can bring those strong leadership qualities back to our school systems, many of the big problems that are bringing down our next generation will go away. Martin Luther King, Jr. was a man of principles and values, and he was prepared to (and did) die for his convictions. In a speech in Detroit in

1963, he said, "If a man hasn't discovered something that he will die for, he isn't fit to live." I would have been honored to meet him.

There are times when you need a strong friend to stand with you in the face of tough decisions and circumstances. This friend is not there just to give moral support and offer help in the third person, but is really **with** you. The help may come in a way and at a special time for which you will forever be grateful and will never forget.

In 2001, our board decided to sell our campus to the University of North Texas. We had agreed to the price and terms, but had not established the closing date. The truth was that the University kept postponing the closing date, and using their state bond monies to fund other projects. We simply kept getting pushed to the proverbial "back of the line." My dear friend and school development consultant, the late Mr. Rob Clark, told me one day, "Rodney, go over to UNT right now, and tell them to set the closing date, or you are pulling your school off the market. I will go with you, or will wait in your office until you return." I decided to go alone. Rob waited in my office. In a couple of hours, I came back with a date, and the future and life of our school changed. That day was a turning point for our school, and I know it would have not have happened without my friend's encouragement. There are few days that go by that I don't think about Rob and miss him.

I am blessed to have several board members who I know will patiently listen to any of my frustrations. Historically, as an employee of the board, if I asked a member for their opinion, I felt obligated to accept their "suggestion," as all administrators would. Sometimes an administrator just wants to spew. He really doesn't need an idea, solution, or suggestion, he just needs to vent. All of my present board would make me that offer, and it is a wonderful and rare gift. I have their cell phone numbers, and they would be offended if I needed them and didn't call.

A very dear friend, Dr. James Kitchens, a published author and counselor, told me that often his patients need to hear their thoughts spoken out loud. He phrased it something like, "Often, people have thoughts that are like a back-lashed, open-faced fishing reel. They have to get the line out before they can get those thoughts straightened out." Jim and his wife, Rachel, are two wonderful friends that have helped with their financial support, prayers, and words of encouragement. If you are running a school, be it private or public, and don't have at least one Rachel and Jim in your corner, I honestly believe your future looks bleak; that is just the way it is in a leadership position in the school business. There are so many passionate issues, and so many good friends you want to please, but that is actually an impossible goal.

Before I go further, I want to explain to the reader that the dollars I'm about to refer to may seem out of reach for some. In all honesty, they were out of reach for us for almost twenty years. I remember a family selling a parcel of inherited land and bringing the school $5,000, and I thought we had hit the lottery. A parent named Elmer Cox always brought in $5,000 every November. I can't begin to tell you how many of those "long nights" we all have had, when Elmer's gift seemed like a life raft. A father who was a physician came in one day and handed me $10,000; it was like manna from heaven. But if you have a vision, and don't make compromises, the gifts will slowly grow into a different stratosphere. The school's finances will change gradually, but you will experience life seeming much easier. You will still have disappointments, but they will not seem to destroy all that you have worked for.

But the non-heroes do take a mental and emotional toll on administrators. In 2006, we had finished building the first and second phases of our campus. The cost was in the $25,000,000 range. I was very distraught over several large donors who were not honoring their pledges. I have to believe that they intended to pay their pledge when they made it. The problem was that they never told me that certain financial events had to line up for them in order to be able to give the amount they had pledged, or that their pledge had a "hook" in it. To the former, it would have been better for them to pledge a reasonable amount, and give more if their "ship came in." To the other group, I say it would have been much better and more honorable to tell me there were strings attached, so I could decline the "gift" immediately and respectfully.

During the campaign, I remember waking up in the middle of the night clutching my pillow very tightly. I was dreaming that several families who had pledged a total of $10,000,000 were not going to pay their pledge, and we had spent those pledges in anticipation of receiving them. Historically, Liberty had a solid track record of pledges made that were paid—it was nearly 100%. In fact, one year we collected 103% of the amount pledged; families paid their original pledge, then made another.

Now I am writing seven years later, and know how Campaigns I and II actually turned out. We had some large commitments that were never honored. One of the fathers got mad at me, I believe, for **not** firing a band director. He had promised to give $250,000 but walked away without honoring his word. Actually I should have fired the band director, and a few months later, I did; but at the time I believed he was owed an opportunity to improve. But that father never told me that his pledge depended on anything I did or didn't do.

Another family pledged $2,000,000 and simply never paid the pledge and never called. Another couple got a divorce, and paid $400,000 of their pledge of $600,000. That sounds like we don't appreciate the $400,000, and that is not true. The point is that we spent the $600,000, and it would have been so much better if they had pledged what they **knew** they would give.

Another family met me for lunch, and before the coffee and tea came, the wife humorously said, "I know what this lunch is about, and I want to cut to the chase. My husband and I will give $1,000,000." To date, $13,500 has been paid. At another lunch, I asked a family if they would consider giving a gift of $1,000,000. After thought and consideration, the husband said, "We can do that." He reached his hand across the table, and said, "My word is my bond." To date, about $50,000 of that pledge has been honored. A really good friend made a pledge of $85,000, and to date, approximately $15,000 has been paid.

Maybe the most disappointing experience came from a family who made an unsolicited pledge of $1,000,000. The father called me for an appointment and told me that he and his wife had prayed about their gift, wished it to remain anonymous, and were only too happy that they could afford to bless our school. When the steel was delivered to our school site, he called me to tell me he saw the steel delivered, that he knew the invoice would soon be coming due, and that he would bring the check over the next week. It took me six years to obtain $750,000, and finally I had to let it go. Board members graciously stopped asking me if he has paid his remaining pledge, and like the others, we wrote it off. Again, we are so appreciative of the $750,000, but we spent the $1,000,000—not a little "hiccup."

I believe that every one of those pledges was made with the best of intentions. But the sad fact is that we have "written off" over $10,000,000 of $20,000,000 raised in pledges. That hurtful reality may make one a stronger leader, but it is enormously discouraging. I've learned to attach a factor of discernment to all pledges, which will greatly soften future disappointments.

For a long time, I thought the "write-offs" were an integrity issue, but I don't believe that anymore. I think it is something that is akin to a reluctance to give, financial naiveté, maybe an initial exuberance and excitement for the project, or probably a "strings attached" pledge that they didn't think about until they started writing checks. The donors, or non-donors in these cases, just don't realize the extent of elation and celebration over every single pledge; but that the emotional fall, if the pledge is not honored, is just as low as the promised gift was high. Pledges that are not honored are devastating to the campaign leaders. At the risk of losing my "man card," these write-offs made me cry.

In the future, after the pledge is made I will humbly ask them to sign a pledge card and have a conversation about when and how their pledge will be paid. The truth is that the person doing the "ask" is so excited and appreciative of the pledge, that it seems awkward saying anything but "thank you." A word to the "askers": don't be concerned about feeling awkward; genuine donors expect that conversation to happen. If you are the solicitor of the gift, obtaining the details is being responsible to your school, and a sincere donor will appreciate and respect it.

A word to the donors: I would ask of you to **emotionally** trade places with the person who is humbly calling you or is in your presence asking for a donation. He is desperately trying to help **your** child or grandchild. Be thankful it isn't you having to make the ask. If he is not making the "ask," it will inevitably mean several unfortunate scenarios. Your child's teacher may be forced to resign and teach at another school that did have a willing solicitor, your school will not have the funds to stay on the cutting edge of technology, or the facilities your child needs will never be built.

For parents working in industry, think of the development director of your school as your company's sales manager. Without him, there are no orders and that means there is no factory. And every parent and school staff member have to realize that we are all a part of development. All of us have to have an understanding and appreciation of the many ways we can help make our school a better place in which our children can learn. It may be the attitude of our security officer or of the server in the lunch line; we all have a part in making our school a warm and inviting place that encourages all of our families to want to be a part of improving our school.

I think in the overall plan of fundraising at Liberty, we have been very subtle. You will notice that all non-givers will complain that "All they do at Liberty is ask for money. Evidence to the contrary. After our school's Christmas play one year, I was walking across the parking lot with a parent. He asked me, "Rodney, how does a family give to Liberty?"

To be fair, I could list the over 1,300 pledges that were made and came in on time; we have fewer than 1,000 families, so many of them made more than one pledge. The vast majority of our teachers made pledges; out of all of them, **only one** was not paid, and it was for $10 per month for twelve months.

It takes gifts of all sizes to make a capital campaign successful. An important point I want to make is that every family that is part of a private school should participate in all campaigns, **especially** if they are receiving financial aid. Recipients want the financial aid committee to know that no family appreciates the school more than you. It probably will not be a significant gift in terms of amount, but it should be sacrificial and attended by a sincerely worded note of appreciation.

If you are in a public school, there are opportunities to participate in various events, not the least of which is the PTA meetings. I once had a teacher who had been president of her public school's PTA. She told me that at her last meeting there were only four parents in attendance. There may be fundraising events, and I encourage every one of you to participate—your child is watching. As you participate in attendance and/or giving, do it with enthusiasm; your child's teacher and administrator need the encouragement only you can give.

Regardless of whether your child's school is public or private, it goes without saying that if you make a pledge of your time and or money, fulfill it. If an unforeseen situation occurs, have the courage and sensitivity to call the person to whom you made the pledge, explain that you will not be able to pay your pledge, and give the reason. It is just the right thing to do. I learned another important truth, if you made a pledge that was too large, explain and pay as much as you can—it is not an all or nothing agreement. It will say to those in administration that you love your child's school, and want to help to the extent possible.

Generally, parents have no concept as to the enormity of the burdens carried by administrators and development directors, nor can they understand that there are no soft landings. Giving is a way you can greatly reduce their burdens. Administrators are very reluctant to mention money to parents and alumni. I easily understand educators who avoid the tough task of raising money; I promise none of us like it. I have a doctorate degree, and not one education course ever mentioned the responsibility that administrators have to raise money. If they did, my guess is that many administrators would choose another field. But the truth remains that without financial gifts, private schools can't accomplish what every parent wants and expects for their child's school.

And I understand there are thousands of weak administrators who drone on about the obvious and popular policies, knowing it is just rhetoric. Everyone "in the room" knows the real issues cost money, and far too many weary and overworked administrators have had "the ask" beaten out of them. Maybe the administrator and/or board members are in over their head in a number of ways. It doesn't really matter the reason, the job is just too big. If that is the case, please have the integrity to resign.

I think there is a legitimate time for administrators and board members to grow weary, and that is not a shameful thing. If you are tired of the battle, then move on, but speak the truth about it before you leave. When John F. Kennedy was asked how he became a hero he said, "It was involuntary; they sank my boat." Maybe your boat is taking on water, and if it is, I suggest you turn in your resignation and stop torturing everyone involved—especially you.

Maybe you are one of those administrators who has fought a good fight, but now it may be time to send in replacements. Only energized heroes need be in this battle because it is for the minds and hearts of our kids. For whatever reason, too many of my colleagues are not going to say or do anything that might offend or anger anyone, especially a parent who might call his lawyer or threaten to speak at the next board meeting. In 2009 there was a public school in Washington, DC that had 23 concurrent lawsuits filed over discipline issues—and the sad fact is that it is one of many schools without discipline!

The administrator will not confront a teacher who might call the local union boss—excuse me, the "union representative." Most of my colleagues in the field of education have become a fearful bunch. They are afraid of board members, teachers, parents, and some students; and, I'm sorry to say, have reserved a place in the emotional cave of politics.

Rather than take on whoever is leading their school in the wrong direction in verbal combat and fight for what they know is the right thing to do for their students, they would rather just hope the issue goes away. Here's a news flash, it only gets bigger with time. I don't deny there are challenges that have not existed in previous generations. Administrators now must deal with parents who are afraid of not pleasing their own children, or who bow to the god of their child's self-image. This is a relatively new sociological phenomenon that administrators historically have never had to face. The conversation was more like, "If you get paddled at school, you can expect the same at home." As a side point, I think that is double jeopardy and unfair to the child. But the point is that the strength of administrative support from the home has virtually disappeared, and that is not just sad, it is disastrous.

"But wait, what about the inexperienced, emotionally immature or, God forbid, the sexually perverted that are employed as administrators, teachers, and coaches? How can we as parents be categorically supportive?" You are absolutely correct; another reason not to have contracts. But as was said so perfectly by the late Paul Newman in the movie *Hud*, "Don't go shooting all the dogs because one has fleas."

Chapter 20

Higher Salaries—Catch the Wave or Drown

There are many aspects that determine whether or not a school will be able to keep its great teachers and coaches. Let's talk about a few of the most important.

As the president of Liberty Christian School, the responsibility of meeting the needs of our staff rests with me. I have a wonderful board, but they are not the ones our staff looks to for their financial needs. Entering the school year 2009/2010, we had an approximate 96% re-enrollment rate, and were ranked the #1 school in our division by the Texas Association of Private and Parochial Schools; our staff is doing a great job. The question is, "Am I doing mine in the area of fair payment for services rendered?" This ties in with previous chapters, but its level of importance compares to plague level at the Center for Disease Control, so it deserves a chapter of its own.

In the shadow of our success is the sad fact that some of our current salaries are still slightly below the local public school market, and should be above it. We are taking care of that problem slowly, but "slowly" is just not good enough. What surprises me is that we have more applicants for teaching positions than we can interview, and almost no staff turnover. For the school year 2009/2010, our lower school had zero teacher turnover.

After acknowledging that financial responsibility, I want to point out that professional educators, whether classroom teachers or administrators, never chose that career for the money. They chose it for the opportunity to teach, coach, and affect kids' lives. A great teacher, coach or administrator was most likely their role model and inspiration at a time in their lives when money and benefits were not even a blip on the screen of their life's radar.

Today, there is a new financial pressure that is being felt by educators that was never significant before. It may be that they want their own children in a private school, or that their child will want more than a bachelor's degree. It may have to do with our nation's level of inflation as it relates to a moderate standard of living. For the same reasons that our school parents have to make more money, our educators have to as well. It is just a reality that school leaders must face, and face it "yesterday."

Although it is true that most educators do not feel the pressure to "keep up with the Joneses," the desire to do better is a factor that is very real. Mercifully for administrators and boards, it will be close to the **"desire"** level as long as they can pursue their dream of educating. But if they can't live that dream of changing a child's life, it will hit the **"need"** level of salary and benefits in a shorter amount of time than you can say "gangs." That is exactly what has happened in many of our public schools, and will happen in our private schools if respect for authority continues to diminish. Has anyone noticed that the teacher unions started raising the issue of salaries as a front page story about the same time that schools lost control of their students' behavior?

My experience is that money will become the issue when the teacher or administrator isn't supported in his effort to teach or administer. If I don't give my teachers, staff, and coaches my wholehearted support, and that will mean standing with them in the face of intimidating parents and lawyers, then I had better find a load of money for salaries, because their hearts will have just become hardened, and their time very expensive.

Sometime in the summer of 2001, I interviewed a couple who were interested in enrolling their two sons at Liberty. Both parents worked in a public school system. After a short time of getting to know them, the father related an experience he'd had that spring with a student. The young man was walking across the basketball court with shoes that created black marks on the school's beautiful wooden floor. He respectfully asked the student to walk around the perimeter of the court, and the student rudely responded with the "F bomb." The teacher/coach sent the young man to the office for discipline for inappropriate response to a teacher. Two hours later, the teacher passed the student in the hall, and the student just gave the teacher a disrespectful "smirk." This teacher/coach was a very valuable part of the school's staff, but because of the lack of administrative support, he actually applied and was accepted as a teacher and coach on our staff after the interview.

Education majors never expected to make "real" money. They gave up that option when they chose their college major. Their friends were majoring in finance, business, real estate, law, medicine, etc., and it was understood there was a tradeoff for doing what you really loved, or being in it for bucks. Some college students loved medicine or law, and the dollars just followed, but I'm sure you get the point. Being able to be a part of a kid's life, not having to be away from home, being able to continue to "play," and teaching a subject one really loves provided the "carrot" needed for us to make the conscious choice to let those in the other fields make the money. That is the way it was supposed to work, but generally speaking, that is no longer the way it is, and hasn't been for over thirty years. Those that entered the profession of education are not being permitted to educate, and that must change!! Educators deserve to make more money, but that should never be the driving issue; if you don't believe that, volunteer to be a substitute teacher for **one** day. My hope and prayer is that the right people will read this book, take it to heart, and things will change.

For several years, Liberty had in place a "work detention" rather than a "detention hall." The student with the detention reported to the janitor or maintenance supervisor when school was dismissed for a task that was appropriate for the offense. When finished, he would call his parents and tell them he had completed his "assignment," and he was dismissed to go home. But if a student was as disrespectful to a teacher as was the young man leaving marks on the basketball floor, he would have been **permanently** expelled immediately—as in not permitted to finish that class period. Expulsion differs from a suspension, as a suspension is for a specific length of time—expulsion is until Jesus returns.

Being "called to the principal's office" is to be called to make bold, difficult, quick decisions, and to not be afraid of making a mistake. It's guaranteed you will make plenty of them. I tell my teachers at the beginning of every year, "If you and I don't make mistakes, we are not working." But if you don't have the "right stuff," you'd better go in a different direction with your life. Most of your days are going to be very tough, and the first year of teaching requires burning a lot of midnight oil.

I think good educators and administrators have to be great communicators, sensitive, loving, and supportive. Emotionally, they could have qualified as a member of one of our country's special forces teams. Good board members, administrators, teachers, and coaches who genuinely care about children and serve as role models with strong family values are my true heroes. Let's find a way to pay them what they are worth, or at least closer to it.

Chapter 21

"Choice"—Not Really a Choice

There are some tough choices that we have to make for the survival of our children. Let's talk.

I had the great experience of leading and growing a successful textile company for eighteen years, and have enjoyed leading a school from virtual infancy to successful adulthood since 1983. There is one thing that I know to be true: to be successful you have to be surrounded with great people. In the school business, public and private, it is about intelligence, of course, but just as important are the traits that are more difficult to measure: emotional maturity, character, work ethic, and integrity, to name some of them. I do my very best to hire people I believe are smarter than I am, and when that happens, my job becomes easier and more enjoyable. I tell my staff every year, "You guys are really making me look good; you are the reason Liberty is a great school." The following portion of this chapter will eventually make sense; just follow me for a couple of paragraphs.

I am sensitive regarding the plight of our minorities in America, but quite honestly, there is no place for racial or ethnic balance or any of those good political and cultural goals in staffing a board or a school. The education of our children is too important to lay their future in the political arena of adults trying to fix a very old problem. The truth of the matter is that we are in a battle for the minds, hearts, and future of your children—no matter your race, gender or religion. I really believe we are on the same team, and I hope that after you read this book, you will know that the success of a school is all about the intelligence **and** character of school teachers and leaders, plus the support of parents and school boards, and has absolutely nothing to do with the color of anyone's skin. In the world's educational race, we are out of time, so I humbly ask any who may be offended to set aside the "good cause." A child's education doesn't have to be sacrificed to obtain equal anything.

I can assure you that if the best candidate for a teacher is of color, I'm going to do my best to hire him. If the members of our math department are all African-Americans, it means that the best applicants I had from which to choose happened to have the same skin color, and it was black. In my opinion, it would be in the best interest of all races to close any organization in America that is trying to equalize opportunities for their race—the world market has accomplished that goal. All employers with longevity are trying to hire the best candidate; if they don't, competition will soon drive them out of business.

I suggest closing the NAACP, and there are some highly respected African- Americans who agree with me. It goes without saying, that the best candidate for board membership or school staff should be elected or hired based on qualifications; no other factors need be considered.

But Dr. Haire, "What about having role models of the same race as the kids in our community? How are they going to get a vision or achieve success if the board president or principal isn't of our race?" Great question. First, there is no "they," only competent and incompetent. Secondly, the world is a little larger than your community. Your community now includes Seoul, Beijing, Hong Kong, the finest prep schools in America and Europe, etc. Thirdly, the power players see the task of staffing their companies, private schools, etc. as a color-blind issue—you have to get that! If parents of minority children are even mentioning color as a limitation to their child's success, then they are way behind the fact curve. Successful schools and companies are desperately looking for the best candidates. How about inspiring your child to be a hard worker, have the reputation of being a respectable boy or girl, make right choices, hang out with the right friends (and we all know what that means), be a person of integrity and character, make good grades, etc.? The new key word in good education is "rigor."

Where are the parents who very firmly say, "You are not going to leave the house wearing that outfit!" The predictable response from the child will be, "Then I will have no friends!" Your retort: "Then you need new ones."

If you are waiting for your school administrator to make sure your son's hat is straight, his jeans are at his waist, or your daughter's skirt is of decent length, you could be waiting a long time. Parents who are allowing their children to run their home are the only voices that administrators are hearing. Nothing has really changed; parents who want their children to make good choices are making sure their children are making good choices.

A few years ago our family took a trip to New York City. We were having lunch when I noticed a crowd gathered around the stage entrance to a theatre. The actor signing autographs was Denzel Washington. I noticed he was wearing a black baseball cap—and it was turned straight. He was wearing jeans with a tee shirt tucked in, and his jeans were at his waist. I remember thinking, "I hope some young men are observing that the 'gangsta' look is now out of style. Denzel changed it."

And akin to that parenting role, I ask, "What are moms and dads thinking who allow their child to talk lazily. These are kids who talk so fast that their entire sentence can be said in two seconds. I suggest that when parents hear that form of laziness, they make their child write out the sentence, and make sure they write neatly and legibly. (And while I'm on laziness, to you fast food managers, what are you thinking letting a person your customers can't understand take orders in your drive-through window? Give the lazy talkers a mop or a pink slip; either way you will have a "new staff" the next day.)

If the citizens of your community have elected a member to your school board for any other reason than that he is qualified, then as a parent in that public independent school district, you'd better get a second job if you have to, and enroll your children in a private school.

Some private schools are playing the racist game regarding the "balancing" of their board membership, but that is rare and most likely is to pander to foundations for money. They are under the false assumption that if they have a person of color on their board, a foundation will more likely consider their application with favor because their board is multi-cultural. Any private school willing to "sell" a place on their board for any politically correct reason will lose respect from staff and parents. If a school wants a good board member, recruit the smartest guy in the room with great people skills—done.

A private school will rarely hire a minority to teach or coach in order to do a balancing act for political purposes. It's just too important to deliver the educational product that their parents are going to demand. Parents with their child in a private school know that education will not be a racial equality issue; it has to be a best person for the job issue.

Another important issue applies only to the parents of public school children. If you are a minority in a poorly run school, you had better call your congressman and tell him to vote for school choice or he will lose your vote and support. But Haire, "You are just taking money out of the pockets of our public schools and putting money into private schools. A little bit self-serving isn't it?" That is definitely one way to look at it, but as Dr. Phil often asks, "How is that working for you?" (By the way, I have no idea where Dr. Phil stands on this particular issue, but I can make a good guess.)

Our congressmen are being led around by the nose by the teacher union lobbyists, politicians, and civil rights organizations. Most of our congressmen vote the way the union officials tell them to vote—very few exceptions. Two of the strongest lobbies in Washington are the teachers unions. They are consistently pressuring their congressmen to vote against "school choice." That means your school property taxes are used to send your child to the local public school, regardless of whether it is actually educating your child or not. As long as the unions are running the show, they are going to have a racially balanced teaching staff, a racially balanced board, contracts that prevent the administrator from firing incompetent teachers or coaches, acceptance of low SAT and ACT performance in the majority of schools, a nationally high drop-out rate, the whole wonderful ball of political correctness wax.

A valuable strategy that could have enormous potential in meeting your child's need for a quality education is the use of a school voucher, birthed from the freedom for parents to choose the best school for their child. This voucher would have to be carefully examined to make sure it contained no hidden agenda or controls from the provider. If you can then take your school voucher and use those dollars to obtain for your child the best education in your area, your child wins—BIG TIME! The real opportunity for you (at least it should be an option) is that assuming the private school tuition is $12,000, and you have your school voucher, let's assume it is worth $4,000; you add $4,000 of your own money and receive $4,000 in financial aid, and you are "IN, BABY!" You may not need the financial aid from the school, but for most Americans, the tuition burden for family budgets is heavy, so help is normally available from private schools if you ask for it and qualify.

Private schools should not exist just for rich kids. That was never anyone's plan. But as long as the public schools are run by unions and politicians, they really will not stand a chance of competing with the privates. It is the same regarding our government. Is there a more **inefficiently** run organization in the United States than the United States Government?

But school choice **could** be a very bright light at the end of the tunnel. If our public schools have to compete with the privates, then the game changes immediately. Now the school board has to hire the best administrator, and he has to hire the best teachers. Why? To stay in business. If your school has a non-motivated teacher, that person gets fired regardless of skin color. No more seniority, and certainly no tenure (which in a practical sense means it is almost impossible for the administrator to fire the poorly performing teacher). If "school choice" becomes the law, a staff member will get to keep his job only if he does his job, regardless of color or gender. You get to keep your job—if you deserve to keep it. You get hired if you are the best candidate.

Parents, your children are competing with kids not just from American private schools, but from schools all over the world. Your public school has the best facilities, best equipment, more library books and computers, and better athletic equipment. They have a huge head start, so they should win the race. But **if** there is no race, and no competition, your kid loses, and loses huge. To quote columnist Walter Williams, "A school choice system, in the form of vouchers or tuition tax credits, would go a long way toward providing the competition necessary to introduce accountability and quality into American education."

Recently, the public schools in Detroit gave all fourth graders what is often referred to as "The Nation's Report Card." Sixty-nine percent of Detroit's public school fourth grade students scored at a level evaluated as unable to demonstrate a **partial** mastery of fundamental academic skills that could be expected from fourth graders—69% FAILED! Move up to the eighth grade, and 77% failed. This story is virtually the same for Philadelphia, New York, Los Angeles, and Washington, DC. Call your congressman today and tell him he has a choice—vote for choice or lose your vote.

True story. A private school in Texas had about 20 girls who wanted to start a soccer program. Because the private school's board wanted to serve their families, the administration was permitted to add the sport. Two years later, they added boys' soccer and had 45 boys going out for approximately 20 positions, so the school's AD started a junior varsity team as well.

The local public school competing with **that** private school had not been able to fund a soccer program—until **then**. After the private school added the soccer program, voila—the public school kids had soccer added to their athletic program. Why? My guess is because that public school couldn't afford to lose state funding if their soccer-minded students applied and were accepted to the private school. The risk of some of their families moving to the private school so their child could play soccer was a real and present danger. May be coincidental, but I doubt it. Pass school choice legislation, and extrapolate that same soccer scenario to the classrooms, labs, gyms, athletic fields, band and choir halls, theatre and drama departments, etc. across our nation, and everybody wins—except the public school administrators, teachers, and coaches who are in way over their heads, and of course, are no longer protected by the unions.

I fired a teacher during my first year in the school business. He was brilliant, had a master's degree in laser science, but was not a good teacher. He continued his career in education by writing curriculum—a perfect match for his skill set. We have some really bright people in our public schools who are simply not teachers, coaches or administrators. And my bet is that the day they get fired is the day they get set free of a career that is making them miserable.

While I had my companies, I contracted the consultant services of Dr. John Shirley to give me advice as to what steps I could take to make our companies more profitable. He told me a true story of a company that had a sales manager who had employed his best friend as a salesman. The friend was bright, had great communication skills, and was a diligent worker. One day the sales manager drove out of the company parking lot and noticed his friend's car parked on the side of the road just outside the company parking lot. Of course he stopped to see if his friend needed help. He found his friend behind the wheel of his car crying, "I just hate calling on customers." The sales manager told his best friend, "I'm going to do you a great favor. Please tender your resignation because this just isn't the right job for you." Our schools have some wonderful people working in them in every area—the only problem is that it is the wrong job for them. (More pertinent advice from Dr. John Shirley is shared in a later chapter.)

Private schools can't accept below-average staff because the competition with other private schools in their geographical area is fierce. Parents simply are not going to pay private school tuition and accept mediocrity—in any category.

If our politicians ever get the courage to legislate "choice," our nation will move up the academic food chain faster than we can imagine. But it will take a willingness to change and lots of guts—two very rare commodities in our world of Washington's good ol' boy system of protectionism.

Chapter 22

Top Gun

There are some actions that boards can take to ensure the longevity and stability of the administrator, and some ways administrators can encourage teachers—these are inexpensive and easy, but make sure they get done.

If your school administrator is competent, he is going to make some very tough decisions, and will ruffle some feathers. If he can't do that, board members are going to have to start an administrator job search in a couple of years, and I promise that process is just as costly as when a company has to replace the unproductive sales manager.

Better to invest in quality from the beginning; you will get a huge return, and the children will be much more likely to get the education that frankly, board members owe them. Remember, your "top gun" is going to have to make some unpopular decisions. He may have to fire a popular coach or a teacher with years of experience, or expel a board member's child from school. He will have to fire a teacher who has been complaining about almost everything for a very long time. Teachers must be positive, always looking for the best parts of the school to talk about, but if they are of the "critical type," they will simply have to spread their "joy" elsewhere. If you have not hired character and integrity in your administrator, you are going to "waffle" when it is time to support him, and odds are you have just lost him.

That bit of advice is not only for board members, but also for parents. If parents do not support the administrator, something very predictable is going to take place in your home. Your child is going to clearly observe that you have seriously questioned your administrator's judgment, and the subtle message to your child is that **all** authority is questioned, not the least of which is your child's teacher. You may indeed have reason to doubt the maturity or judgment of the administrator's decision, but you need to handle it very discreetly, making certain you have **all** of the facts before determining that your child has been treated unfairly, and only then would I address it and then discuss it privately.

By the way, that same principle holds true for all adults who want to encourage their kids to have a healthy respect for authority in general. I will never forget a very unwise discussion my wife and I had one Sunday afternoon after church. I said something very clever about the weak sermon that our pastor had just delivered. I went on to comment that I wished we had stayed home. Something very sad happened **in that moment**, because from that Sunday on, our kids lost some of their respect and love for our pastor. All of us are going to have days when we are not on our game, and that includes your pastor. But if you take a cheap shot at his humanity in front of your young and impressionable child, who never misses a thing, you have just cut a piece of your own authority flesh away from your parental bone.

In 1983, our private school was affiliated with a church in Denton, Texas. The pastor of the church was and is a man of character. At that time, he was also my boss, as is the case in most church/school governments. On a given day, I had a serious problem, and, fortunately, the pastor proved to be a man of emotional courage and strength.

One of our teachers was also a board member of the church. That relationship in this case could have really gotten ugly. The teacher was a wonderful man, but teaching was not his talent or gift. I went to the pastor's office, and told him I was going to have to fire a teacher. Unfortunately this individual not only was a faithful member of the board and church, but one of his best friends. The pastor made the decision to support me, and, in my opinion, took the highest of roads. He did not interfere with my decision to dismiss the teacher/board member, and on that day, the kids won. I did not realize for several years what a courageous thing that was for a pastor to do, but to this day, I proclaim my admiration for the pastor. (Thank you, Gary.)

Running a school is often a very lonely job. You have to be sensitive about teachers knowing they are secure and protected, but the teaching profession can never be about teacher job security. It is a very fine line. Teachers have to always "bring their A game," and have to understand that they must teach in order to keep their jobs. Teaching is, and always has been, about making sure kids learn. That line is not gray. But as an administrator, you just have to make the right hiring and firing decisions as many times as you can, and not worry for a second about the political fallout. That takes a very strong leader who has board support.

If your school is accredited, the administrator must hold an advanced degree; but make no mistake, this job is about more than advanced degrees. And that truth is particularly real when the administrator hires teachers and coaches. I believe your administrator should hire a Master's candidate over a Doctoral candidate if the former is a better communicator. Here's a flash: any teacher with a Bachelor's degree has enough formal education to teach any high school level course in his major, assuming he was a good college student. Teaching is all about organization and communication skills, common sense, integrity, courage, and truly caring about the students (and the students must know it). But if your teacher is not assured of the support from his administrator or the board of trustees, he can't live out those rare traits with any level of confidence and effectiveness. He must know that at the end of the day, his decisions will not be overturned and will never be used as a cause of embarrassment for him and the school.

The public schools have saddled themselves with a requirement that all teachers must be certified. That means that a great engineer or scientist who always wanted to teach math or science could not do so in a public school without being state certified. While this qualification seems smart, it is actually insane. Certification primarily means that during the teacher's college or university training he experienced a semester of "Practice Teaching," and was observed and approved by his professor in the education department. Can you imagine having to observe a business for four and half months before receiving a degree in Business Administration? (What if the company he observed went into Chapter 11 months after his observation? What if the teacher being observed should have been fired years ago?) We have some bright and mature candidates in our country's brain trust who want to teach—let's fire the incompetent teachers, and replace them with the bright guys who really want to teach.

Back to administrator and teacher support. If total support is not the reality of your school's formal and informal infrastructure, the next very predictable fact is that your excellent hire, be it an administrator or teacher, will be sending out his resume to other schools; or as in many of the cases today, will leave the education profession altogether.

I recently played golf with a fellow administrator. Like me, he started and built a private school beginning in 1983. We were reminiscing about the difficult days of the beginning; never enough money, our terrible hires, etc. He was regretful, but had decided to resign. He said, "Rodney, it is so hard to find good board members, I'm just tired of it. I'm going to change professions, and even at my age of sixty-three, I'm going to begin a new career." The school he built and was planning to leave is a highly respected private secular (meaning a non-religious) prep school. The field of education does not need to lose good men like my friend.

A very common scenario in the board-administrator relationship goes something like this. It normally takes a person with a decent amount of money to finance a run for an elected position on a public school board. In a private school, it is common for a person of wealth to be invited to serve. (I know of a private school where board membership is highly valued. To be offered a place on the board costs $1,000,000.) Both cases are completely understandable, but there is a serious flaw in each.

Many people of wealth are running a company. They are the leader, and when they move into the position of a school board member, nothing really changes in their minds. They drive out of the driveway of their company and into the school parking lot for a board meeting; in their minds, they are still running things. Most are Type A personalities. They are of the opinion that if you want something done right, you have to do it yourself, and are saying in their minds, "Let's get on with this board meeting. My time is very valuable."

What has to happen, but so often does not, is that these board members have to mentally move from the "captain" of the ship to one of the "rowers." (Everyone in the boardroom is a rower.) And in all fairness to them, that is a tough transition. Making the mental shift from team owner to team member is very difficult.

If they are an elected public school board member, they ran a campaign with a definite agenda and feel that they owe it to their constituents to fulfill their promises. Sitting on the sidelines is just **not** a part of their DNA. The hook in all of this is that a board member has to know when to "lay an issue down." We all know about promises during times of an election, how everything is now on tape, etc., but the truth is that every office holder has limitations, and in a board room it is that he has only one vote.

Most administrators I know absolutely dread board meetings. They know that a clash of many really good people is imminent, and that the administrator has the most to lose. In the hundreds of private and public schools with which I am familiar, the administrator never has a vote. That is not the case at our school, but we are very different in most respects regarding governance, and for that I am most grateful. **I can't recommend our system highly enough.**

Typically, our board meetings are held five times a year; you can meet too often. In the public school forum, this is the time that members get a chance to show that they know how to run an organization. They are free with advice and wisdom that would astound Solomon. Their audience is their board colleagues. If the policy of the school is an open meeting, the public is invited, and the voters will be impressed by the strong leadership representing their district. The problem is that the administrator is often not a part of the conversation. He is placed in a very awkward, weak, and sad position. If a board votes wrong, obviously with the best of intentions, the administrator has the miserable job of implementing that decision.

Recently I read a study that stated that administrators spend over 20% of their time lobbying board members to make sure their vote is an informed one. If a board member has an agenda, like making sure racial balance is in place on the teaching staff, or the girls' basketball team has the funds for an exotic trip to play in Japan, the job of running a good school just became impossible, and very demoralizing.

But here is the solution. As a board member of a public or private school, picture the CEO of your company as the school's administrator. Instead of telling him what has to be done, your new and best strategy is to ask him if there is anything you can do to help him. **He should be your only hire, should be a voting member on the board, and must believe and know down deep that you are bringing him water and bullets for the foxhole life he walks into at the beginning of each school day.** Leave your ego at the door and show him that you have confidence in him. If you can pull that off, your administrator will leave the meeting on cloud nine, knowing he has real men and women who have his back, and he will face the next day with confidence instead of defeat. And don't forget the meeting **agenda**—it's his protection from being blindsided.

If in a public school, you may need his help in developing a strategy for getting an important bond issue passed, but be careful. He has a full-time job running the school or schools, and if you use him up in politics, what you have left is a burned out administrator. Use his collateral time wisely.

The board does have a fiscal responsibility to oversee the budget, but your administrator should deliver a budget based on his experience and the counsel from his principals and business manager. As a board member, you can't rubber-stamp the budget; that is not ethical or smart. But to "nit pick" it is just as irresponsible. If your administrator has the necessary maturity and wisdom, then he should also have your confidence. He may need you to watch his back and, for instance, not let a super influential staff member shove some nonessentials into the budget. In a closed door session, just ask him outright if he needs you to be the "heavy." He may be concerned that you might see his acceptance of your offer as a weakness, but assure him that you view it as being a good partner, and your offer may be the best strategy.

Any school budget is a moving target, so please be understanding if he is over budget in any given area. Let him know that you understand that his main job is to motivate teachers, and if he is unable to hit a financial goal on the number, strongly encourage him by telling him you could not have done any better. That is the truth.

He may need your help in deciding how to deal with a lawsuit, and never let him feel alone in that area. Most of the suits should be given to your insurance company to fight; it is a sad sign of our times that we live in a litigious culture. Get proper legal counsel, and be prepared. That is something you can do as a board member for which your administrator will be grateful. A private school in the Ft. Worth, Texas area has two lawyers on retainer. Unfortunately, that is not uncommon.

It is important for one of the board members to call your administrator occasionally to find out if he can do anything to help. Every semester, send his wife and him out for the best steak in town, and ask him if he wants to invite a few colleagues. This is a line item expense in the budget categorized "Board Initiative Fund." For your only hire, it is such a great feeling for him to know he is not alone in the battle.

Additionally, I want to emphasize the value of parents who may not have served on the board, but take time out of their busy schedules to share their appreciation for the role the staff of your school plays in the lives of your children. Any school that has families who are encouragers is blessed indeed.

I have observed that one of the most important contributions made by parents has been their kind words or notes to their child's teacher. At times they were like oil on a wound. To the administrator, teachers, and coaches nothing will improve your school like your **acknowledgement** of their sacrifice and love for your children. I can honestly say that without the support of these appreciative moms and dads, Liberty might have lost some very valuable teachers and coaches.

Recently I was in our lunchroom, and one of our teachers recalled an encouraging moment. She remembered that about four years ago a parent had called me to tell me what a good job the teacher was doing, and how much their child was enjoying school. I then picked up the phone, dialed the teacher's extension, gave her the general facts of my conversation with the parent, and told her how proud I was to serve with her. She said at the lunch table that those words of encouragement lasted her for **two years**! (Note to self: Do that more often!)

Chapter 23

SWATS—"What Are They??"

If a student is allowed to intimidate a teacher or parent, or bully a fellow student, then bring an AK-47 to the knife fight—there are some battles you can't afford to lose.

Your administrator has so many issues with which to deal, that you cannot even imagine how important his "righteous indignation" is to your school. A perfect example happened to me in the spring of 2006. I was sitting at one of the staff lunchroom tables having a conversation with two of our high school teachers. One of them mentioned to me that she had to hurry up and eat because she had to move her car before the end of the lunch period. I asked her why the rush. She proceeded to tell me that one of her students had gotten angry with her and had threatened to "key" her car, and that if she moved it, it would be unlikely that the hostile student would find it.

As the administrator, my position, fortunately or unfortunately, depending on your comfort level with authority, wields a great deal of power. For me, it's a very good thing; I don't think you can properly lead a school without it. She went on to tell me that everyone was afraid of this girl, and even the office staff didn't want to confront her. I knew the student, and was, quite honestly, angry that she had been permitted to intimidate any member of our staff. It is important to know that this lady is a great person and teacher, and something was very wrong with this picture. For whatever reason, the teacher believed it was in her best interest not to confront this student **or** her parents.

I informed her that she should enjoy her lunch, and that I would have the girl sent to my office immediately. The student would have no time to get to the parking lot. I remember the surprised look on her face when she realized that I was not afraid of the girl, and frankly, I was surprised at her surprise.

This may be a good time to speak the obvious, but private schools are not a bubble. Frankly, bubbles do not exist. There is not a perfect deacon board, church, school board, administrator, teacher, or family. Never send your children to a private school because you want them in a perfect school. There are enormous differences, but one is not perfection— we will get into that later.

I met with our counselor and the girl in my office immediately after lunch. I asked the girl in the presence of the counselor if she was having a problem with her teacher. The student said she felt that one of her papers was not graded fairly, and she was very angry. I took time to listen to her version of the story, and then told her that under no condition was she to leave the building, but to report back to my office **immediately** after the last bell of the day.

I immediately called her mother and told her to be in my office twenty minutes **before** the end of the school day, that we were going to solve a serious problem, and that together we would develop a plan of action. At the meeting with only the mom, I explained the situation and insisted on her support, or she would have to withdraw her child from our school.

At the meeting immediately after school with everyone present, I began by being very clear that I was not angry with the student. This is probably a good time to tell the reader that whenever a school administrator tells you he is not angry, he is most likely "boiling." But I kept my cool, and was very clear to the student and her mother, that any expression, much less action, of anger through intimidation or threats toward **anyone** was not going to happen on my watch.

I gave the mother and her daughter two options. The father was not active in the home, or I would have insisted that he be there as well. By the way, in my experience, the absent father is at the core of many of our school-related issues. The philosopher and writer George Herbert (1593-1633) may have said it best, "One father is more than a hundred school masters."

The first option was that she could withdraw from Liberty Christian School immediately, and I clearly expressed that that was my preference because I just don't allow threats of violence anywhere or anytime. Second, if she chose to stay, and that was an offer temporarily on the table, but ever showed any sort of disrespect to any staff member or fellow student, failed to turn in her homework on time or had unexcused tardies, she could expect to be immediately **expelled** or, in the presence of one of our female counselors receive swats, her choice. If a student "withdraws," it is not a reflection on their permanent record; if expelled, that is not a good thing.

Her mother was shocked at my bold position, and asked, "What are swats?" Her daughter explained that I was referring to a paddling. Her mother stated that her daughter was in high school, and that she was too old to be paddled. I responded that I totally agreed, but that she was too old for "time out," and probably would cherish a few days of suspension from school. In a brief moment, the mother actually sensed a huge relief to know that someone other than her rebellious daughter was in control.

I may be mistaken, but I think I observed that I had the mom's complete support, maybe even a hint of admiration.

If I could have read the mind of the daughter, I would say she was relieved as well. I asked the girl if she understood that my ground rules were nowhere near a bluff, and did she want to stay at Liberty or leave? She didn't hesitate; she wanted to stay. Our conversation was well documented by our girls' counselor, the student, and her mother; and we all signed this personally designed "document of understanding."

Let me tell you very candidly, I could never have taken that strong a stance if I had been insecure regarding the total support of my board of trustees. I presently work with a board that has proven their support of me in the tough times. They are busy in their respective professions, and do not have the time or desire to interfere with the day-to-day operations of our school. To my knowledge, not one member of our board ever knew of this meeting—nor should they have been bothered.

Kids have a basic need to know that someone is in control. It sends them the subliminal message that they are protected and loved. In many situations, when a principal or a teacher doesn't do his job of managing out-of-control students, it's because the teacher fears that his decision will be overturned. He will allow the student to show disrespect if he even suspects his support is weak. He concludes that too much of his day is wasted in trying to obtain the control and respect that he should have always had and, I might add, did have in previous generations.

Can any of you remember the times when, if you got into trouble at school, you were also in trouble at home? In our current society, that is unfortunately a very rare exception. When kids are disrespectful or disobedient in school, their parents seem to feel an insidious need to become their child's defense attorney. Most believe that if they can establish a "shadow of a doubt" argument, their child will get off without a record. The classroom has not been, nor ever should be, a democracy. The teacher has to be judge and jury. If the teacher or coach is emotionally immature, or you cannot trust his judgment, he should be fired—the job is just too big for him. I would take this action regardless of how advanced the teacher's degree might be; there are a lot of smart and well educated teachers who just are not savvy enough to be a teacher or coach.

Recently I had a teacher applicant in my office who was teaching second grade in a public elementary school. I asked her why she would take a cut in salary to work for Liberty, and her answer was that she couldn't teach because of the chaos in her classroom. She told me it was February of that school year before she got the last child not to stand on the table in her classroom. Simply put and grossly understated, the atmosphere was not conducive to teaching.

I asked her why her principal wouldn't assist her. She responded that he was not emotionally strong enough, and the "red tape" was just not worth the trouble. I asked her about support from the child's parents, and she said their response was, "We have problems of our own; can't you control a second grader?" So she was applying for a teaching job with us because she was one of our alumni and knew she would be supported and would be able to enjoy the profession for which she had spent her college years preparing. She had not given up on her dream.

If a teacher does not have support from the administrator, it is likely that very little teaching will take place at any level or grade. Too many administrators have sent a clear message to the teachers that all discipline problems should be handled in the classroom, and that is just wrong. One of the reasons the administrator is there is to support the teacher. It is a fact that some students will push the rules to the limit, and if the punishment is only a "time out" or an "in-school suspension," order will never happen in the average classroom—guaranteed.

Some of you are saying to yourself, "Dr. Haire is promoting hitting children." Please, that is like saying your surgeon slices on his patients. Hello! What we have now is not working! And don't let the liberal educational establishment redefine terms to fit their failed theories. Paddling or spanking is good discipline; child abuse is not. I feel just as adamant against child abuse, and that **would** include hitting, as I do about not loving your child enough to properly discipline him. The terms defining the action are important in that they convey the spirit of the action. Paddling or spanking is not hitting; it is not of the same spirit or intention. Our athletic director, Coach Greg Price, would never hire a coach who would grab a football player's helmet, shake a player, or curse at him. Kids are God's children. He is very protective of them and proper love and discipline are part of the training process. Too many schools have forgotten that, and too many classrooms are chaotic. And we have no one to blame but ourselves and the cowardly public officials that we elected.

In my experience, the issues cover the entire spectrum of ages from preschoolers to twelfth graders. A few years ago, I had to expel a **four-year-old**. This little boy bit, hit, and tripped anyone who got in his way, and that is not permissible at Liberty. The parents were very cooperative and encouraged us to take whatever action we needed to take to make sure their son obeyed the rules. We just could not allow that boy to intimidate our other children, and had to tell his parents they had to remove their son from our school. Liberty does not paddle preschool children, but if we did, I believe this little boy would have responded and obeyed. Spanking a young child when it is appropriate and administered with love is almost always effective and everyone is happier that the four-year-old is not in control of the classroom. His parents wanted us to paddle him, but we see that as strictly a parental responsibility at such a young age. We lost a great family and a chance to correct a very young little boy, but you just cannot win them all. (Note to self: Revisit the policy of not spanking preschool age children when the request to do so comes from the parents.)

On the positive side of this very controversial and volatile subject, a teacher told me about two young men, who happened to be athletes, who were being disruptive in her math class. These students were in middle school. I called them into my office within the hour and gave them three options. First, they could return to class, and immediately after the class was over, apologize to the teacher for their disrespectful behavior and become her best-behaved students starting "tomorrow." Apologize is really not the correct term. They had to ask the teacher if she would **forgive** them. The distinction between asking for forgiveness and making an apology may seem narrow, but apologizing in today's society will, in many cases, be reduced to a quick "Sorry"—meaning they wish they had not gotten caught. Asking if the teacher will forgive them has a dimension of repentance added, which is good for the soul.

Their next choice, or "behind the second door," they could report to their coach after every class disruption, and explain to him that they just could not abide by classroom rule number one - that of obeying and respecting the teacher. (They understood that this choice would get them paddled.) Or third, that in order to return to class, they would have to be accompanied by their parent or parents for as long as it took us to feel confident that they could behave (that's a word we don't hear very often). They chose door number one and, not surprisingly, things went fabulously.

Several years ago I did have a student that chose door number three. His parents were both professors at the University of North Texas, and were only too happy to support my authority and their son's decision. All of the adults in this scenario were surprised at the boy's decision. I honestly think the boy either thought it was going to be cute, or he thought it was a bluff. After the first hour, with Mom sitting in the desk next to his, he came in and asked for door number one. He was truly repentant.

Recently a student from a "Blue Ribbon" school in Texas applied for admission into our school. I asked her why she was transferring, and she told me that there were a couple of reasons. First, she explained that her parents wanted her to make good grades in order to be accepted into Texas Tech University in Lubbock, Texas. Secondly, she had a chemistry class that had thirty-five students in it and the teacher was never able to answer her questions. When I asked her why, she said that the teacher was always trying to get control of the class. Thirdly, she would go in early for tutoring, and the teacher would rarely show up. This in a "BLUE RIBBON" school in my beloved State of Texas!! I know of few educators who believe that "Blue Ribbon" is **not** a sham of a designation, and publicly very misleading.

A classroom teacher should be professionally observed regarding classroom management skills. Let's assume the teacher has strong knowledge of subject matter. If his classroom management skills are weak, the administrator should immediately help train the teacher, expect observable improvement quickly, or fire him. Classroom management is a tough skill for teachers to master, but disrespect for a teacher cannot be tolerated. All in the profession must be able to manage any classroom without losing teaching quality. However, if there is a need for a stronger arm, then there needs to be that person available immediately, and his title is Administrator.

When our school was smaller, I did all of the teacher observations. A teacher can have excellent classroom management skills, but still have a bad day. On any given day, a good teacher can have a lesson that does not go as planned. Maybe his child is sick, maybe the teacher is not feeling well, etc. I had a password for my teachers to use in case it was not their best day. It was understood that when I walked into the classroom, and this was "one of those days," they would simply say, "Thank you, Dr. Haire, for joining us today," and that was my key to leave as soon as possible—the observation would take place on another day. Our teachers understood that these thorough observations were part of their permanent record, and I was on their side if they were having an exceptionally bad day.

As our school grew, I discovered that I was actually unable to objectively observe our teachers. We have staff devotionals at least two times per week, and I became aware of personal issues and situations during those times, making it almost impossible for me to evaluate a teacher as well as was expected. We employed Dr. Lloyd Campbell, who held a PhD in Education, to perform the function of evaluating our teaching staff. We continued with Dr. Campbell's services for several years. It was our decision to give our teachers three observations during the year. The first one was announced, the second and third were not. I discovered that great teachers loved to be observed and professionally evaluated. I'm not sure how poorly performing teachers feel about evaluations; I fortunately don't have one at this time. (That last sentence seems arrogant and haughty and I don't mean it to be; I just couldn't pass up an opportunity to brag on our staff.)

Chapter 24

Are You All Hat and No Cows??

I want to suggest a job description for board members that is a valuable tool and may prevent a "train-wreck."

I know a public school administrator who spends a lot of time in the school's bookroom, presumably taking inventory, to avoid unpleasant parents who are always ready with suggestions or the ever-present, "Have you got just **one** minute?" Board members, administrators, and teachers get the same thing at ball games. Leadership territory is very demanding—but the payoff is grand if you can handle the pressure.

I hope this book will empower my colleagues who occupy the administrator's office to speak and act courageously and speak loudly. You are the ones with the privilege and responsibility to restore dignity to your office—just do it!! Be the gutsy leader you know you can be, play offense, and do not think, "What if they fire me?" or "What if they talk badly about me?" If you are right in your convictions, you are going to gain the honor and respect of anyone who matters. Make no mistake, if you are serving a "wimpy" board, you could go down. You may get fired—oops, "asked to resign," because you said or did what you knew to be right. If you lose your job, do it because you said and did the right thing. Trust me, another district is looking for YOU. I recently was contacted by a "headhunting" firm for private schools, and was told they had forty openings for an administrator and only six serious candidates. Speak the truth and make no apologies.

Many of us have the title of "Dr." in front of our name, and some don't, but we are all called "educators," and should only use that title if we deserve to wear it. It implies we have many of the answers and possess the leadership skills to implement them. So STAND UP and be the leader that so many teachers are crying out for. Otherwise, hang up your clipboard and whistle. Our educational system, both public and private, is in serious trouble. It's going to take serious educators to correct those problems, and we are the only professionals who can do it, but as they say in the South, "You can't be all hat and no cows."

Decisions are sometimes difficult because you don't know for sure you are right. But if you are fortunate enough to know you are right, you have to have the courage to fight it through. The truth is that education is an art, not a science, and there are many more questions than answers. This book is about uncovering the answers we do have, possessing the courage to act, and realizing there is no time left to pull any punches.

I feel very badly for school board members who have been promoted or elected beyond their level of competence. Many of America's public and private schools have board members who are great pilots, accountants, entrepreneurs, etc., but they have no idea or training on how to run a school. And here is a real shocker: you can't send a recently elected board member to a three-day seminar and expect him to be a "certified" educator. What if I were sent to a three-day seminar on piloting a plane? Anyone want a quick trip?

You know by now that I like to cut to the chase. So permit me to be very clear: if you have been elected to a school board it is because we are blessed to live in a free country. And while we have the best political system in the world, it does have some drawbacks. For instance, if you are on the board of a school, odds are you know very little if anything about running a school, and my guess is that no one knows it better than you. To say otherwise would be like a person saying he knows how to build a car because he has a driver's license. So with that being said, let's make it work. The board should have a minimal number of tasks, but those duties are very important—no, HUGE!! The board should do the following things:

1. Hire the best Superintendent (public school term) or President or Headmaster (private school term) you can find. This person should be employed, and you will have to "pirate" him from another school. This task is the board's primary responsibility, so it has to be right. The board's hire should be a strong leader and motivator, who is of the highest integrity, possesses great people skills, and exudes the confidence to hire principals who are as good or better than he is at running a school. He should be a person of courage. Hire the "race horse," and have the common sense as a board member to get out of his way and let him run.

2. Approve a common sense budget. Make sure that all purchases over a reasonably large amount have three competitive bids. That can be done with an executive committee of the board, but is not necessarily a board meeting agenda item because the board is not in the purchasing business at this level. The board buys land and buildings, not office furniture, computers or shoulder pads.

3. Deal with all bond issues and the raising of money. Your "race horse" is running the school or schools. In a private school, the headmaster will have to see the larger donors. Those donors have a right to know that their money is spent wisely. Administrators

of private schools are expected to make "the ask" when major donors are involved; it is a difficult task, but this role is part of the culture. If you are a board interviewing a headmaster who has an aversion to raising money, my suggestion is to move on to another candidate.

4. Form a committee only at the request of the administrator. This might include setting geographical boundaries for schools within the district, meeting governmental regulations, etc. The administrator should be strong enough to tell you when he needs your help, because you are his support system. Recently we needed to examine our transportation policy. I got a call from a board member who asked me if he could help by researching a good transportation strategy and reporting back to the board. This board member realized I had a need for assistance before I did, but his offer was in a "Can I help you" spirit, and I greatly appreciated his help. The administrator should look forward to all board meetings. Hopefully, he knows the board will not pass up an opportunity to encourage him. He fights battles on the front lines for the district or the school for which each of you is responsible. Your job is to bring him bullets and water.

5. Give him, his principals, teachers, and coaches credit for the good, and you (the board) take the heat for the bad if you can. He is going to make mistakes; you want him to, otherwise he is not working.

6. Make sure he has the credentials to meet all accreditation requirements. While this is crucial, it is the least important aspect regarding criteria for a successful hire. There are a lot of MBA's

in Chapter 11, and the same principle is prevalent in the business of education.

I suggest having a round-table discussion with your board to add the above responsibilities in a way that fits the culture of your school. I would also be open to the strong possibility that by making some changes in the board's responsibilities and boundaries, the school's culture might improve. Public or private, you are talking about an amendment to the by-laws, not a publicly held referendum.

Board members, please read carefully. Subjects to avoid talking about with parents include, but are not limited to, the following: the playing time that their child received in the game, students' grades, cheerleading tryouts, and morning traffic problems. And they certainly are not agenda items for a board meeting. Do not let them come up on your "screen."

Let me get very personal and specific about an issue that comes up regularly in board meetings that nobody wants to talk about. In almost 100% of the meetings of both private and public schools, a member is going to intentionally or unintentionally place the administrator on the spot. Maybe it's asking a question that the administrator can't possibly know the answer to, like, "Dr. Haire, do you know why fourteen out of the twenty students in 'Mrs. Abercrombie's' class failed the last Algebra I exam?" Another member chimes in, "I heard the same thing from my child. And you can bet one thing, my child is not perfect, but he is not a liar!" Another, "Dr. Haire, did you know that the drama teacher had our kids rehearsing until 10:00 p.m. last Wednesday night, and the kids had an English exam on Thursday?!" In the minds of far too many parents, the only potential liars in any scenario that pertains to their child are their child's teachers or coaches. Now is the time and here is the place for the chairperson of the board to remember the AGENDA!

First, most of it is not true. On a good day, all of it is out of context. But what is going on in the mind of the administrator? He has to sit in the board room and hear about rumors that have no substance, and he can't do anything about it. He can't defend himself, even if he doesn't care if he gets fired. He has to protect "his young" and his staff. We administrators have to hear this kind of thing all the time from parents. When it comes from a boardroom, it does damage somewhere very deep in our souls. This room is the place where we need to come for support, encouragement, and wise counsel, not to defend the latest garbage being circulated.

A few years ago, we were having a meeting at the home of one of our board members. One member had a son who played on the football team, and let's just say that the boy was not a "starter." This board member asked me **in the meeting,** "Did you know that my son didn't even get in the game last Friday night?" By coincidence, I remembered asking the head coach before that game, if we got ahead in the score, to please make sure that all of our kids had an opportunity to get in the game. I asked him specifically to assign that responsibility to one of his assistant coaches.

In response to the board member's question, I told him that I would check into the situation and get back to him. (For those of you who are wondering, this question occurred before I discovered the enormous benefit of the "agenda rule.") The coach told me he clearly remembered asking the boy if he wanted in the game, and the boy told him he did not.

I couldn't tell the dad that his son was afraid to play—I just did not have the heart to say that to a father, or do that to a boy. So I called the dad back, and told him that I was so sorry about the oversight, and that I would make sure to do a better job of instructing our coaches to try to make sure, if we got a comfortable lead, all got to play. I threw the coach and myself "under the bus," but it was better than the boy losing face in the eyes of his dad—administrators make those decisions all the time. But this is an example of what can happen in a board meeting, and it will destroy your board's effectiveness and your administrator's morale.

The solution is to have an agenda, and don't let go of it. Warning! After the meeting, a member may ask, "Can we have some time off the record, just a sort of round-table discussion?" The answer from the **chairperson** should always be, "I'm sorry, but no. If you guys want to meet at a local restaurant, feel free, but "Dr. Smith" has a school to run. Thanks to all of you for attending this very productive meeting. Do I have a motion to adjourn?" I'm telling you, it will happen from the very best of people with the best of intentions.

Chapter 25

Don't Talk About the Money, Show It to Me!!

Every school has needs, all the time! The larger your school, the bigger the needs—big horses eat more than little ones. If you are on the board, get your very own short list of donors—it's easy.

In any private school, there is a constant need for money for **relatively** small items, in the cost range (in 2010 dollars) from $2,500 to $15,000. Until October of 2007, I had never asked a member of our board to help and been denied. On this occasion, I heard a "No" from one of our board members, and it was to fund the last of a $4,000 project. Our need to reach the goal was **$500.** If you are on the board, it really is imperative that if you do not have the money, you are able to get it. The right answer would have been, "Rodney, I don't personally have $500 right now. I will make a phone call or two, secure the gift, and call you back with instructions of who to send a thank you letter and a tax-deductible receipt." The important thing is for the administrator to know that any one of his board members can raise relatively small amounts of money that the school needs to finish a project. That was a sickening phone call, and I strongly suggest you never deliver that message to your administrator.

But that valuable tool in your board responsibility arsenal must be cultivated. At a proper time, you will meet a dad who you know has capacity to help the school with projects. Some of the projects might be large, most will be small. Before the need arises, directly ask the parent with whom you have a trusting relationship if he would be willing to help fund a school project should the need arise. And don't assume people with money are your best candidates. People who are willing and want to help may have very little in the way of financial capacity, but they will give what they can, and **every** gift is needed. One of your jobs as a board member is to identify the "givers." They are easy to identify: they have a good relationship with most of the other parents—they would have won Most Likely to Succeed or Class Favorite in high school. And dads who are givers tend to hang out with other givers. As a giver, he will be honored that you asked him to help; giving is what "makes his clock tick." I have observed that people are divided into two groups: "takers" or "givers." (And we are all one or the other.) I have also observed that the givers are generally happier people.

I have helpful couple friends who have called me several times to ask if they can pay the tuition for a disadvantaged student. I can't even begin to share the encouragement of parents calling on their own to offer support. Administrators typically put their hat in their hand and "make the ask." It is always for another parent's child, a computer printer, a needed musical instrument, etc., but having to **ask** is just hard. (Thanks, Doug and Linda, for blessing the lives of kids!)

A relatively new family to Liberty asked for a meeting with our development director and me. They wanted to know how they could help. I told them of a dream we had to build a sanctuary that would be a place of Godly worship. They said they would help, but would also like for us to meet his parents, as they had a heart to give as well. From the two meetings, our school now has the gift to begin raising money aggressively for the sanctuary, and three children who need financial assistance are having their tuition paid by this family. (Thank you, Lee, Donna, Lee, and Terri.)

I recently had a single mom who desperately wanted her two children in our school. The problem was that she didn't have the necessary funds to make that a reality. She said, "Dr. Haire, I am so ashamed to have to ask you for financial assistance, but I have to keep reminding myself it is for my children." She said, "I have most of the needed funds, but after cutting my budget everywhere I can, I am still short." I responded, "I know exactly how you feel. I ask for money on a regular basis, and it is never for my personal gain—it is for the children. I'll be glad to make some phone calls, and I'm sure we can raise the amount you are short."

The administrator has to be the chief fund-raiser for major gifts, and most of us have had no training. I know of no university course that offers "The Art of the Ask" in their educational degree program. In fact, most educational departments are void of even mentioning school politics or fundraising.

Another supportive family at Liberty sees a need and just fills it. In 2007, they upgraded the girls' softball field, planted beautiful trees and shrubs, and built an outdoor mall for our students to enjoy during lunch on nice days. All given without "the ask." (Thanks, Craig and Tonya.)

Another dad has been an enormous help in assisting us with gifts that give large projects real traction. He is a dependable giver, has determined to do whatever he can do to help, and is so appreciated by so many. (Thanks, Ken.)

Our trees, shrubs, and grass on our campus remind me of an interesting boardroom story. We were in a board meeting, and the discussion of being over budget on our capital building project was a topic on the agenda. When you are in a building program, "over budget" is always on the agenda. One board member said something like, "I think landscaping is very important; if we don't plant grass, trees, and shrubs, our new campus will look unfinished." Another chimed in, "I agree. I think we are looking at $75,000, plus or minus." The first said, "I'll match whatever you give." The second said, "I'll take half." The first replied, "Done." This conversation happened in less than two minutes. We ordered trees, shrubs, and grass, and sent each an invoice for half. That is the way good board members handle things when you have men in the room with capacity AND a heart to give. No vote, no discussion. (Craig and Jack—I owe you each a "white hat.")

We have a very special couple who are alumni parents, and they saw that the boys' baseball field needed to be improved, and poured approximately $60,000 of their own money into the project. They never had to be asked for the money. They wanted Liberty to continue to be a school of excellence. This project was on their heart, and it will benefit hundreds of young men for decades. The father has been a loyal board member for many years, and his wife has chaired our PTF. (Way to go, Don and Patty!)

Other parents obtained several hundred thousand dollars for various construction projects, and additionally took on the sizable job of running our Warrior Booster Club. These families love our school, and will do anything within their power to help—they have shown it many times with love and their financial support. (Thanks to the Gannons, Lochs, Fitzgeralds, and Woodalls.)

A grandmother of three great young men who are Liberty students lives in Florida and has been a wonderful and faithful donor to our many building projects for years. I have never had the pleasure of meeting her. (Thank you, Mrs. West.)

For the last several years, an alumnus of 1987 sends several checks a month to the school—we use those funds to help single moms with tuition. We have used Harlan's and April's gift to help single mothers afford Liberty—thanks, guys.

We have a board member who gives of his time and talents in very unique ways. He is trained in land development and building projects. He knows the best way to build a facility for the highest and best use. (Bob, you are appreciated.)

Another board member owns a carpet company and truly loves to give of his products and services to our various school needs and also to needy families in the community. It doesn't require a lengthy presentation, just let him know the need. (Thanks, Michael and Audrey.)

These families and hundreds more are a help and an encouragement to so many. We are incredibly fortunate at Liberty to have an abundance of committed parents, alumni, and grandparents. Although I would like to mention every one of them, I will say that I believe all givers will receive rewards in heaven for their generosity. (And none of them expected nor asked that their name be mentioned in this book.) I mentioned them to bring to the reader a level of personal identity to the importance of giving, and to let all know that gifts of all sizes are of tremendous value and will ensure the future of your school. Your kids may not realize the importance of your gift, maybe not this side of heaven. But being a good parent is all about "doing" without recognition—no one said life was fair—but giving is enormously rewarding. At a PTF meeting one year, I asked the audience, "What would your life be like without Liberty

Christian School?" Maybe it is a good question for the reader as it pertains to **your** school.

In the public school arena, the support is different, but a positive and helpful parent's and/or board member's attitude and encouragement is worth millions. There may be giving opportunities, but you will have to take the initiative to ask. Before Liberty, Judy and I had our two kids in a public school. During an Open House, Judy told me that the encyclopedias in the school's library were out of date. The year was in 1977, and Bill Gates hadn't changed the world yet. I told the principal to buy a new set and send me the bill. I never heard from him.

Warning to board members: for all of the opportunities to help, the possibility to undo all your good can happen with an innocent overstepping of your boundaries. It is worth repeating: you can set yourselves up for a terrible dilemma if you start trying to solve problems for which you have been given no authority. If you fall into the trap of trying to solve a parent's problem that has to do with day-to- day operations, you have put yourself in a no-win situation. It will take a war room type of board meeting to get you out of the jam, and worse, it leaves your only hire and soldier, the administrator, on life support.

When a disgruntled parent calls, thank him for the call, but tell him the board does not deal with personnel or operational issues, only fiscal issues and general policy. Explain that his best solution is to go through the proper channels. The parent may tell you that he has talked to everyone, that you are his last hope. That is when you explain that the board has voted unanimously NOT to get involved in school operations. I suggest telling him how sorry you are that his child is disappointed, and that you hope she makes it next year. Parents may tell you that they regret the day they voted for you, and never to call them for a favor, **a donation,** or call you their friend. Welcome to the world of school board politics. And please hear this: you are not serving on the board for anyone other than the students. This is not your stepping stone to the US Presidency, so just get tough-skinned and do the right thing. You can't expect your decisions to be any more popular than the administrator's, so pass the heat on to him—he will have to face it eventually anyway. There is only one boat, and we are all in it.

Chapter 26

Exactly When Do We Want To Start the Improvement Program?
Or
What Are You Waiting For?

Is your school worth asking itself the tough questions?

I know I told you that this is not going to be a "how to" book, but I can't resist the temptation—I desperately want to throw myself a slow pitch over the plate. Try this at your next public school board meeting. I suggest an **informed** group of parents attend the next school board meeting **with permission** to publicly address the trustees. The group spokesperson has to be a person who is well-respected. He is going to politely ask the school board to research the following ideas and policies **before** the next school board meeting. Have the issues in writing, and a copy for each member of the board and for every member of your group (no more than 20 or 30).

1. Consider a policy whereby the Board can only hire one person, the administrator. The administrator may choose to delegate some of his hires to the principals, vice principals, academic chairs, etc., but that is not the role of the board. However, at the top position, probably called the Superintendent, the Board does the hiring and no preference is allowed on the basis of race, color or creed. **The most highly qualified person gets the job.** That may mean that a white male is hired by the board to run an inner city school, but if

he is, it is because he was the most highly qualified candidate, not for any other reason. Ask the board members, "Do you want your heart surgeon because hiring him met the hospital's racial quota, or your airplane pilot flying the plane because **she** balanced the gender quota?" Why should we settle for anything less from the person hired to run our children's schools? (Answer: a rhetorical question.)

2. Ask the board specifically how the teacher unions serve the best interest of your children. (Answer: they don't.)
3. Ask why administrators and teachers have contracts, and are those contracts in the best interest of our children? (Honest Answer: "Because of the unions; second reason, we have always done it that way, and finally the answer; no, they are not.")
4. Ask how the Department of Education in Washington, DC and in the capital of your state benefits your children. (Answer: they give us money. Your follow up question, "At what cost to our freedom to run our school efficiently? And by the way, how much money, and what per cent of our total budget do they give—exactly?)
5. Ask if anyone has considered privatizing your public school, and if not, would the board form a committee to research that alternative. You would appreciate, in exchange for your support and vote in the next election, a report back to your parents' spokesperson prior to the next meeting. Considering new ideas may be of great value to the residents of your school district.
4. Ask, "What is the penalty if our district ceases to give the state standardized test, and allows our teachers to teach the curriculum (textbooks), instead of teaching to and or administering the test?"

Be very clear that you expect, in exchange for your vote at the next election, a complete report before the next board meeting. Offer to help them do the needed research if they say they don't have time.

Privatizing your public school sounds a little like spitting on the flag. I really get that. However, the public schools we send our kids to today are far different from those of the previous generations. In Texas, as in most states, there is a state-mandated achievement test that is **not** "scope and sequenced" into the curriculum. For instance, at Liberty we teach multiplication and division in second grade, and introduce algebra in the third grade. If we took time out of the planned scope and sequence to prepare our students for a standardized test, our students would not be ready for the introduction to algebra that has been designed to fit into the child's learning sequence of third grade.

Public and private school textbooks are written and planned on a nine-month teaching cycle; they have been for generations. If the state government mandates that the local system not only give this test, but make the results of it a determining factor in the amount of money the state will send to that local school, big guess as to what you can expect. Virtually all teachers will teach to the test; in most districts, it's a scheduled class. Some teachers feel pressured to give their students the answers to the test. So we are now not only taking time away from the sequenced curriculum, but teachers are feeling pressured, and have stooped, in many cases, to cheating. Can you imagine what that does to the morale of the thousands of good and honorable public school teachers?

To add insult to injury, the Dallas Independent School District just reduced the level of academic standards to ensure that more students would succeed. The Dallas Independent School District, in the year 2008, approved significant changes in school policy. According to the Dallas Morning News, here are some of the highlights:

1. Homework grades should be given only when the grades will raise a student's average, not lower it.
2. Teachers must accept overdue assignments, and their principal will determine if there is a penalty.
3. Students who fail a test can retake the exam.
4. Teachers cannot give a zero on an assignment unless they call the parents and have made "efforts to assist students in completing the work."
5. Teachers who fail a given percentage of their students will need to develop a professional improvement plan.

I thought it interesting that this new plan to **improve** the Dallas schools was publicly announced on August 16, 2008, too late for parents to enroll their children in a private school if they so chose. This is one decision where I believe strongly that the school board should overturn the superintendent's decision—never thought I would say that! About a month later, the superintendent had the terrible responsibility of informing the Dallas School District Board of Trustees that the DISD would have a shortfall north of $84,000,000. In my opinion, this is not a "rounding error."

Parents, since your public school is run by the board of trustees, you have to ask them the really tough questions—your child's future is at stake. The list of competitors for placement in highly respected universities is exhaustive, and will include graduates from the finest prep schools, and dedicated students from all over the world. America's public schools have to get competitive, and get there fast. Approximately ninety percent of the children in the United States are in our public schools, and if we don't get it right, not only is your child's future earning potential at risk, but our country's brain trust will be bankrupt.

On August 7, 2008, Oprah Winfrey did a full segment on her talk show on some of the problems facing public education. She invited Bill and Melinda Gates to share their common passion for the general plight of the public schools in the United States. Anderson Cooper did the on-site reporting from various schools. If memory serves, Oprah Winfrey stated that the US is ranked 24th overall in the world in math. (I believe this program was originally produced in 2006, but I am deriving that from comments made during the show; I could be wrong on the date of the taping.) I want to make a few comments about that show that will illustrate my overall evaluation of this very dire issue.

Mr. and Mrs. Gates and Ms. Winfrey more than deserve to share their views. I don't know if any of the three are trained educators, but all three are generous philanthropists, and have earned a place at any table of public concern. They put their money behind issues that are not only a problem to America's citizenry, but to those in other parts of our world. I believe that Anderson Cooper is a first class journalist.

Anderson Cooper interviewed two African-American young men who were high school students in a dilapidated school building in Washington, DC. Cooper went on to interview a principal, apparently employed in the same school, who appeared to me to be emotionally defeated. He showed Cooper a copy of a "work order" to repair a ceiling that was literally falling down; the work order was dated several years prior to that interview. Both the students and the principal seemed to me to be very depressed, and I believe had given up the fight. The two fine young men and the principal just could not understand how their school building was "left behind." The ceiling literally had holes in it, some entire windows were missing, some bathrooms were so badly damaged that they were unusable, etc.

Another segment of the program showed an interview of a very nice young lady from a public school in Tennessee. (I could be wrong about the state, but in reality, it could have been any state.) This student graduated with a 4.0 GPA, the valedictorian of her high school graduating class. She went to a university and discovered that she was totally unprepared for the academic demands.

All of these dots do connect, but in my view this particular Oprah segment totally missed an opportunity to deliver what could have been a powerful show. The question "What?" was clearly addressed—kudos to the Oprah producer. But the "What" questions are frankly answered by observations and statistics. We all know that too many of our public schools are in physical disrepair and too many teachers are doing a poor job of teaching. But the solutions are in the answers to the "Why" questions. **Why** was the building **not** repaired (or condemned and torn down), and **why** was the valedictorian not prepared?

One at a time. In my view, Anderson Cooper should have interviewed the two young men during a normal school lunch period and in the hall during a passing period, not when there were no students in the building. Cooper should have gone into a classroom in session, and stayed long enough to be a "fly on the wall." He should have interviewed a teacher and guidance counselor. He then would have left his research assignment with answers to the "WHY" questions, been able to prepare Oprah for another show or extended segment, and been ready to share solutions.

Mr. Cooper should have spent some class time in the physics and Senior English classes in the school in Tennessee. He should have asked those teachers, "In your opinion, **why** wasn't your valedictorian ready for college?" In my opinion, the obvious answer is, "We had to 'dumb down' the curriculum." Is anyone asking, "Why would we ever dumb down a school?"

In fairness, if Cooper had interviewed a certain **private** school in Texas, he would have found that for the school year 2007/2008, the administrator approved six freshmen students to take physics. All six students received an "A." For those who have never taken a physics course, much of the math required for physics is Algebra II and beyond, none of which any of these high school freshman had taken. Think there was some dumbing down in that private school's physics course? Without a voucher system in place, many public school parents will not be able to afford the luxury of transferring their child to a **good** private or better public school that truly performs and competes academically on the world stage.

In Washington, Cooper should have asked the school board chairman, "**Why** are there holes in the ceiling in one of your high schools? And **why** are metal detectors needed? **Why** have you allowed a principal to remain in office at a school with inoperable bathrooms and missing windows for over five years?" Cooper should have asked the president of the PTA, "**Why** haven't the parents been in the face of the school board chairman asking **WHY?** **Why** have the parents not stood up in force and recruited proactive parents who know how to build buildings to volunteer to fix up their children's school?" I have a feeling that if Microsoft was in the condition of those schools, Mr. Gates would be asking "**Why?**"

To the applause from her audience, Oprah announced that the schools in Washington, DC were going to receive $1,000,000,000 (BILLION) to repair the public schools. Two thoughts: first, that will certainly and temporarily answer the "What" issue; and second, can you imagine the "good ol' boy" system at work in those contracts? My guess is that those contracts will be the sweetest deals for connected contractors that they have seen in a very long time. (I would love to be wrong; just show me the invoices and work completed for the $1,000,000,000. I'll send my e-mail upon request and apologize.) But in truth, in three years or less, unless the "Why" is addressed and solved, the district will need another billion, and then another.

The dots connect at the leadership positions in all cases—that is the common thread. The principal of the DC school should have been in the face of the school board, and threatening to call a press conference and name names if the first repair order was not completed in 60 days—not five years (and his job never been in jeopardy)!! The principal in Tennessee should have turned his faculty upside down, and made them teach the curriculum or fire them. If our public school crisis is about money, then it's about fraud at worst, and mismanagement at best—we all pay more than enough taxes. The issue facing our public schools is about people in power being afraid, not making the tough decisions, and not having to answer the tough questions.

Both private and public schools are in trouble, but the American public system is so badly broken that it does not even resemble the more productive and competitive public system that was common in the 1950s and 1960s. Even additional computer labs, beautiful buildings, and higher salaries have only netted our public schools a lower place on the academic food chain. We have to wake up and smell the watered-down coffee.

Interestingly, Oprah has recently (September of 2010) aired another show on the subject of fixing our schools. Joined by guests including Bill Gates and Davis Guggenheim, the director of the documentary *Waiting for "Superman,"* the program served as a call to action to turn our country's schools around. Many of their proposed solutions have much in common with this book because they are based on the common sense principles of hiring great teachers and principals and "putting the power on the ground," to quote Mr. Guggenheim.

It may be a surprise, but nobody in the **public** school arena is asking, "Why are parents paying school taxes AND paying thousands of dollars in tuition for their kids to attend private schools? What is the draw?" Here are some hints. It is not about "white flight" or a desire for segregation, prayer in schools, Bible courses, or better curriculum. Every private school of which I am aware would like to have more diversity, students are going to pray as long as there are tests, all Christian schools are looking for a better Bible curriculum, and finding better textbooks is always on the front burner of all department heads in the private school sector.

But there **are** several reasons—the question is where to start. First, parents want their child in a safe environment. They have told me they have a guilty conscience for dropping their child off at a place where they would be afraid to work. There is a lack of confidence in the basic ability of administrators to ensure that their child will simply have a "good and safe day at school." I had a mother enroll her child at Liberty in 2008 in our sixth grade. Her son was threatened every day of the previous school year, and he told me that because he was always fearful of getting beat up, he "really didn't think he had learned a thing." He had passed the sixth grade with all A's and B's, but still believed he needed to repeat the grade.

Parents want to give their child a chance to "surface," to be a part of an activity that they enjoy. A public school official asking any private school administrator, "What can we do to improve our public schools?" would hear, "Make sure enrollment never exceeds approximately 175 students per grade, and no more than 23 students in a core class." Larger is not better in the school business. At Liberty, we work very hard to keep our class sizes in grades seventh through twelfth in core courses less than 20 students per teacher. Admittedly we can't always meet that goal, but we get very creative and our capable counselors spend countless hours trying to make sure our classes are smaller rather than larger. (Thanks, Toni, Norm, and Tim.)

Another response would be that good private schools don't keep teachers who are not talented. Our parents will simply not pay for an **average** teacher. Additionally, private schools that are successful endeavor to place a role model in every classroom. Our job is to make the parents say to themselves, "I really can't decide which teacher is best for my child; they are all wonderful."

I fear that this chapter, as it relates to improving our public schools, could be a waste of your time to read and my time to write if the educational establishment has too much pride to ask the private schools for advice. It is the same reason that our federal government does not ask Warren Buffet or Ross Perot what changes the government needs to make to run a profitable country. Do you think Buffet or Perot would allow one of their companies to continually run a deficit? It is all about institutional pride. When my wife and I started Liberty, we asked the best private schools in the country, "What did you do that you wish you hadn't done; and what didn't you do that you wish you had?" Many opened up their wisdom, and we took notes as fast as we could write.

I taught a course at the Association of Christian Schools International in their Dallas convention for about four years in the period from 1998 to 2002 on "How Not to Run a Private School." I gave it different titles, but the message was virtually the same. The first year there were about 15 administrators in a room that would hold 100; I was both humbled and embarrassed. The last three years it was standing room only. That last year, I remember a board member who was seated on the third row walking out of my seminar—actually, he stormed out. I was explaining how board members should not run schools—who knew?? (And I thought I said it with such sensitivity—guess not.)

Chapter 27

Prayer Out, Evolution In—We Finally Got it Right!!
(Only if you are an atheistic para-educator)

Will someone in the academic community have the courage to admit that they have no idea how man got here? And now it is about global warming—what in the world could Al Gore know about global warming? (I hope God doesn't send the earth the beginning of another Ice Age in the middle of one of his speeches.)

So many parents want to make the issues of prayer in school and creation vs. evolution the main difference between public and private schools. The issue is not that anyone is going to have less of a relationship with God because he is not permitted to pray in school. Your child is not going to get behind in his scripture reading because he can't carry his Bible to school (which, by the way, is not against the law).

If your child is in a public school that happens to be led by a principal who is fearful of the liberal left, is an atheist, or is easily intimidated by the ACLU, you may have a "rights" issue with which to deal. But if you publicly disagree, it could be difficult for your child.

Many years ago, about five of our seniors got their courage up to hand out a simple, Christian-based tract called "The Four Spiritual Laws" to students at the Denton High School in Denton, Texas. Our students were standing on the sidewalk, an area that was not blocking anyone from doing anything, handing out Christian tracts. The principal told them to leave, and then wrote me a letter telling me to cease all efforts promoting religion on HIS campus. I knew it wasn't "his campus," but

Denton was a smaller town then, our school was new, and frankly, I did not want to start a fight. Today, I would take the issue to court, but we were the proverbial new kid on the block and in reality and retrospect, I think I got pushed around by the local schoolyard bully.

The real and larger issue is that the federal government has expelled God from public schools. It is not that God can't take up for Himself, and thus we need to write our representatives and senators to protect Him. The God of the Bible, who is the only one alive (Buddha, Mohammed, and Joseph Smith are still in the grave, and not in great shape) will not be wonderfully ecstatic if our Congress **allows** Him back in public schools. If Biblical history is a predictor of the future (and I know for atheists it may not be), for God to take notice and forgive our lawmakers, several things will have to take place that are a very "long shot."

Starting with the Supreme Court Justices and moving down the political "food chain" to the local school board members, a change of heart will be required. If they pray and repent fervently for not giving God **first** place in our public schools, He **may** forgive them. Remember the children of Israel, after they had been slaves to Pharaoh for 400 years, had to earnestly repent for worshipping their false gods before God sent Moses to lead them out. I heard an old preacher say one time, "If God can't drive, He won't ride." Christian parents, I suggest you leave the issue of prayer in schools to the lawmakers. When all of our Supreme Court Justices and all members of the Executive and Legislative Branch get on their knees and repent, we may once again see God's face and enjoy His presence in the halls of our public schools, and maybe even Congress. A simple vote, as **important** as your vote is, the last time I read the scriptures, is not going to impress God—the problem is bigger than that.

We have to get the right candidates in, and that means we **do** have to vote. Ultimately, the job of protecting our nation's greatness does lie in the men and women who write and pass our laws. But at the end of the day, our elected representatives have to answer for their own crazy idea of expelling God from America's public schools in the name of religious freedom—good luck!!

I'm sad for our African-American brothers and sisters. After they finally obtained the right to attend white public schools, legally ending the era of segregation, seemingly almost on cue the Supreme Court took prayer out of our public schools. When that happened, the core of what made our schools great began to rot from the inside out. It **always** starts from the inside, and now after several decades, you can see that our once excellent public schools have become a war zone. We never had violence or blatant disrespect for authority before that law passed. That is a phenomenon that happened after God was legally informed He was not God. The African-Americans were so happy to finally get onto a level educational playing field, and who could blame them? The first ones were not thrilled, they were frightened. But later, after they were actually accepted, not just admitted, they fell into a system that had been spiritually "gutted." Remove the Bible from the process of taking oaths on the stand, or take the chaplain from our Congress, and we will observe a downward spiral at an exponential speed, as we saw in the schools. Our country is great because it is a Godly country. A book written by the late Marlin Maddoux, *Public Education Against America* is a must read. Mr. Maddoux did the extensive research and presented the facts, and I believe **every** parent should read it. My bet is that the Maddoux book will never see the shelves of a public school, and, sadly, very few public libraries. Parents, this is a MUST READ—but it is not for young kids; don't make them a part of our fight. They are still in training.

"But Dr. Haire, what about the separation of church and state?" May I remind all that our founders were predominantly devout Christians—twenty-nine were pastors. In the Virginia Bill of Rights, Article 16, from June 12, 1776, the authors wrote " That religion, or the duty which we owe to our Creator, and the manner of discharging it, can be directed only by reason and conviction, not by force or violence; and therefore all men are equally entitled to the free exercise of religion, according to the dictates of conscience; and that it is the mutual duty of all to practice Christian forbearance, love, and charity towards each other." The second President of the United States, John Adams, affirmed, "The general principles on which the fathers achieved independence were…the general principles of Christianity." It was very clear that their intent was that the government not be permitted to interfere with our freedom of religion in any way.

I picture our founders and writers of the Constitution turning over in their graves at the stupidity of the Supreme Court in forbidding prayer in schools. They intended to openly worship God in **every public** place. The first textbook in many of our American public schools was the Bible. Did you know that Harvard was named for a Puritan minister? Are other religions welcome? Of course they are—that is one difference between a free country and one that is not. Try publicly worshipping Jesus in Iraq or Iran, and my guess is that you will be "late for dinner."

Just a quick word regarding evolution vs. creation. The truth is they both take faith. I am not going to try to convince anyone of my faith in creation. And I am not going to accuse my friends who are evolutionists of being atheists. They may be, and if they are, for their sakes, I hope they are right. If they are wrong… The honest truth is that nobody knows for sure how we got here. Aristotle was a very reluctant atheist, and was troubled to his last day with the issue that he referred to as "the first mover." In his mind, he could never come to an intelligent answer to the question, "Who pushed the first stone down the hill that started the process?" I tell our students that God created the heavens and the earth, and He didn't tell us how He did it. Let's turn the page—we have diseases for which to find a cures. There is plenty in science to discover that we need not spend time trying to answer a question we are never going to really resolve. Meanwhile, other countries are "cleaning our clocks" academically, so "CAN WE PLEASE MOVE ON?"

I mentioned it earlier, but let me reiterate, if I were an African-American or Hispanic parent, I would insist that my Congressmen vote for "school choice" YESTERDAY! Why? Because our public schools are failing; and if statistics are correct, the **average** minority family in America is not going to be able to afford a **good** private school. I am saying that "school choice" will make **all** schools better; competition just does that—period. I think "Choice" will actually improve all schools; we just have to vote the politicos out of Washington.

And it is going to take some time before all of our public schools are going to be able to compete. I would guess somewhere in the range of three to five years; it all depends on the leadership. If you have a strong superintendent, it may happen sooner rather than later, but **you** don't have years. Your superintendent has to get the bad teachers out and replace them with good ones, which will not happen overnight. After our public schools are forced to compete with the good private schools (and "good" is the operative word here), the issue of "choice" will go away. "Choice" will need to stay, legally, but after a few years of having to compete with private schools, the difference in public and private schools will primarily be religion, and that is a good thing in a free country. If you are an atheist, you should be able to send your child to a non-religious school with quality not being a factor of money. Good luck on the "Rapture," but hey, to sum up one of Lawrence Peter (Yogi) Berra's famous quotes, "You came to a fork in the road, and took it."

The private schools in America have had to deal with **choice** since their inception. Our school competes with other private schools in an approximate twenty-five mile geographic range. But today, geography is becoming a less important issue for the educated-minded parent. It is very common for a family to make an appointment to interview with our school, and be accompanied by their realtor. They are first going to find the best private school, then purchase a home near the school. The breadwinner of the family will drive a surprisingly long distance to work in order to provide the best school for his children. Presently one of our fathers is commuting to New York, another to Orlando.

Good schools have several elements in common. For instance, the counseling department has to be staffed with emotionally mature counselors. In lower school, much of the counselor's time is spent assisting parents in making good decisions and in the difficult times of raising their children. There are the stages of development that are easy enough to research for any parent, but we all know that it is just not that simple.

In the middle school, counselors are key players during these transitional years. The counselor's role is to help students build a relationship with other students and deal with issues with their parents. Counselors in upper school play a critical role in helping our students position themselves for admission into the **universities of their choice**, and work hard to obtain the maximum number of scholarships and grants for our grads. These professionals must earn the respect and admiration from our students, their parents, and their peers. Our parents expect their child who qualifies for admission, to be accepted and prepared for the university of their choice. At Liberty, that means that our graduates are prepared spiritually, academically, and socially.

For the year 2007/2008, in a graduating class of ninety students, our counselor over seniors helped obtain over $3,500,000 in scholarships and grants. During the summer of 2008, we sent our staff of counselors to a seminar hosted by Harvard University in order to broaden their vision and build a networking outreach to better serve our families.

We offer athletic programs too numerous to list, a performance-driven fine arts program, and a staff in which over one-third hold advanced degrees. We send our teachers to advanced training seminars. For instance, in the summer of 2008, Dr. Sarah Lippe, our English department chairperson, took her team to Oxford University in England for a week-long seminar. Elements like these are common to good schools.

There are over one hundred private schools in the Dallas Fort Worth metroplex, and I know the ones with whom we have to compete. The other schools are not competitive, and will soon go out of business. My point is that, because our children's education is at stake, a standard of excellence should apply to our public schools as well. If school choice becomes law, the process of survival of the fittest will immediately become operable and our children will win. Competition will force all boards to hire the "best" superintendent, schools will be looking for the best teachers, and success will follow quickly. I'm not suggesting for one minute that any school administrator would not look for the best candidate to fill any position. But I am saying that when competition enters the ring, the elevation of expectations and performance is greatly enhanced.

A solid objection was recently expressed on the radio by a conservative talk show host. He was against "choice" because taxpayers who do not have children in school are currently paying taxes to the public schools—how would we determine how those tax dollars would be distributed? I suggest those dollars be distributed to the schools that have the highest percentage of high school graduates, but there may be a better idea. But because we have a challenge, let's not "throw the baby out with the bath water."

And what will happen to our ineffective school principals, teachers, and coaches? They will **not** be able to get a school job, and that is as it should be. There would be no demand for poorly performing administrators and staff in America's schools. Why should we settle for less? As long as parents keep sending politicians who accept funds from teacher unions to our state and national congresses, the message to our elected officials is clear: if you want our union block vote, you must vote

"No School Choice," and, friends, our kids are sold down the political river.

I am unable to even read all of the job applications that I receive every year, much less interview all of the candidates. The litmus test, after proper credentials are in order, for hiring a teacher at Liberty is simple: "Would we want this applicant teaching our own child?" That is a very high bar an applicant has to "clear." But why should any school settle for less? Requiring a master's degree to teach almost any grade or subject in lower, middle or high school is an academic overkill. BUT, to hire teachers with tenacity, organizational skills, communication skills, and self-discipline makes sense. Those are a few of the personal attributes that were required to obtain that advanced degree and, accordingly, made the teachers more valuable.

Chapter 28

The Right Guy Runs the School—Wrong Guy Doesn't Get an Offer

We have too many administrators running schools and teachers teaching classes who are incompetent at their jobs. Can someone explain why? I'll try.

Just a few words about the most important responsibility you have as a board member: HIRE THE RIGHT GUY!!! I know, I know, "Haire, you have already talked about this." Well, it's a big deal. I want to warn you board guys not to be too impressed with educational interviewees who seem to have all the answers. Degrees don't necessarily make an effective leader. Educators are notorious for writing papers and books that have a reading level of post-doctorate, ones in which the reader thinks he knows what he just read, but isn't sure. The conclusion follows, "This guy must be really bright, especially if he holds multiple degrees." Go a little slower on the "Wow, this guy must be really bright!!" part. There is a huge difference between a man who is "educated" and one who is "bright."

I suggest he interview for the top job, and all board members agree to a simple interview process that I must credit to an alumni dad of Liberty, Jim Charles. After the interviewee is comfortable with the board and both have had time to ask questions, the board chairperson presents an important challenge to the candidate. The conversation might go something like, "Mr. Administrator Applicant, there is a piece of art hanging on the wall right behind you; it is a print. Please take a few minutes to gather your thoughts and **sell** that print to us. I realize that this is an unusual request, but we must know our administrator can express his ideas and goals clearly." Your applicant may respond, "You have to be kidding. I hold a Master's Degree in Education!" Board chairperson responds, "We all greatly admire and appreciate your academic achievements. But we have to know that you can communicate your ideas and goals. Please take three minutes to think about your presentation, then tell us why we should buy that print. Your three minutes of preparation begin now." If he freezes, he will not be able to sell his plans and dreams to a staff of principals and teachers, and I would genuinely thank him for his time. IF you find he can communicate and think on his feet, continue the interview. Look for confidence, joy, creativity, and a sense of humor—all are needed to be an effective leader. A "presence" is important, and a reminder to board members: this is your most important responsibility, and your only hire. "Haire, that is the most unprofessional litmus test I have ever heard of; I'm embarrassed to even suggest that." If you disagree, then fine, I'm just saying…

Running a school is all about motivating others to do what you know needs to be done. Degrees are necessary for your school to meet accreditation standards. But that being said, university education departments no more prepare a student to be an educator than an MBA degree prepares a student to be a successful entrepreneur. I don't deny that both programs are valuable and have merit; my point is that it is just not that simple. And please don't insult anyone's intelligence by adding gender or color of skin to the criteria. Please, give me a break!! People of any gender or race can do the job if they have "the right stuff."

I've had two careers in my life; the first one in business, the other obviously in education. My textile companies were successful. They took eighteen years to build. I sold them in 1984 in order to direct all of my energy to building the best Christian school I could. My wife, Judy, and I did not come from wealthy families, and maybe for that reason, never lived too extravagantly. When we started Liberty Christian School, we knew there was never going to be a financial reward that would ever compare to my income in business, and we understood and accepted that. We got into business to make money, but got into the school business because we wanted to help kids become all that they could be. We knew in our hearts that there would be rewards greater than money—and we were right.

Establishing the school would be a much harder challenge than running my textile company ever was, and as I mentioned earlier, that was a huge surprise to me. I thought running a school, compared to running three multi-million dollar companies, would be a snap, especially a relatively small school. WRONG! I thought that giving up the headaches of running a very competitive textile business was going to be a relatively even swap: money and a hard day at the office in exchange for little money, and a fun, spiritually edifying day. Well, not exactly. Both professions have rewards. I know that the rewards I have now are eternal, but the job is a great deal more challenging. When you are dealing with other people's kids, it gets very personal, and can get extremely intense. If high standards are to be held, it is much tougher than running a profitable company. I'm sure Jesus had something clearly in His mind when He said, "My burden is light," but I'm almost certain He was not referring to the school business.

Another surprise for me should not have been a surprise. I knew that a degree in business did not necessarily make a good businessman, but was surprised to learn that a degree in education did not necessarily make a good teacher or administrator. I have interviewed hundreds of people with education degrees, and many with advanced degrees, that I would not hire for any position in our school. This business of administration and teaching is a tough assignment, and it takes the same courage and tenacity to be a good teacher as it does to be a good entrepreneur.

You have to have the credentials in education to get hired. It is part of the accreditation requirement. In my opinion, it is close to the bottom of the chart in predicting success. Further, I've learned that a candidate with a bachelor's degree who is a great communicator and approachable, is a better teacher than one with a master's or doctorate degree who is condescending or "arrogant."

The truth is, we are all salesmen. Some sell houses, others math. And in my opinion, it takes a better salesman to sell math to most students than it takes to sell a house to most buyers. The house buyer is typically a "warm market." They probably want to be there, are probably even excited. I guarantee there are not many excited math "customers" in our student body. The teacher has to create enthusiasm, inspire a good work ethic, enforce discipline, etc. Just having an advanced degree won't even come close to fulfilling what it will take. That athlete is thinking about the game Friday night and the girl is hoping for a smile from the handsome young man who has a locker next to hers. This is serious competition for any teacher.

If I were the president of a university, I would add a course in the Department of Education entitled something like "Preparation for Battle

101." I'd warn the new recruits about the tough days ahead. I would hire professors to teach the course who had "been there," and would instruct them to not be shy about telling the education majors that their biggest challenges will have nothing to do with their major subject area. These very valuable college professors might be expensive, because they would be in high demand by the best universities.

The professors of "101" would tell their students that subject knowledge and lesson plans are absolutely required, but will do you no good if you don't prepare a great strategy to deliver them. Most classroom management and administration courses at the college level are weak. There is too much theory, and rarely do you obtain information on how to deal with controlling school boards, fearful and insecure teachers, and "child-centered" homes.

I don't totally agree with Darwin's theory of evolution, not only because it opposes God's Word, but also because I could never figure out why, if we evolved from monkeys, do we still have monkeys? But I do agree with his "survival of the fittest" model as applied to school administrators and teachers. Many who are weak leave the profession for "family" reasons. But most hang on, are demoted or fired, or if they happen to be "twisted," may end up imprisoned. There are perverts among us because we live in what Christians call a "fallen world," but there is something that wounds our heart when such a person is found to be in the calling and profession of the clergy or education. On a personal note, God did call me, and while I have had many very hard and lonely days, He prepared me for the educational battles through my business experiences, and I would never even think of doing my life a different way.

But my fantasy course, "Preparation for Battle 101," will be very difficult to get into the education department of any university because most education department chairs think they know it all. That makes me crazy. Remember, our school is very highly ranked among private schools in Texas. Many years we have sent 100% of our students to colleges and universities. Many of our graduates are accepted into the university of their first choice. We enjoy a great reputation with a number of universities. I offered to teach the "Preparation for Battle 101" course **pro bono** at one of our local universities, and got this response: "Sorry, we just don't have room for that type of course in our schedule." I believe it should be **mandatory** for all educational majors, and only taught by administrators with school experience, preferably a lot of it!

There is a very strong belief in most universities that they have all the answers, and that is particularly true in the departments of education. In the meantime, the USA enjoys an embarrassingly low place on our world's educational chart—go figure. The schools of education are also loaded with professors with too much pride, considering the pitiful job they are doing in preparing our young people for the great profession of teaching. Recently I visited the College of Education at a university, and everyone referred to everyone else as Dr. Jones, Dr. Smith, Dr. Bighead, etc. I really thought I was on a show like Candid Camera; I couldn't believe those professors were that insecure.

The field of education has this insulation thing going on. They insist you call them "Professor" or "Doctor," and nobody is talking about the lousy job they are doing in preparing our teachers to be successful. The university education departments need to have an interview process in place in which the candidate is allowed to enter if the admissions committee believes he would make a good teacher. We all know teachers and administrators who should not have been offered a job in a school. Take a step back and make sure the university candidate for the school of education is approved for entrance.

Let's hear it for knowledge and mastery of subject and material, good lesson plans, and solid educational principles. But let's also hear it for integrity, character, emotional maturity, and communication skills required to deal with unmotivated students, demanding parents, a weak administrator, unsupportive board members, gossipy peers, etc. And let's not forget to teach the raw politics that are woven into the fabric of our public and private schools when preparing this course curriculum of "101" that shamefully will never be taught, or at best, is light years away. On second thought, it might be taught sooner rather than later if our elected officials find the courage to vote "Choice."

Chapter 29

All On Board—Hear This!

Board members have to get the right administrator in place. He has to be a fit for the culture of your school and has to have great hiring skills—guidelines for board members to live by in this chapter.

Every year during our Teacher Orientation, I tell our teachers, "Concerning everything you say in your classroom, you can assume there is a loudspeaker on the dining room table of the home of each of your students, and little "Heather" is repeating a **part** of what you said in class that day." She is going to leave out the context, and will only tell the parts of it that make her look like she is trying to survive the hardest course ever, or the embellishments needed to make you sound like a teacher from hell. Most parents will buy the story "hook, line, and sinker," and it will be discussed further out of context in the football stadium or gym on Friday night. What can the administration or board do to stop such a destructive pattern of gossip? Nothing, absolutely nothing. But you can expect it to happen, and when it does, don't "let it in." However, I would boldly let the messenger who brings it to you know how destructive even having that kind of conversation is to the school. Pros seem to always be talking about ideas and plans, while the mentally and emotionally stunted talk about people and non-events. There are some serious issues with which we must deal, so I let the chatter slide. If the staff member who seems to always be talking negatively has proven he is a gossip, I'd fire him.

Schools have to be full of franchise players at the administrator, teacher, and coach level. These positions have to be hires that are players who are emotionally mature. Here's an example: I interviewed a family for admission several years ago. Present in the interview were the mother and her fifteen-year-old son. The mom started telling me about how abused her son had been by her former husband as he was growing up. She related the story of her husband walking down the hall one day, passing her son, who was just learning to walk. The toddler stumbled and fell in front of his dad, who grabbed his son by the hair, threw him against the wall, and kept on walking. At the end of her story, the son turned to his mom and spit on her. This conversation happened during my first encounter with this broken family. The parents had been divorced for several years, but the emotional wounds had not yet healed. I invited the mother to be excused to go into the restroom to clean her face, and I began to talk to the son. He started crying, but even in the apparent moment of frustration, I told him that his disrespectful action demanded a heart-to-heart plea for forgiveness, and he assured me that he would make that plea to his mother. When she returned, he did indeed ask for her forgiveness.

After they left, I called a counselor friend and confided in him what had just happened in my office, using no names of course. He explained that there is 50% of each parent in the soul of every child, and it never goes away. The mother had probably told the truth. But after a length of time, her son was unable to stand further condemnation of 50% of his very being. The mother had just gone too far. Some conversations need never take place in the presence of a child.

The point of this story is that school leaders must deal with situations every day that test the emotional maturity of the administrator, teacher, or coach. The administrator must consider the tremendous sensitivity of issues for which he and his staff may not be trained. But **if** the school staff member has the savvy, he can defuse a volatile situation with minimum damage.

In 1987, I met and hired a really great social studies teacher for our high school. One day, he was teaching his students the value of serving others, and the importance of being honest and humble as that truth relates to the leaders of our nation, past and present. His lesson included the evil that too much power can bring to our leaders, and that power draws too many of them away from being the servant leader we elected. To drive home his point, he washed his students' feet— in class! He went on to become a wonderful principal, and what I appreciate most is that he will get in my face if he thinks he is right and I am not. One of his students, who upon graduation from Liberty accepted an appointment to West Point, said about him, "He is the greatest man I have ever met." Dr. Noto, you are the man!

In 1983, I hired a couple, the husband as a science teacher, athletic director, and head football coach; the wife as a math teacher. I like to hire couples if competence is not comprised, because teaching and coaching become a large part of your life, and sharing it with a spouse who has the context of firsthand knowledge is enormously beneficial. (I have had to field the "nepotism" ball more than once, but good judgment is always champion.) This man is one who changes boys into men through teaching integrity and a solid work ethic; I am truly honored to serve with him. His wife soon became a master teacher in math, directed our cheerleaders for a number of years, and is a beautiful role model for our young ladies. I have evaluated each of them over the years, and cannot say which one is the best teacher. The husband was seen standing on his desk in order to teach a science theory, while the wife is more reserved. Our school would not be what it is without Mark and Patrice Bowles.

In 1988, I hired an English teacher. I hesitate to say that she is the best in the world, but am comfortable saying she is the best in the country. She has taught twelfth grade English at Liberty since 1990, and has brought a level of academic excellence to her classroom that has raised the bar for our entire faculty. Prior to our students' senior year, they are very fearful of her English class, but just weeks into it are in love with the challenge she brings to the table. Along with her students and their parents, I have grown to admire Dr. Lippe tremendously.

I believe it is a tragedy for parents to allow their child to take a course in summer school to avoid a challenging teacher. It sends the message to their child that they (the parents) don't think their child can do well with an academic challenge—so sad. Liberty does not offer a course in summer school to a student unless the student fails that course. The reason is that if a student makes a 55 in a subject and fails the course, at least he obtained 55% of the knowledge of the course. Summer school can supplement what is really a review for him in order to receive what he needs to learn from the course. We have to remember that a course is about gaining the knowledge, as well as receiving credit.

In the early 1980s, I hired two of the most talented, gifted educators you can imagine. I knew they would be good, but had no idea! One taught fourth grade and the other taught kindergarten. They were truly role models for the other teachers, and anchored our lower school with a level of maturity and leadership that was astounding. I knew it would be difficult to replace their level of excellence in the classroom. I will tell you that promoting them to principal and vice principal respectively was a very tough decision. However, they went on to display an even greater level of leadership as administrators. I'm honored to serve with Mrs. Watts and Dr. Nicklas.

Here are five hiring truisms that my years in the field of education have taught me:

1. I would never hire a male teacher to teach below fourth grade. You have to sell that decision, and it will never pass the "makes-sense test." I don't have to hear that this is not fair or politically correct. You are right on both counts. But that does not change the fact that it has the "strange" factor, and that is a reflection on the person who made the hire.

2. Being a parent is the PhD in education. There is nothing in the college experience at the undergraduate or graduate level that will compare to what rearing a child teaches you about educating kids. All things being equal, hire the applicant who has reared a child.

3. Teachers below fourth grade have to have the "mommy thing" going at their core. Teachers at and above fourth grade have to have the "authority thing" going for them. It's an understood part of their presence. Somehow you leave your first meeting respecting the patience of those who teach below fourth grade, and holding a high degree of respect for those teachers of fourth grade and above.

4. Never hire to balance a racial, religious or gender quota. If you have hired for any other reason than **quality**, you have cheated those students that you have been given the authority to educate. This

may be in conflict with board policy, so board members, rewrite or eliminate the stupid policy. By the way, the less you put in a board policy manual, the less you will have to defend in court. If you have a "bean counter" on your board, he may insist everything be in writing, but somebody remind him he only has one vote. The thinner the manual the safer.

5. Remember, you are always hiring a salesperson. Your best teacher candidate could have easily majored in marketing or advertising. He is selling his course to a normally cold audience. After puberty, the girls are primarily hoping that a boy will call them, and the boys are dreading rejection. (That emotional roller coaster actually happens before puberty in many cases.) Either way, memorizing the Preamble to our Constitution is not on their radar. Your hire has to have the creativity and the charisma to establish classroom interaction. If you have hired a teacher who is a little strange, you blew it. (You have to know "strange" when you see it in any business.)

6. Be very cautious regarding hiring friends or relatives—you may have to fire them. Never hire someone you can't fire. That is a tough position when you hire couples, so raise the bar in the interview process to include that aspect. As I said earlier, I like to hire family members, but only if the spouse is the best candidate. (Recently a board member brought up the issue of my hiring relatives, and said it looked like nepotism. I warned you of this possibility earlier. I gave him a list of the staff who were related, and asked him who on the list he would fire. He said, "None, these are all good hires." Make sure your critics have no case.

Hiring teachers is the most important aspect of the administrator's job (I trust at this stage of *CALLED*, the board hires only the administrator. If you, the administrator, have delegated further hiring to a committee, I strongly suggest that you observe whether the committee is competent **in hiring**. Many good teachers and department heads are far too accepting of an applicant's subtle weaknesses. If they don't have strong hiring skills, for whatever reason, you **must** override their decision. You will appear to be micromanaging, but you are the captain of the ship, and if it goes down, it's because you have allowed the wrong people to steer. I would **gently** disassemble the committee and start over. It will not take you long to find out if your committee (of no more than three) can hire successfully. Until you know, insist that you give final approval on all hires. If your committee is emotionally mature, I would invest some of your time and train them on hiring the right candidates.

Hiring is an art in any business, and that is especially true in the business of education because we are hiring the trainers of our country's brain trust. I had a principal one time that had no idea what to look for in a good teacher. He would send me candidates whom I would never hire for any position. On the other hand, I now have leadership in place that never sends me a poor candidate. Our principal of our upper school may be the most gifted administrator in hiring that I have ever met—Ed Cook's choices are pure genius. Our vice principal, Mark Bowles, has the hiring skills to see into an applicant's intent—so very rare. These gifts within the administrative structure are invaluable, and crucial in the success of our school. That is why the idea of turning hiring selections over to a school or deacon board is, how can I say this gently, INSANE!

Chapter 30

Are You Sure the Call Was For You?

There may not be a more important job description than that of an administrator. Let me show you a great one I doubt you have ever seen before.

If you are "called" to serve as the school administrator, that can either be a great thing or the worst experience of your life. Your job description SHOULD read something like I am about to describe. If it doesn't, renegotiate or get out while the getting is good, and remember that it is never too late to "bolt." Many school boards may need to rewrite the job description for **their only hire**, but at the end of the day, it needs to be signed by all members of the board, as well as the new administrator. If you have **not** committed it to writing, you will lose the war as soon as the first shot is fired across the "political" bow. Here's the nearly ideal job description and personal description of a school administrator:

1. Possesses an exceptionally high degree of character and integrity, and will not ever be expected to compromise those standards.
2. Encourages, supports, and inspires the continuing training of his staff. He is always supportive of his teachers, and is always willing to help them in any way possible.
3. Is a natural leader, a great communicator, and understands he must earn the respect of the staff.
4. Loves to see children succeed. He sets healthy boundaries for his staff and students, and is very predictably consistent. He is lavish

with praise. At Liberty we have "Praise Reports." The student is "written up" by one of his teachers for doing a good job or an exceptionally good deed. He is called to the office and our administrator calls his parent on the speaker phone and joins the child and his parents for a time of celebration. Many fathers cry.

5. Is not afraid of anyone, especially members of the board, teachers, parents, students or the media; not only because he is a courageous person, but also because he knows the board will always support him.

6. Hires the best staff he can find, regardless of race, sex, color, or religion. If you are the administrator of a Christian, Jewish, Catholic, etc. school, you may have some special qualifications to navigate, but make no mistake, your success will depend on the quality of your hires. It is your most important task by a long shot, so work on getting **all** reasonable restrictions removed. (I have a good friend and relative, Mrs. Sherilyn Jones of Houston, who is a Gentile and has successfully taught history and English at a Jewish school for years. But I would not hire an atheist to teach in a Christian school.)

7. Has the authority to hire and fire all staff, and no staff member has a contract of employment—not even the administrator (for now, that may not be a practical idea for you—but it should be a goal, and implemented as attrition and board courage allow). No teacher should be tenured. Teachers and administrators should be invited back each year based on their evaluation and performance. For proven pros, this will be a formality, almost a time of light celebration for a job predictably well done. If the

administrator so chooses, he may delegate any of these decisions to staff committees, but reserves the authority to make the final decision. By the way, asking high school students to give a teacher an evaluation is a terrible idea.

8. Can expect board support as long as his decisions are consistent, fair to all, and made in the spirit of improving the school. The board understands that the administrator will make mistakes, but as long as the good faith effort is present and he does his best, he will never have to second guess the support of the board.
9. Possesses the academic credentials required for the school's accreditation.
10. If the administrator is in a private school, it is understood that he is the primary and most effective major gift fund-raiser. He can expect every board member to assist him in raising money by personally giving or assisting in obtaining major gifts. Each board member realizes the gravity of his fundraising responsibility, and will help in any way possible.

In my opinion, this is close to the perfect and ideal job description that would fulfill the common sense management principle of balancing responsibility with authority. The school administrator would know what is expected, and have full authority to accomplish the goals for which he has been hired.

The honeymoon period will last until a parent of influence, teacher, or coach has a problem with the new administrator. A staff member (that you probably inherited or should not have hired in the first place) will approach a board member friend, and supposedly on behalf of "many" say, "He just isn't what we expected," or "We (the 'we' referred to here is the other two teachers who should never have been hired either) have never done it this way before." If the complaint comes from a parent, he will always open with something like, "You know, I don't know why everyone calls **me** with these things, but trust me, there are many who believe like I do… " (the "many" he is referring to is the other parent whose child didn't pass the test either). And of course there is always the three-page letter to the board that is anonymous—I suggest those go in "File 13."

It will be about the third or fourth board meeting when the fine print of the administrator's agreement that was dressed up in several pages of philosophical, legal, and wordy jargon is pulled out of the manual. It will be loaded with many different ways to change the spirit of the original agreement, will trap the administrator, and sadly, will lead to what is today in the USA, a very brief tenure of a school administrator. A story in the Dallas Morning News by Joshua Benton probably reported it best. He honestly discusses the frustrations of a teacher who has worked for five administrators in six years. Benton writes, "The folks who study how kids learn say that stability is key to a good learning environment."

If the board hired the wrong administrator, then they have to own that poor decision and fire him. But I would get a very strong confirmation that there was actually a deal-breaking mistake made by the administrator before taking sides. Get this supportive data from your best teachers and most respectable and emotionally mature parents before even considering making a change. And if you made a good hire, I would show your unwavering support for your administrator.

I am sure all board members know that a public forum to resolve a problem is a terrible idea. Only with permission from your administrator should you hold a meeting with an executive committee of board members and the disgruntled person or couple alone. If parents want to come in a group, tell them no. I realize that many public and private schools have an "open to the public" meeting policy—change the policy. Parents who want to express their opinion can do so privately with the executive committee if they have already met with the persons directly involved. Never meet with more than one family at a time. That goes for administrators, teachers, and coaches. And NEVER have a meeting regarding the competence of any person in authority in the presence of a student.

Essentially, we are talking about situations that cause disgruntled parents to surface, creating frustration for the administrator. They are the parents of a child who did not make the team, didn't make the cheerleading squad, didn't get enough playing time, was accused of cheating, has accumulated excessive absences, or just did a dumb "kid" thing. It amazes me how a well-meaning parent will **not** take the failure of their child, who made an error in judgment, and use that failure as an opportunity to teach a life lesson that is invaluable. The student can learn at any age the lesson of accountability and disappointment. That learning experience will create enormous value for children that will benefit them for the rest of their lives.

Recently, a father of a girl who did not make a varsity team told me that all he really cared about was that his daughter was happy. He blamed the coach, the assistant coach, and the athletic director. The truth is, nobody was to blame. His daughter was simply not a good enough athlete to make the team, and the father was in denial. By the way, over the years I have been offered large sums of money to fire a coach who was doing a good job. I have never taken a bribe; I'm not perfect, but am just not for sale. If you have taken a gift from a parent to make a decision, I would confess it to your board as soon as you can call a meeting. You have to get that off your mind, and truth will indeed set you free. If you ever take a bribe and let it remain unconfessed, it will happen again and again, and the price of your integrity will just continue to fall.

Another complaining parent had a daughter who was a good basketball player who did not make the required grade to be athletically eligible to play for a two-week period. The problem was that there was an overnight trip to play in a tournament during that period of time, and he didn't want her to miss the trip. I tried to "sell" the value of teaching her to take responsibility for her actions, but he was not interested—it was a concept he would not consider. I insisted she miss the trip, and I don't think the dad has spoken to me since.

I will never forget a very wealthy parent who sat in my office and told me that because his son did not get enough playing time in a football game, he was not going to give our capital campaign "a frigging dime." Sorry, just not for sale.

I was saddened for every one of these kids and their parents, because there is a much larger lesson to be learned by facing the truth, one that can benefit their child for life. Actually, a very low percentage of high school athletes play at the college level, and less than 1% will play in the pros. But a very high percentage will be mothers or fathers, wives or husbands, or someone's employee or employer. And every one of those crucial roles takes sacrifice and the tenacity to continue in the face of disappointment, adversity, and failure. Our children have to learn those lessons from life, and it is so much easier to teach them while we can help them up, not prop them up.

I've observed that in today's schools, both public and private, disappointed parents who are dysfunctional will do a lot of "mouthing." And unfortunately, a large percentage of the parent body has to listen to them. You know the type. They will not go away and nobody wants to see them coming. In the private school business it's less of an issue because we can "ask" a family to leave.

We had a wonderful young man who attended Liberty and happened to be a gifted athlete. However, his father was extremely critical of the coaching staff. I told the father that he had created a problem for us, and that our coaching staff and I, frankly, "hated to see him coming." Because of the dad's pride, he decided that it was best for his son to withdraw from Liberty. His son had some great friends and did not want to leave, but the pride of the dad was not able to stand the honest criticism. (If I could redo that conversation, I would have been more sensitive in my choice of words to the father, and protected the son. But I never dreamed he would make such a self-serving decision.)

As I am writing this chapter, we are in the interview process with a family who has a son who loves to play football. We already see the strong possibility that the father will be in the face of our coaches on a regular basis. It really looks like it will be a no-win situation. If we take the boy, our coaches will have to work overtime trying to please the dad. In the meantime, the boy will make good friends and we will grow to love him. We will probably not admit him; the signs of bad things to come are just too pervasive.

It is a very edifying experience to observe a parent who will allow his child to take an unfortunate fall, and not make excuses or try to change the rules. Let your child live through the crisis. It will make him a much happier and mentally stronger person. We know as adults that life is very hard and not fair. But we adults know it's not the unfairness that will determine our child's success in life. It's how we train him to deal with it. It takes a tenacious person, a tough adult, to make a job work or a marriage last. When are they going to learn how to not quit or how to finish a job they started if we keep catching them in our parent net? Answer? They won't.

Another group that can cause real headaches for administrators is unprofessional teachers. These are not the perverts you read about in the newspaper. The ones I am referring to virtually never make the news. These teachers will rank very low on an emotional maturity scale, and normally take their complaints to the break room or the proverbial "water cooler," and worse, into the classroom. When I was principal, every year I would tell our teachers that I would not tolerate some things, and it was only fair that they know what my "hot" buttons were before the year began. I also acknowledged that all of us have areas that we consider very important, and that I wanted to know what theirs were as well. Respect that is one-sided is nothing more than "bullying," and will never accomplish the desired goals. The most important issues for me may be different than yours, but here are a few that over the years have proven to be "deal breakers" for me:

1. Do not gossip—the Lord hates it and so do I.

2. Never tease another person—**especially** a student. If a teacher wants to tease, it must be at his own expense—a young person doesn't "get" sarcasm.
3. Return parent phone calls or e-mails in 24 hours or less—the problem grows with time. Winston Churchill said, "When you turn your back on a problem, it doubles in size."
4. Always assume there is a loudspeaker going from your classroom to the family dinner table. Never say something you would not want repeated to any parent.
5. Never be intimidated by a parent or a student—you are the authority, and have the grade book. But remember that there are two things a teacher or administrator must never be: a bully or a coward.
6. Always be respectful to parents and students, and never be afraid to ask for forgiveness if you have made a mistake—it's a great opportunity to model character.
7. Don't show films in class unless there is a related lesson that **strongly** applies to the subject. Always give a test on any film shown. I am suspicious of a teacher who shows more than two films per semester—too reflective of being a lazy teacher.
8. Never give study hall time during your class. You are getting paid to teach, not monitor a study hall. Of course I realize it can be beneficial to allow a little time at the end of class for students to start their homework so you can answer questions pertaining to the given homework assignment.
9. Give homework that is **purposeful**: to prepare for the next day's lecture and discussion in English and history; to practice

what you taught that day in science, foreign language, and math. All homework should be returned to the student promptly. If it is not important enough for you to grade in a timely way, you can't expect the assignment to hold value to the student.

10. Remember that a teacher is **always** a role model—in school and out. That is intrusive and maybe unfair, but it goes with the territory of being a teacher and a leader.
11. Dress properly at all times. Ignore the dress code that your union negotiated if it causes you to appear unprofessional.
12. You are a part of the school team. If one of your athletic teams is playing that night 200 miles away, have the common sense to lessen the homework due the next day. And never whine and play the "athletics is more important that academics" card. It is, at times, more important to most students and their parents, so move on.

The staff members I have had problems with were those that I instinctively knew I shouldn't have hired, or should have fired. The lesson for administrators is to follow your instincts. Blaise Pascal (1623-1662) said that "The heart has reasons which reason knows nothing of." If you have a "leading," or instinct, follow it. Scripture tells us there is wisdom in Godly counsel. If you have a trustworthy colleague, include that person in the interview and evaluation process if he can be helpful.

Chapter 31

Wait—Don't Pull the Trigger Just Yet!!

Your school is not a democracy, and that is a good thing; but make sure all know the rules of engagement. If you don't set forth the rules, others will set them for you, and that is a terrible thing.

I have to share a great story of a teacher that I hired from a school in California. In one of our weekly teacher meetings in October, "Mrs. Jones" spoke up and said that she disagreed with my decision to do a certain thing, and would like to have the staff discuss it. It was **not** one of those topics for which I invited input. It was a clear directive having to do with our teacher dress code. I politely thanked her for her opinion, and stated that we would move on to the next topic.

After the meeting, I privately asked her to meet me in my office. She was there in five minutes, and I said, "Listen, I hope we can work together until the end of this semester, but you should be making applications to other schools immediately." She was shocked, and responded, "Dr. Haire, what have I done wrong?" I explained my perception of her blatant and public disrespect for authority, and said that when I wanted opinions, I would ask for them. She was utterly amazed at my response to her "suggestion." She said that her previous administrator wouldn't have even considered her comment disrespectful. She apologized and asked if I would let her have another chance.

I totally forgave her, but thought to myself, "That school administrator in California is trying to run a democracy, and he doesn't know that form of government will not work in a school structure." Respect for authority is an essential part of good leadership. I have to respect my board's authority, and the principals have to respect mine, the teachers have to respect the principal's, you get the picture. Respect has to start from the top, or it will never happen in the classroom.

So if the board has hired the administrator, and he is weak, then things get very political, and the spirit of the school will deteriorate faster than you can say "petition." Everyone runs for the boat of survival, and starts playing the blame game. The media wants to attend the board meetings, the newspapers give front-page coverage, and the administrator is left feeling very alone. If his job is to please the right people, that will get really ugly really fast. If the board doesn't have the courage to stand with their administrator, he simply can't survive. He may try to adjust, request that a coach try to give a little more playing time for a player, maybe arrange for special tutoring for the angry parent's kid, but all of that is a "band-aid" to the real problem. Parents with character are the strength of the school. They tend to raise kids with character, and we have all witnessed sad exceptions. The really great teachers, those any school wants to keep, and those wonderful parents, can easily see the compromises and the school loses some of its greatness. In reality, there slowly evolves a new job description, and the school administrator will be expected to adhere to the following **unwritten** standards:

1. Will adhere to board decisions without question, and will patronize all board members when called upon.
2. Will always take the initiative to participate in community organizations, even if the organizations are ineffective and accomplish nothing.

3. Will always make every effort to cooperate with the teachers and their union officials, even at the expense of the students.
4. Will make every effort to placate all parents, ensure that their child advances to the next grade and that, in the process, the child will feel good about himself. Self-esteem of the student shall always take precedent over actual accomplishments.
5. Will be willing and prepared to take full responsibility for all school failures to meet the expectations of the board, community and state.
6. Will keep employed on staff any person that the board wants to keep, regardless of competence and evaluations.
7. If the school is private, the administrator will be the only fund-raiser, because all board participation is voluntary. If the school is public, the superintendent will participate in any and all efforts made by the PTA, booster club, band club, or any other organization trying to raise funds. This effort may be personally demeaning and very time-consuming, but the objective is to offer full cooperation, regardless of the benefits to the school. (I have to say that I think it is "not cool" for an administrator to sit on a rooftop, have pies thrown at him, or sit on top of a pole to get kids to read books, attend school, or the myriad of things that good students are **supposed** to do—but that's me.)

After the "honeymoon" period of six months (maybe shorter), this second job description "kicks into high gear," at least in most school districts—thus the reason for the average brief stay of administrators. The real answer is that when the board finds a good man, their support, their respect, and his personal dignity must be preserved at all costs. If this is not the way the board functions philosophically **and** practically, the administrator will become a discouraged and ineffective leader. And now, my friends, the trickle-down effect begins. His countenance will change, his confidence level will drop, his decision-making will take on that ever so slight hesitation that the "franchise players" will notice, and a common question in the minds of those who know him will be, "I wonder what is wrong with Dr. Smith?"

I'll never forget a board meeting years ago when a nightmare of an experience happened to me. One of my board members called me and suggested that my wife not attend the meeting that night. In the early years, Judy always attended our meetings. I have always served as chairman of the board because in my business training, the person who knew the most about the organization was the chairman and CEO. That model has served our school very well since 1983 with few exceptions (I'm about to share one of those "times").

I thought the request for Judy not to come was strange, but trusted him. I was a young administrator and very naive. Upon entering the meeting, one of the members who I knew **could** be a problem asked me, "Who is actually running this school?" He went on to say that he had no idea who was in charge of any area, and wanted things changed. It was then that I understood the reason for the call requesting that my wife not attend. In retrospect, it was a kind and sensitive phone call that saved my wife and me humiliation and embarrassment.

My response was unexpected by the whole room. I got in his face, and told this member that if I ran our school the way he ran his company, we would be out of business. I went on to say that I had recently been in his business establishment, wanted to give him my business, but couldn't get a straight answer from any of his employees. Further, that I was not about to run our school that way. That in fact, my staff members and I knew exactly who was running what, and that our school was performing extremely well.

The man who warned me not to bring my wife to the meeting knew about the surprise attack, but my retaliation was unexpected by all—even me. The guy wearing the black hat apparently failed to obtain the support of the rest of the board, and in fact, was left standing alone. He soon resigned. If a board member is a problem to your capable administrator, he is a problem to the board, and should be asked or forced to resign by a vote of the board. In our school, our by-laws state that a majority can remove any member, and no reason has to be given. (Thankfully, we have never had to call for that vote.)

When board support for a competent school administrator is solid, the board must protect him at all cost. If he has made a mistake, help him clean it up, but never make him believe you are not on his team. When a good administrator is in place, the school will see a positive and upward move of the morale of the entire staff. If you remain solid in your support, you will see an increase in momentum from the ground up. You will obtain larger gifts for the school, and they will be much more frequent. I'm telling you from experience, when the administrator is confident of his board's support, the whole school will take on a new and enriching dynamic—and parents, staff, and students will really not completely understand why. An easy way to evaluate the effectiveness of an administrator is to observe the turnover rate of the good teachers. A Master Teacher will not work for an ineffective administrator very long.

With that said, a supportive board will enjoy good meetings, stay focused on issues, and be able to help the administrator come up with good solutions. The length of the meetings will be two to three hours. **The meeting should be run by your administrator**. It is very common for a board to meet too often. It is necessary to have stated meeting dates, but schedule them so that serious issues that need board attention are the only topics on the agenda. We have about six meetings per year. The school calendar can dictate the times when meetings are vitally important. I don't think you need a meeting in May, June, July, August, November or December.

This may be a good time to remind parents, board members, administrators, and teachers that none of us can do all of what is expected of us all of the time. For instance, I do a lousy job of setting school board meeting dates far enough ahead so that all members can put the date on their calendars and avoid conflicts. By this time, they know that is a weakness of mine, and I think probably say, "Rodney has a hard time with that one." My assistant, the genius Carmen Goodson, has to contact all members to get the best date possible. There are some challenges that all of us can win easily; my advice to me—"Don't miss an 'easy putt'; get the dates out."

Chapter 32

Can We Talk??

There must be mature adults in charge of every aspect of your school. If not, bad things <u>will</u> happen.

When board support is in place and a problematic teacher or parent is called to the principal's office, a whole new and positive and proactive scenario is going to take place. The administrator will be on the offensive, protecting the school's mission and vision, and the staff will feel more confident and secure. It may not be a wonderful experience for the complaining parent or staff member, but it certainly will be a confidence building experience for the school as a whole. Remember, parents with a bad attitude normally want to meet in mass, and if granted, I promise that the meeting will head south—and get there very quickly.

Parents deserve to be heard, and problems have to be addressed, but if you allow parents to meet in mass (more than one family at a time) their "agenda" takes the place of the real issue. My experience is that if there is more than one family in the room, you will primarily be listening to opinions that do not pertain to the issue. But a family bringing a problem that needs to be corrected or an opportunity that holds great potential for improvement will much more likely be able to clearly express it in a closed meeting. You want to really **hear** what they say, and you can't do it in a state of confusion.

On the other hand, it is almost always the case that when a bright and rational parent actually hears himself express his concern, he hears the solution as he speaks it out loud. If the parent is dysfunctional, and that primarily means that he has a "child-centered" home, he is not going to settle for a realistic solution, so just get through the meeting, and move on to the next challenge. Homes where decisions are made either exclusively for the child, or made by the child, have increased along with the number of failed or troubled marriages. The child's wishes become the currency that attempts to buy each parent's love, and that creates a dysfunctional home. The real problem is that the child, in an attempt to continue to receive unhealthy parental focus, will be allowed to make demands, thereby keeping the world centered upon him.

Most of the school administrator's day is about solving problems. If you are a parent, and get a call from the administrator, it most likely involves a problem that you or your child caused. If you are a teacher, it probably was something you did that was a "What was I thinking?" If you are a board member, it could be a **request** to stop doing whatever you did or said that caused the school a problem. I wish I had more time in my day to make positive phone calls that express my appreciation to the hundreds of parents and board members who have helped make our school so successful. Unfortunately, the "urgent" takes precedent over the "important."

The story of the life of a student really begins with the story of the family. To say that our schools will not excel until our parents become standard-bearers for excellence and start demanding more from their children is a cliché. There has to be good communication and a solid relationship between teacher and parent before most children will even approach their potential. This is not to say that the parent and teacher have to like each other, although that is the most desirable relationship.

The goal is to train and educate the child, not build a parent-teacher friendship. If the teacher will not respond to the parent, then the administrator has to facilitate and force that communication. If the parent will not be reasonable and supportive of the teacher, then the administrator must step in, support the teacher, and deal with the parent directly or in tandem with the teacher. If the teacher refuses to communicate with a supportive parent, then the teacher should be properly warned, should apologize to the parent, and immediately learn some basic communication skills or be fired. I had to fire a really good lower school teacher a few years ago because she did not know how to apologize, and that weakness "poisoned the well" in her professional relationships.

The point being, most children will not learn without the parent and the teacher being supportive partners because they have to interact for the benefit of the child. The greater cause is the education of the child, and thus the future generations of our nation.

I have to tell you a humorous story of a fine teacher and wonderfully supportive parents. Early in my educational career, one of my kindergarten teachers sent a little girl to my office to be paddled. I'll call this child "Sally." She was in trouble for repeatedly not remembering to raise her hand before speaking. The teacher had discussed the problem with her parents (they expressed total support of whatever discipline the teacher recommended). The teacher had punished her with "walking time" during her recess (that is our equivalent to "time out"), but nothing was getting through to "Sally."

The next step of corrective behavior was that she had to be sent to my office. Now when a kindergartner is sent to the principal's office, he or she is normally in tears before leaving the classroom, but not so with "Sally." She walked into my office with what I'd describe as almost a swagger, more with confidence than a bad attitude. When "Sally" arrived, I asked her to explain why she was sent to my office. She told me it was because she kept forgetting to raise her hand for permission to talk, and that she just couldn't remember to do that. I explained that her teacher had sent her to my office to be paddled. She very eloquently told me she would really try to remember, completely understood the rule, but could make no promises that her future behavior would be different. These transparent responses make it very difficult for administrators to keep a straight face, and that certainly was true in the case of "Sally."

Before I began to give her three light swats, "Sally" stopped me, and told me she wanted to tell me something. She said, "Mr. Haire, did you know that I'm the littlest person in the whole school?" I told her that I hadn't really thought about that, and thanked her for telling me. Just as I resumed this very unpleasant task, "Sally" stopped me again, I said, "What now, Sally?" and she said, "Mr. Haire, did you know that I'm going to Disneyland this summer?" I replied, "No, I didn't, but what in the world does that have to do with your getting paddled?" She said, in the most serious way, "Well, Mr. Haire, I was thinking of inviting you to go with me." "Sally" did eventually get paddled. I think she may have cried a little; I can't remember for sure. But I'll tell you, my bet is that "Sally" is running someone's company today, or owns her own. She sure seemed to be in control in my office that day. "Sally" was the real winner that day because her teacher and parents were on the same page and had the same goal—that "Sally" win the race of education through good training. She was never sent to my office again. That leads me to another important facet in the structure of a successful school.

Sometime from the 1960s to the 1990s, our American culture of child rearing shifted to the left. This is not a book on sociological trends, but somewhere in that approximate time frame, parents started courting the favor of their kids. Today, I hear parents say, "Johnny, time to get ready for school, **ok**?" Did your parents ever **ask** you if you wanted to get ready for school? They might have asked you if you desired chocolate or vanilla, or if you wanted to wear the blue shirt or the white one, but most training took the grammatical form of a directive.

Parents must wake up and stop giving their children permission to become flakes. God doesn't say, "Now Rodney, don't steal, **ok**?" I remember the time when, if you were paddled at school, you got another when you arrived home. I haven't heard that in years. Again, I happen to consider that level of discipline too harsh—it's double jeopardy. But the pendulum went too far to the left for your child's own good, and the line dividing right from wrong has gotten very fuzzy.

Those were the days before students were allowed to form gangs, wear "colors," talk disrespectfully to teachers, treat each other with a violent attitude, and communicate with curse words. As adults, we have some very difficult decisions to make, and one of them is to decide if the changes we have made in childrearing and teaching are working for us. As mentioned earlier, a related phrase that has developed in recent years is "a child-centered home" and, unfortunately, we now have "student-centered schools."

The causes for both are two-fold, and I don't think they are really related. First, there is an element of fear on the part of the administrators that has to be faced boldly and eliminated. Your administrator must be empowered to enforce school rules, or you will be in court sooner rather than later. Secondly is the tragic breakdown of the home. With a fifty percent plus divorce rate, our term **family unit** is an oxymoron. If parents are, even subconsciously, competing for the love of their child through a permissive approach to training, the child and both parents lose. All of the adults in the life of a child are settling for too little from themselves; the school staff knows they are not going to be supported and thus, are unable to protect and train their students. If teachers ever totally accept a student-run school, terrible things are predictable.

One of the most horrendous examples happened in a school near Dallas. At a middle school, an occurrence that, if true, should call for some "heads to roll" happened in the boys' locker room. From the Sheriff's Department came a report that one or more eighth grade boys had sodomized and tortured some smaller seventh grade boys for an entire school year. I'm not sure if it was just one boy or several who were the victim of this unbelievable behavior, but that is not really the point.

According to a Dallas Morning News report on July 27, 2008, editorial columnist Rod Dreher wrote a story uncovering the series of year-long tragic events that allegedly had happened in the boys' locker room. In Mr. Dreher's very excellent and transparent article, he went on to write that a far less harmful event happened to him in school, and he admitted that he was not certain that the damage caused by that experience to him had yet or would ever heal. These stories are all too familiar to many of us, and strong leaders must stand up. If not, more stories like this will continue to surface. In my opinion, if the reports that I read are true, where were the adults who were supposed to be in charge? I can't imagine that those coaches could not have heard the screams, or been made aware of reports from the other students or from the victim or victims.

Not every applicant with a certified teaching degree should be hired as a teacher or coach, and in my opinion, this situation certainly calls for an investigation! A few years ago, I assigned a coach to monitor our boys' locker room because the boys thought towel popping was "just good fun." The coach may have had a paddle with him the first day of his duty, I'm not sure; all I know is that the reports magically stopped.

I think that before every school year begins, a thorough examination of **every** school's staff should be reviewed by the administration from top to bottom. Those who are not emotionally mature enough to lead a classroom, bright and creative enough to potentially be evaluated as an indispensable staff member, and caring enough to protect the students from harm must be fired. Staff evaluation, while ongoing, should begin formally every February. This year, I will have an administrative meeting with only one topic on the agenda, "Have any of us made a questionable hire?" If the administrator has a staff member who has great potential but needs proper training, then by all means, he should keep him and train him!

Chapter 33

You Been Daddy Wolfed??

Our kids have to be trained to survive—maybe we can learn some things from "daddy wolves."

It was in the spring of 1983, and one of our great parents, Mrs. Betty McCrae, came in to see me. She had a wonderful daughter whom she was raising by herself, and doing a phenomenal job. She asked me, "Rodney, did you ever hear of parents who *daddy wolfed* their kids?" I told her that I had never heard the phrase. She went on to tell me that parents have a responsibility to guide their kids in the same way that a daddy wolf guides his pups. A daddy wolf will teach his pups how to survive in the wild: to drink water that is moving, to walk up slowly on prey, to avoid detection by not walking on dead twigs, and to watch out for humans. You get the picture. We are failing miserably at "daddy wolfing" our kids. It seems to me we are either "catching their prey" for them, or letting them learn the rules of the jungle alone; neither of which is good parenting.

For instance, we have to do a better job of teaching them "timing." You would never ask your boss for a raise on Monday morning or Friday afternoon. Your child should be taught never to ask for a raise in their allowance toward the end of the month.

We have to teach our sons that they should always shake the hand of their date's father with a grip that tells him that if he has a flat tire, he is strong enough to fix it. The gold standard for this training was exemplified by one of our sophomores in 2009. He called the girl's father to ask if he could take his daughter on a date. The father said he would like to get to know him, and that he would like for the young man to join his family for dinner prior to the date. During the dinner, the dad asked the boy how long he had been driving. The young man told him almost two weeks. The wise dad said, "I'd like for you to take me for a ride." After proving to the father that he was a good driver, the dad asked, "When are you planning to have my daughter home?" The young man said, "My mom wants me home by 10:00 p.m., so I'll have her home by 9:30." The dad said, "Good, I'll look forward to seeing her then." The dad and the young man had a clear understanding, both had satisfied their responsibilities, and all lived "happily ever after."

We must teach our youngster that when he gets that part-time job, he should treat it like a full-time job. He has to hear that it's important to report a few minutes early, and stay a few minutes late. And when turning in a paper at school, because he signs his name in the top corner of the paper, it should reflect his best work, and his paper should never be "dog-eared" or wrinkled. Our kids are not programmed to survive, and that's our job as parents, teachers, coaches, and school administrators. We have to "daddy wolf" our young. They are not programmed for successful survival in this harsh world.

Can you remember when parents were not concerned about being the only ones who said no to a bad idea? Today, if one child can get a parent to give permission to do something, that "sign-off" becomes the standard of acceptance for all of the parents in their social circle. Parents are fearful that if they say no, that could mean their child will be excluded from some "club," or worse, that the parents will be labeled too conservative or Christian or Mormon—whatever. I can't tell you how badly our children are crying out for parents to "step up" and be parents.

I had an eleventh grade boy walk into my office one day. He had accumulated an excessive number of tardies and said, "Mr. Haire, would you please paddle me? I deserve it." He actually hadn't yet been called to my office; he just had a guilty conscience. He went on to say that his parents didn't care what time he got home at night; he was literally crying out to me for boundaries. In a child's subconscious, healthy boundaries are interpreted as protection, not walls of confinement. Not many kids will ever verbalize that, but at some level they know it's true. I just could not give him swats. I told him that I deeply cared for him, that I desperately wanted him to make good choices, and to visit me anytime he needed to talk. His parents never did really get it. They never connected good discipline with love. Several years later, one of his classmates told me that he died in a motorcycle accident. I often wonder if he died from not having learned the self-discipline that parents, doing their job, should have taught. We will never know.

I've recently noticed that more and more kids are wearing their "strict parents" like a badge of honor. "My parents are so strict, they won't even let me go to the mall to just hang out" has become a statement of pride. The message that their parents care enough to help them decide who their friends are and when they are old enough to go on a date becomes a not-so-subtle message that their parents love them, and sometimes have to say no.

Recently the father of a ninth grade girl told me of an event that he and his wife had just experienced. Their daughter had invited a friend over to spend the night. About 8:00 p.m., a group of four boys showed up without his wife or him expecting them. As it turned out, neither did his daughter. The parents knew the four boys and welcomed them into their home.

The kids went upstairs to watch television, and later the dad went up to check on them. He found that the girl guest was in a chair with one of the boys. The father said to the couple, "I suggest if you want to make out, you go over to the girl's house, and get in **one** chair in **her** parents' home. Now one of you move to the sofa!" He went on to say to the three boys who were behaving themselves, "Did you know that you had been invited to our home to give your friend a ride so he could make out with a girl who is a guest in our home? Do you think that is fair to our family?"

This scenario, while very admirable, is not totally unique, nor is it especially book worthy. But the part of the story that is interesting is that one by one, each boy and the girl came downstairs and sincerely apologized to the dad. The series of events was simple: he went back to his study, and one at a time, each boy and the visiting girl quietly knocked on the door asking, "May I speak with you a moment? Please forgive me for being dishonest—it will not happen again." The father forgave them, and as the boys left, the leader of the four said, "Sir, you rock!"

If we don't "daddy wolf" our kids, someone in authority in the life of your child will do it for them, and it will not be a pleasant experience. I had a wonderful sister, the late Mrs. Lynda Adleta, who lived in Dallas. She was all about her grandchildren, and loved being a part of their lives. One of her granddaughters expressed a strong interest in becoming an actress. Lynda, along with her daughter Shelly, took her to an open audition. It was run by a highly respected and well known organization, and the leader of the evening's audition was very direct and professional. There were several hundred girls from the age of 12 to 15 in the audience, all with a dream in their hearts for the "big screen," and desperately wanting to be one of the 50 who would be invited to Las Vegas to contend for the next "cut."

The first thing the leader said was, "All girls with a tattoo anywhere may leave now." Next he said, "All girls who have a piercing anywhere but in their earlobe may leave." And then the shocker. He said, "All moms who have had breast augmentation, or are wearing a tee shirt or blouse more than one size too small, you and your daughter may leave." His last point was made because he wanted the mothers to understand that for their daughters to achieve their dream, a strong, confident, and mature parent was a must, and his years of experience proved to him that to allow any of the above to stay was a waste of everyone's time and money. My sister was proud that her daughter and granddaughter were allowed to move on to the next level.

Most parents try so hard to be friends with their kids that they fail in their duty to train them. It sometimes takes direct confrontation, an honest dialogue, and for certain, accountability. Kids are having parties with no parents present. Parents leave liquor cabinets open, allowing kids to bring in whatever they want, and do not even question them for fear of embarrassing their child. From personal observation, kids of all ages want supervision. It may be subliminal, but they want it because they need it for their survival, but more importantly, to know they are loved.

I encourage parents of children of all ages to give parties for their children and their friends, and if they get right in the middle of it, all will have a better time—the only thing "cooler" than a fun parent, is a fun parent who has the courage to say no. By the way, if you host a party for kids eighth grade and under, make every effort to invite all who are in the class—don't leave out the kid who has no friends. If your school is too large, that may not be practical. Just consider how you would feel if your kid were left out.

I see an increasing rate of parents who are running their companies brilliantly, and letting their kids raise themselves. If they ran their companies with the dereliction of duty, denial of existing problems, and acceptance of poor behavior on the job, they would be broke.

Rearing kids is a tough business, but if done right, brings great rewards. Rearing them, and evaluating their friends, demands that you risk not being a popular parent. You can be demanding **and** loving; you can have high standards, and the reward is respect. Nobody respects wimps - not even your child.

I'm not suggesting that parents "die on every hill." Choose your battles carefully. Saying no or saying yes is not the issue. It's a matter of the importance of the issue **to you**. You can over-parent, and if you make that mistake, you will bring up a child with no self-confidence. Some therapists describe that child this way: "The child has no furniture in his house." It's like this: we have to train our kids to make good decisions, and they have to learn to do that as we allow them to make decisions that are **age appropriate**. They have to make decisions in order to learn that they have to live with their choices.

For instance, we have a policy at Liberty that allows a student to drop a class within a five-day period after signing up for it. After that, they are in it for the entire year. A few years ago, one parent came in at midterm and requested that her daughter be allowed to drop a course. The reason given was that she simply did not like the teacher, and would often come home crying because the teacher was just too demanding. By the way, it's a good idea to explain to your child that the term "conflict with my teacher" does not exist. One of your child's primary responsibilities is to make sure that a "teacher conflict" never exists.

After trying to persuade the parent to support the rule of their child not being able to drop a class, a **former** administrator very unwisely folded, and allowed the student to make the change. I must say that had I been consulted, the drop would never have occurred; but when those things happen, we all move on and make the best of it. It was not a hill I chose to die on.

Another student requested a move from a different class, also based on "a personality conflict with the teacher." This time the administrator talked to the parent, explained the benefit of staying the course and the value of the lesson of learning to live with our decisions, and this time we all won. The parent fully supported the administrator and the policy.

Now here is the "kicker"—both students have been at our school for several years. I know them both. The first child has no personality; she is not just shy, she has not said ten words to me in eight years. She has no self-confidence because she has never had to work through a problem—she has always "just dropped the class." The second student speaks to everyone—"lots of furniture" in her emotional house. The payoff for being a healthy parent is huge—JUST HUGE!

If you make a bad decision as a parent, no—make that **when** you make one, just move on to the next opportunity to do it right. And when you make a mistake, it will be a "blip on the screen" if your child has heard you often say, "I love you."

A second grader was sent to my office to be paddled, and it seemed to me that this boy was being sent too often. Typically he would be disciplined, I would give him time to regain his composure, give him a hug, and tell him, "I love you." It occurred to me that he might be doing things to be sent to my office to feel loved. To test my gut feelings, I started seeking him out in the halls, putting my arm on his shoulder, and saying, "Billy, how are you doing? I've noticed you have been doing really well in class—congratulations, I'm very proud of you!" His trips to the office stopped **completely**.

Aren't we all that way? Don't we respond much better to affirmation than criticism?

Chapter 34

"But What about My Baseball Cards??"

I have an idea, let's add a bull elephant to the herd and see if things don't improve.

When I was growing up in the 1950s and 1960s, the parent was **always** on the side of the school administration. Case in point: it was 1955, and I remember getting kicked off the school bus for fighting. I had a very good reason—"Johnny" had taken my baseball cards. These were not just any old cards; I had nearly all of the starters on every major league team! I had Mays, Mantle, Berra, Ford, Williams—even Stengel.

My walk home took about two hours longer than the ride would have taken. After I got home, my mother told my dad about my "little episode" on the bus. I will always remember what took place after we finished eating dinner. Dad's response was not to ask any questions of me. He didn't care about my baseball card collection as much as he cared about his son's behavior. I had been in a fight, and my responsibility was to get back on the bus—period. My sister and I were not allowed to have a personality conflict with an authority figure, and on this night, the bus driver was at the top of that list.

When we finished dinner, he simply told me to get ready. He said we were going to visit the bus driver at his home. Dad happened to be president of the school board in Addison, Texas (the Addison School is now the Magic Time Machine restaurant on Beltline Road), but his political clout was not an operative term in our home. His first goal was to raise a son, not be chairman of the board. He drove me to the bus driver's house, and I had been told in no uncertain terms that I owed him an apology for disobeying the rules of riding the bus. In the '50s, one knocked on the door, then stepped off of the porch to show respect for the man and his home.

Dad insisted that I go to the door alone. I sincerely apologized, and remember how relieved I was that "Mr. Jones" accepted my apology. It meant that I could continue to ride the bus, as opposed to walking or taking a **long** bike ride—EACH WAY! Until that evening, I never thought that riding the school bus was a privilege.

Sometimes I hear parents defending their child's really dumb behavior, and I quietly say to myself, "Thank you, Dad, for that bus driver lesson." But in the field of parenting, and in the atmosphere of today's family dynamics, nothing is quite as simple as it appears. But just because it isn't simple, and may be difficult, doesn't mean we parents have an excuse to not do our job. We just can't allow ourselves to have a "personality conflict" with our responsibilities.

In the former generation, there was a justified trust that existed in the adult population. As our culture has degenerated, and some of that in the name of "progressive education," there is a lingering doubt as to whether those in authority actually have the common sense needed to make the decisions that directly affect your child. That is a doubt that was rarely in question in the parenting world of the '50s and '60s. But things have changed. All progress is not good, and school administrative decisions are now made for reasons that sometimes make no sense to anyone, as well they shouldn't. "Houston, we have a problem."

In today's schools, when most kids get into trouble, the parent helps them build a case that would put good defense lawyers to shame. Parents' distrust and skepticism of their child's school staff is a legitimate concern. Things have become a bit more complicated. Maybe our entire culture is devoid of genuine role models for our kids, and maybe it also has to do with the terrible examples set by some of our governmental and religious leaders. The contributing factors and the unanswered questions are without end. At the end of the day, the simple fact remains that we do not have the confidence in our leaders that we had in past generations. Where that leaves parents today is searching for a school that has genuine leaders in whom they can safely place their confidence to care for their children. Parents are now going to virtually any extent to find that mature leader. We have had dads who passed up big promotions from their company because they didn't have confidence they could find another Liberty Christian School if they moved their family. I pray the same be true for your school. Way to go, Liberty Staff.

But it is not even as simple as the lack of good leadership in our schools. Families are self-destructing before our kids' very eyes, a phenomenon never before seen in our country's cultural history. The ink on the divorce papers has not yet dried when the parent feels compelled to "ride in on the white horse" with the battle cry," My kid is innocent." Driven by the guilt of being an absent father or mother, of not spending time (quality or quantity) with their child, the parents decide the least they can do is defend their child from almost anything and everything.

So when the child gets into trouble, the parent feels compelled to save the day—all the while, really trying to make up for their own lack of parenting or presence. Maybe it's because parents are so protective of their child's school record, not wanting something negative to show up should he apply for college entrance or someday run for President of the

United States. But maybe, just maybe, to further muddy this water of trust, underneath all of the posturing and protecting, a legitimate truth is that the parents lack confidence in their child's administrators, teachers, and coaches to make mature decisions. And they have a "bulletproof case."

Intuitively, the parent knows within the first few minutes if his child is in the care of an emotionally mature teacher and administrator. In today's schools, unfortunately, that issue has real relevance, and has understandably caused parents to question whether their child is in good hands, which is very sad. It doesn't take many bad hires on the part of the administrator or the board to cause the parents to question the administration's judgment. The first and logical place parents are going to begin is to make sure the charge against their child is valid. Sadly, if the shoe fits, we as administrators and board members must wear it.

Ultimately, the school administrator is placed in a situation where he must justify a decision. The venue may be his office, or a legal court of law, but the authority of the school must prove its case. The answer is not only going to be time-consuming and expensive, but justifiably and tragically, it may be at the expense of the bedrock confidence in our educational leaders.

Added to that issue of whether the person running your child's school is truly capable or competent are a few other stumbling blocks that cause parents to feel the need to fight for their child and go against their genuine desire to support authority.

Recently we read of a superintendent of a school district, in charge of a student population in the thousands, abusing the school district's credit card. It is also **common** for school districts to face the humiliating charge of teachers having sex with minor-aged students. Many true—all very sad. In most all cases, and there are many more than any of us will ever know, the school officials defend their hiring decision, adding further doubt as to how cautious an administrator can be to blindly hire such a person, although sometimes there are no clues. The next item on the news is that the administrator, teacher, or coach "is on paid leave" until further notice.

If these were isolated instances, it would be one thing, but as we know, they are common in school districts in many cities and in virtually all states. How supportive can we expect parents to be of an administrator when their child has to pass through a metal detector before entering the school building, sees dogs parading the halls in search of drugs, knows that gangs are allowed to remain gangs and wear their colors, is fearful to go to the bathroom, and hears disrespectful language from student to student, even student to teacher, hardly any of which is stopped by those in authority. I have had many parents tell me that they never intended to enroll their child in a private school, but just could not, in good conscience, drop their child off at a place where they would fear to work.

In 2004, I interviewed a parent who desperately wanted her daughter accepted into Liberty. I asked her why she was changing her daughter's school. She informed me that she was visiting with the public school's counselors regarding her daughter's schedule. While there she observed students in the lunchroom throwing food, the larger kids shoving the smaller ones out of the lunch line, and a noise factor that was unbelievable. She told the counselor, "I just can't do this. I can't place my daughter in a school that **I** would not consider attending myself." That is why she came to interview at Liberty.

A few years ago, I interviewed a parent who wanted her children to attend Liberty. At the beginning of the interview, I asked her the simple question, "Why are you applying?" Her response floored me. She told me that she had noticed that her kids would literally run from the car when they pulled into the driveway at home, and head for the bathroom. She asked them why they didn't use the bathroom at school; why would they suffer the discomfort? They told her that the bathrooms are where kids get beat up and have their lunch money stolen. They would not go into the school bathroom—period. I may be stepping out on a limb here, but I think the obvious solution is for the administrator to kick the bully or bullies out of the school. "Plan B," position an administrator in the bathroom during every break.

Recently there was a study done by a person studying elephants in South Africa. It was observed that there was a herd of young elephants in a particular game reserve with no adult bull elephants in the population. The young elephants absolutely destroyed the fences and trees and were dangerous to each other. The operators of the preserve added **one** bull elephant to the herd, and guess what? All of the destructive behavior stopped immediately.

The issues facing our schools, public and private, are going to require some very difficult decisions by very courageous people. Let's not fool ourselves; the education of our young and the future of our nation are at stake. It's going to take statesmen cut from the cloth of George Washington and Abraham Lincoln to make the tough decisions. We have had all of the people-pleasing, wimpy politicos our kids can take. Harry

Truman was one of those guys who knew how to make a difficult decision. On his desk was a sign that read, "The buck stops here." So where is the logical place to start to remedy this little "issue" of our children's education? At the top!

Chapter 35

WARNING—This Chapter Is Going To Test My Credibility

We have spent serious time talking about hires and their importance in the success of a school. In 1975, about eight years before I entered the field of education, I employed a psychologist, Dr. John Shirley, to analyze the employees that I had hired to work in my companies. I wanted him to evaluate their strengths and weaknesses, as well as their placement in the organizational structure. Basically, I wanted him to tell me if I had our company staffed for success, and ways it could be improved.

One of the advantages that I gained from Dr. Shirley was an understanding that the general tendencies of the personalities of people are, **in many cases,** related to their physical characteristics and to a large extent predictable. He referred to his research and study as "Body Types." I'll explain.

Dr. Shirley's report had great value to me in assessing those whom I had hired, and more importantly, in determining whom I would hire in the future. Nobody has a corner on understanding the personnel market. There are no silver bullets that are going to protect you from making a bad hire, but this study, while not scientific, has been enormously helpful to me. Warning—you are about to enter the weird zone. Leave your attitude and preconceived notions at the door, and just enjoy what, at first, seemed to me to be "snake oil," but later proved to be much more on point than not. Dr. Shirley's report was about seventy-five pages long; I'm going to share the "bottom line" of a few pages of his report.

According to Dr. Shirley, people will tell you a great deal without saying a word. They are going to speak with their body type—thin, average but on the thin side, average, average but on the heavy side, or heavy. This is not body language, but body type.

According to Dr. Shirley, men and women can generally be divided into five different physical body types, and each type has **general tendencies**—the operative word here is **general**. It can be applied to both men and women and to all races. There are many exceptions, so to call this a rule is a stretch. To call it a head start in reading your employee or applicant is accurate.

The first body type appears lean and thin. This is a person that you would best describe as linear. Dr. Shirley named this body type ectomorphs, or "ectos." Ectos have long fingers, a long neck, and appear linear. They don't have to be tall—height is not part of this "scan." They are generally a reserved and cautious group. Their best asset is typically their intelligence, and meeting people is not high on their list of favorite things to do. Ectos tend to be generally more antisocial than social. You will see them attending as few parties as possible. They are physically made to stay away from people and conflicts. When you meet them they would be more comfortable if you would keep a desk or a piece of furniture between you and them. You will notice that they may not offer to shake hands first, but if they do, they would rather not, so don't squeeze very hard.

This person typically makes a good "bean-counter." He will work all day, and be just as strong at the end of the day as he was at 8:00 a.m. These guys are normally very intelligent and make great accountants, technology specialists, surgeons, dentists, and bankers. They generally love research, but would rather not deliver their findings in a public forum. They are generally not risk takers, and if they come up with that "better mouse trap," they will probably need to find a different person to bring it to market. Otherwise, it will just stay on paper. These folks are built for distance. In fact, you can find many of them running marathons.

The next body type is the meso-ectomorph, or "meso-ectos." This person is not quite as linear, not as thin, but very definitely on the lean side. He will appear to be a little more confident, but you will probably not see him running for a public office. After saying that, Denton County has a young man who fits the meso-ecto model, is on the rise, and would make a great president— his name is Andrew Eads—watch for him! Andrew, a Liberty graduate, is very bright and lean, but he is an exception on several fronts. He loves people, is not afraid of making tough decisions, and is eager to convince you he is right.

The meso-ecto is the person who is normally on time, has all of his information together, and always takes care of business. You can hire him to be a science or math teacher, and he is often found in the position of band or choir director, basketball, track, tennis, golf or cross country coach. Normally this person will be capable of leadership, but he has to have the **desire** to lead. These guys will make great Human Resource directors, because they have the detail thing going on and can communicate well to your staff. They can make great teachers if their personality tends to be outgoing. On the very strong side of both the ectos and the meso-ectos, you typically find very conservative men and women with a high level of intelligence, trust, integrity, and character.

The mesomorph, or "meso," is the next body type, and this person is the body beautiful person. This person is physically well proportioned, and is comfortable around people because he is confident. He has the perfect body, and that leads him to believe he can get himself out of any predicament. These types are our astronauts, tennis players, quarterbacks, soccer players, and basketball point guards. Astronauts, because inherently they actually have the confidence that if "the" button doesn't work, they will "think of something." Here is your athletic director, cheerleading director, department chair or administrator. This is a type that can motivate anyone to do anything, and they are often natural leaders.

They take care of themselves physically. Subconsciously, their body will be one of their best assets. They will probably tell you about the best health club in the area, and will know what they are talking about. As I write this book, there are several examples of well-known personalities who fit this body type. They include such people as the Reverend Billy Graham, Ross Perot, Senator Mitt Romney, former President George W. Bush, Governor Sarah Palin, Bruce Springsteen, and the late Elvis Presley in his earlier days—you get the picture.

Next is the meso-endomorph, or "meso-endos." This guy is on the thick side, but certainly not fat. When you see him, you think "thick bodied." He is built for a tough day. He can handle confrontation, probably has a great sense of humor, loves people, and innately believes he has the ability to "take out" any competitor. These guys typically make great anythings, except rarely will you find them in accounting or neurosurgery. Here is likely your best possible candidate for administrator or sales manager. He has definite ideas, and if he is bright, can motivate faculty and staff to follow him to achieve greatness. These folks also make good development directors, athletic directors, and board members. They are natural politicians, love people, want to be president of everything—so give them the job, and get out of their way. In my view, examples of public figures in this group would be Dr. Phil McGraw, Jay Leno, Terry Bradshaw, and Garth Brooks.

The last general body type is the endomorph. Here is the guy who just looks "round." He has a flat forehead, short fingers, flat wrist, and virtually no neck (he hates wearing a tie—in fact, may not own one). He is built for strength, but not endurance. He loves people. His office will be filled with photos of friends and family. He is a family guy, and will have photos of his kids and wife everywhere. He really "moves in" wherever he is hired. This guy is loved by everyone. He is not going to like late meetings, so if you are thinking potential board member, you had better not count on him for attendance in meetings held at night. He is not built for marathons or sprints, but will get the job done.

There are many exceptions. I'll bet I know as many as you. There are great endomorph (round people) band directors, and wonderful ectomorph (slim guys) football coaches. Just use this information to give you a head start. I have said this is not scientific, and it's certainly not spiritual. However, I have used it to my advantage over the years. Quite honestly, my fear is that it will probably appear on the "snake oil" side to the reader, but my hope is that it may be of help to you in the important area of hiring and team building. And if Dr. Shirley's ideas hadn't saved me so much money and employee turnover over the last forty years, it would have been much better for my credibility and ego to have just left this chapter out—but that is not the kind of book I have chosen to write.

In the summer of 2008, my wife and I went to Cabo San Lucas. Picture this: We are lying by the pool. An ectomorph (linear) gets out of the pool, immediately wraps her child in a towel, and then runs under an umbrella to get out of the sun. A member of the same group is a meso-endomorph (thick), and he gets out of the pool and grabs his child and tosses him in the water to play a little longer. He stays thirty minutes or longer, totally oblivious to the sun's rays. He stays for two reasons: first, he doesn't believe anything can really hurt him, and second, he is going to have fun.

Later that evening, we see the same group at dinner. At the head of the table is the meso-endo, and he is picking up the check because this is HIS party, and, I'm purely speculating, but I suspect he probably owns the company that afforded the entire group the vacation. Body type can matter.

In Closing

I'd like to add the disclaimer that we all hear so often, "Any connection to real people is purely coincidental," but that of course would be a lie. My administration experience has been filled with great and talented people, of whom I've mentioned only a few. It's 2010 and I serve with a school board that may well be the best in the world—I'm not exaggerating. And as I look over our teaching staff, I believe that all who are currently teaching will be invited back enthusiastically.

This book acknowledges that getting to a significant place of achievement in any school's development is very difficult. It takes leaders who are not afraid of offending and don't care if they get re-elected or fired—at least not at the cost of making a decision they know to be wrong. And it is a "one decision at a time" business, and it is the **intent** of a wrong decision that is important—not the mistake itself.

As educators, we have to understand the dynamics of what it takes to run a good school. I have explained as honestly and forthrightly as I can what it takes to do that; and to show you as transparently as possible the "stuff" it takes to be:

CALLED TO THE PRINCIPAL'S OFFICE

CALLED TO THE PRINCIPAL'S OFFICE

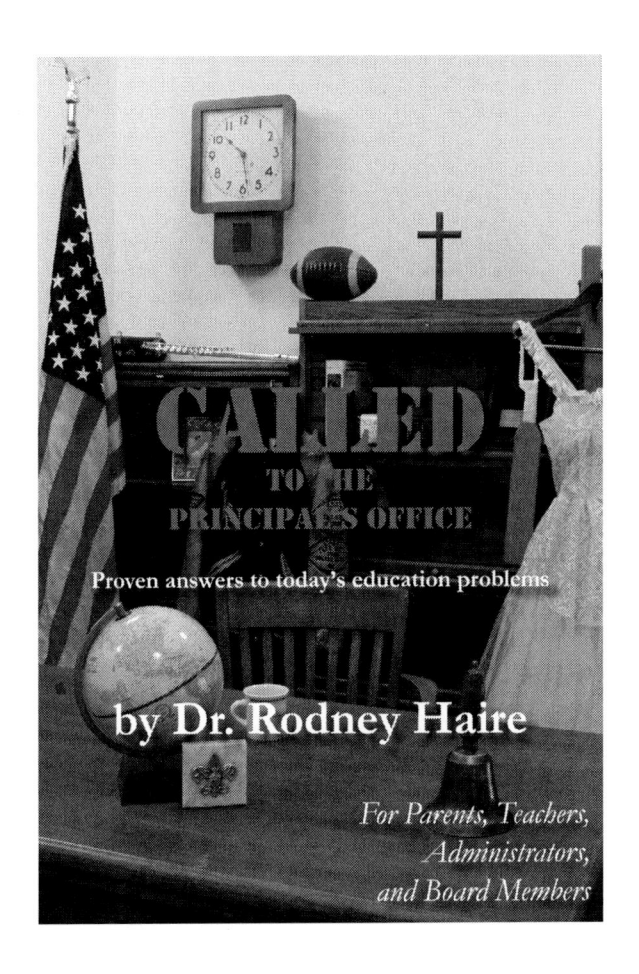

To purchase additional copies of CALLED:

- Web: www.libertychristian.com/CALLED
- Phone: 940-294-2127
- E-mail: CALLED@libertychristian.com